the Joy of Eating French Food

Great French Dishes Made Easy

by Renny Darling

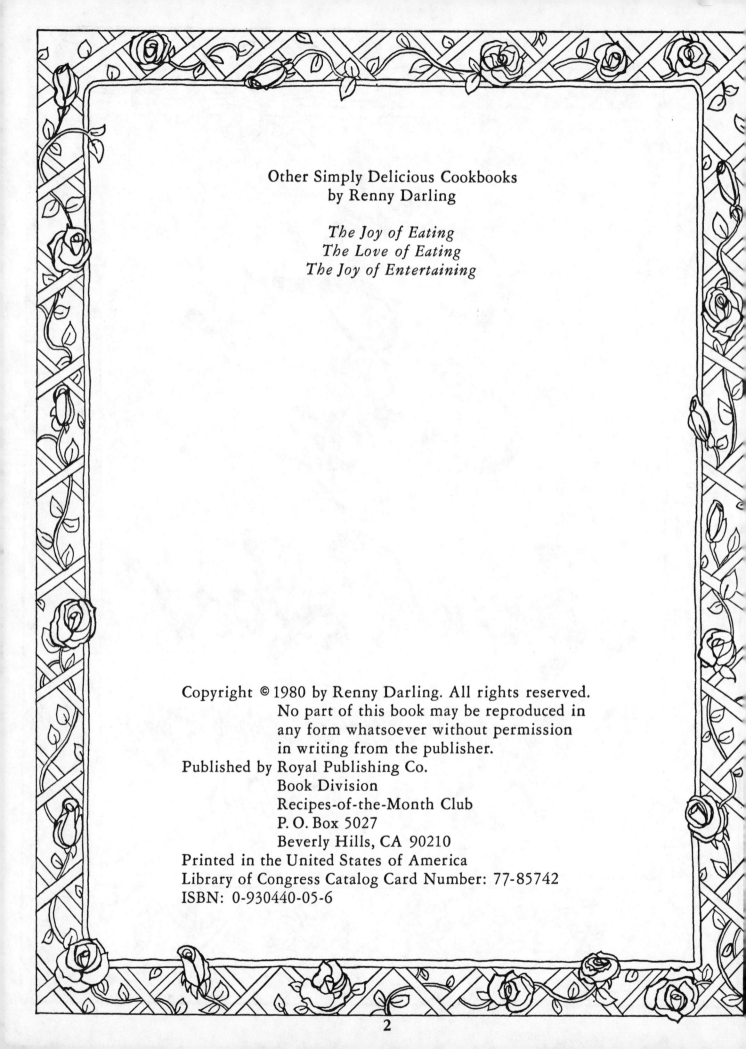

Other Simply Delicious Cookbooks
by Renny Darling

The Joy of Eating
The Love of Eating
The Joy of Entertaining

Published by Royal Publishing Co.
Book Division
Recipes-of-the-Month Club
P. O. Box 5027
Beverly Hills, CA 90210
Printed in the United States of America
Library of Congress Catalog Card Number: 77-85742
ISBN: 0-930440-05-6

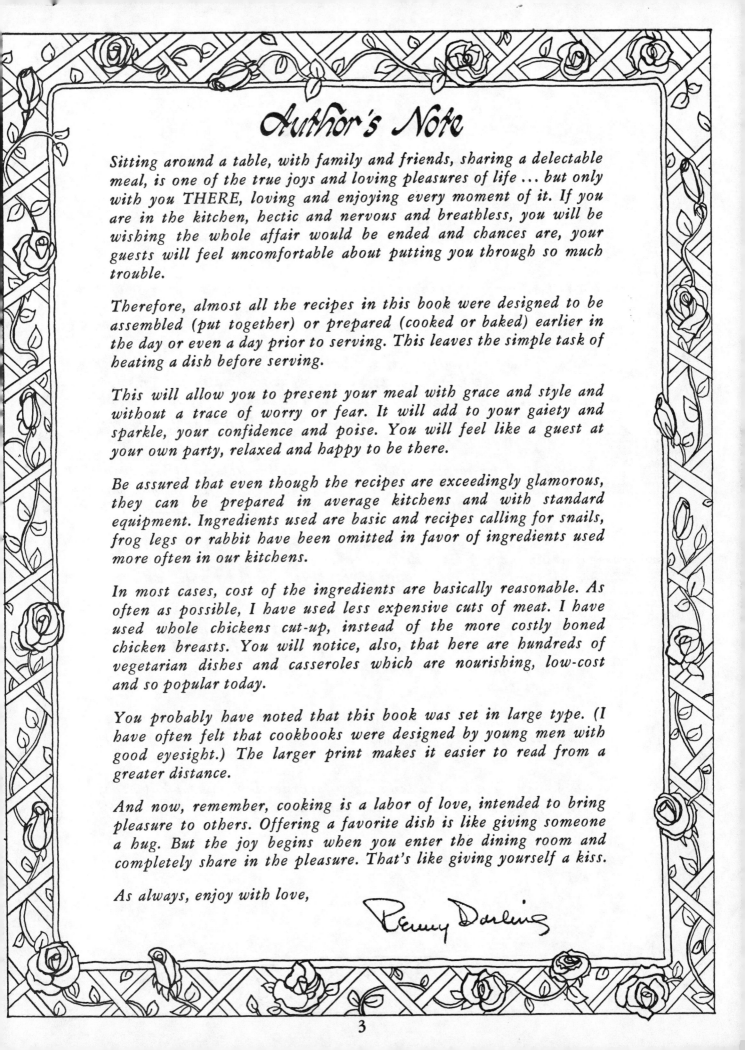

Author's Note

Sitting around a table, with family and friends, sharing a delectable meal, is one of the true joys and loving pleasures of life ... but only with you THERE, loving and enjoying every moment of it. If you are in the kitchen, hectic and nervous and breathless, you will be wishing the whole affair would be ended and chances are, your guests will feel uncomfortable about putting you through so much trouble.

Therefore, almost all the recipes in this book were designed to be assembled (put together) or prepared (cooked or baked) earlier in the day or even a day prior to serving. This leaves the simple task of heating a dish before serving.

This will allow you to present your meal with grace and style and without a trace of worry or fear. It will add to your gaiety and sparkle, your confidence and poise. You will feel like a guest at your own party, relaxed and happy to be there.

Be assured that even though the recipes are exceedingly glamorous, they can be prepared in average kitchens and with standard equipment. Ingredients used are basic and recipes calling for snails, frog legs or rabbit have been omitted in favor of ingredients used more often in our kitchens.

In most cases, cost of the ingredients are basically reasonable. As often as possible, I have used less expensive cuts of meat. I have used whole chickens cut-up, instead of the more costly boned chicken breasts. You will notice, also, that here are hundreds of vegetarian dishes and casseroles which are nourishing, low-cost and so popular today.

You probably have noted that this book was set in large type. (I have often felt that cookbooks were designed by young men with good eyesight.) The larger print makes it easier to read from a greater distance.

And now, remember, cooking is a labor of love, intended to bring pleasure to others. Offering a favorite dish is like giving someone a hug. But the joy begins when you enter the dining room and completely share in the pleasure. That's like giving yourself a kiss.

As always, enjoy with love,

Renny Darling

The Introduction

As I write this, I am gazing out of the window at a 12-foot avocado tree that I planted 5 years ago from a little seed. I am amazed. The sun is drenching the garden with yellow and the leaves are barely rippling from the little puffs of breeze. Last night, I was up late, finishing the last touches of this manuscript and here I am, as always and how ironic, writing the very last words, the introduction.

It is hard for me to believe that it has been only a little over 3 years since THE JOY OF EATING first was published. In so many ways, it seems and feels so much longer. And in this time, I have received thousands of letters from all over the country and other parts of the world, affirming the philosophy behind my three earlier books ... that women and men today want to dine in the grandest style. Yet, they do not have, nor do they care to spend, enormous amounts of time in preparation. They want recipes that taste and present as if they took all day to prepare but with none of the hassle.

And that is the purpose of this book, as well ... to bring the exciting and fabled dishes of the great French cuisine into your home, with recipes that are QUICK and EASY and INCREDIBLY DELICIOUS.

This is a cookbook for everyone ... from the most inexperienced beginning cooks to seasoned and accomplished gourmets. The recipes are simple and easy to prepare and the results will truly amaze you.

It was not my intent to cover the cooking of France in any particular pattern or region. My choices were purely eclectic. What I planned was to include my favorites in the French-style and with lovely accompaniments.

French food has the reputation of being complicated and difficult to prepare. The recipes that follow were designed to dispel any jitters or uneasiness, for preparation is the essence of simplicity.

So, I offer you, here, a few of my favorite things and I hope they bring you and your family and your friends much pleasure and joy.

Toujours Bon Appetit,

R.D.
Beverly Hills, California
March, 1980

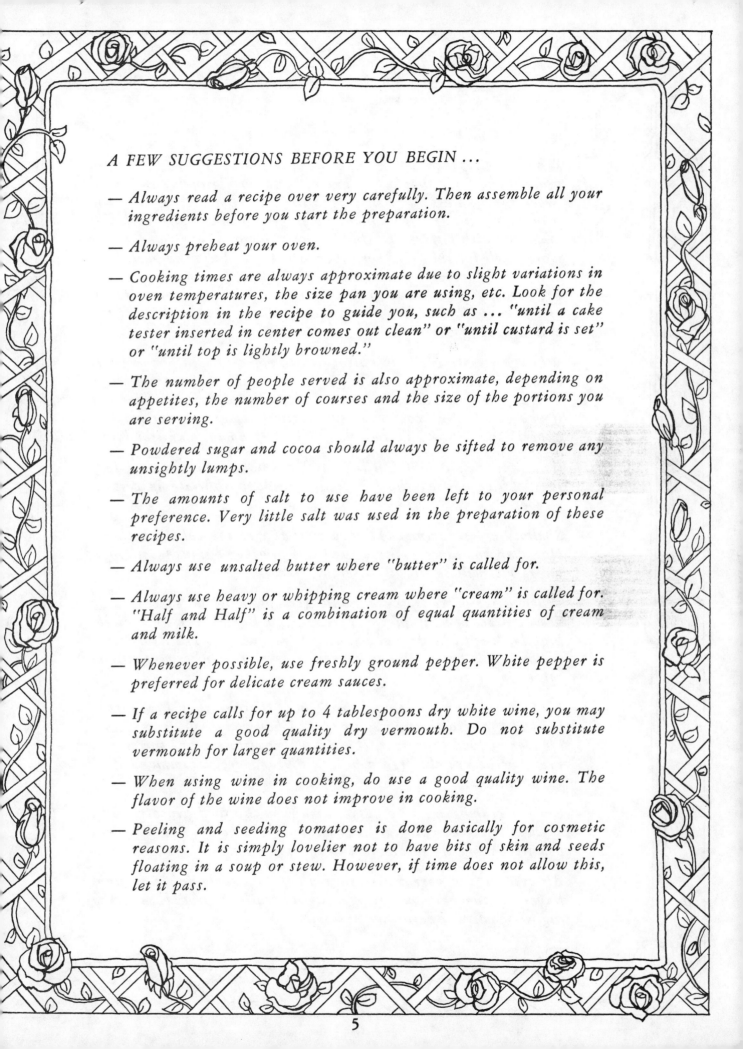

A FEW SUGGESTIONS BEFORE YOU BEGIN ...

— *Always read a recipe over very carefully. Then assemble all your ingredients before you start the preparation.*

— *Always preheat your oven.*

— *Cooking times are always approximate due to slight variations in oven temperatures, the size pan you are using, etc. Look for the description in the recipe to guide you, such as ... "until a cake tester inserted in center comes out clean" or "until custard is set" or "until top is lightly browned."*

— *The number of people served is also approximate, depending on appetites, the number of courses and the size of the portions you are serving.*

— *Powdered sugar and cocoa should always be sifted to remove any unsightly lumps.*

— *The amounts of salt to use have been left to your personal preference. Very little salt was used in the preparation of these recipes.*

— *Always use unsalted butter where "butter" is called for.*

— *Always use heavy or whipping cream where "cream" is called for. "Half and Half" is a combination of equal quantities of cream and milk.*

— *Whenever possible, use freshly ground pepper. White pepper is preferred for delicate cream sauces.*

— *If a recipe calls for up to 4 tablespoons dry white wine, you may substitute a good quality dry vermouth. Do not substitute vermouth for larger quantities.*

— *When using wine in cooking, do use a good quality wine. The flavor of the wine does not improve in cooking.*

— *Peeling and seeding tomatoes is done basically for cosmetic reasons. It is simply lovelier not to have bits of skin and seeds floating in a soup or stew. However, if time does not allow this, let it pass.*

— When a recipe calls for "1/2 orange, grated" or "1/2 lemon, grated" the fruit should be "grated" and not "ground" in a food processor (unless it has a grating attachment). Using the processor with the steel blade releases too much pith and will make the dish bitter. The third largest side of a four-sided grater works well for this. Use very short strokes and use the peel, fruit and juice. Remove any large pieces of membrane. If you use the processor, you will need to remove the zest (the thin outer peel), and discard the pith (the white part). Then you can process the zest with the fruit.

— When you saute garlic in butter or oil, make certain not to fry it or let it brown. Overcooking garlic will make a dish taste bitter and unpleasant. Fresh garlic is preferable to garlic powder but if you can find a "coarse grind" garlic powder in your market, experiment with it. Taste will tell if it is up to your standards.

— As a general rule, unless it is specifically noted, it is not necessary to sift flour. Sifted flour is lighter and appropriate in certain recipes.

— Shallots are recommended wherever the recipe calls for these. However, you can substitute the bulbs of green onions (scallions), but results will be slightly altered.

— When a recipe calls for a liquid (cream, wine or sauce) to be "reduced to 1/2" it means to cook the liquid over moderately high heat, until it is cooked down or "reduced" to 1/2 its original volume. This process intensifies the flavor of an otherwise diluted sauce.

— Fresh bread crumbs are used throughout these recipes. I am rather fond of the results using egg bread. When you make crumbs in a blender or food processor, there is no need to remove the crusts. Fresh bread crumbs freeze beautifully and are recommended to keep on hand.

— Cracker crumbs are very easy to make in the food processor and a wonderful way to utilize leftover crackers. These freeze beautifully and are recommended to keep on hand.

— Always use the very finest ingredients available for maximum flavor ... the best quality meats, the freshest produce and the highest quality of herbs and spices.

The Contents

For Mamma,
   for her golden hands
   and loving arms ...

Breads
&
Muffins

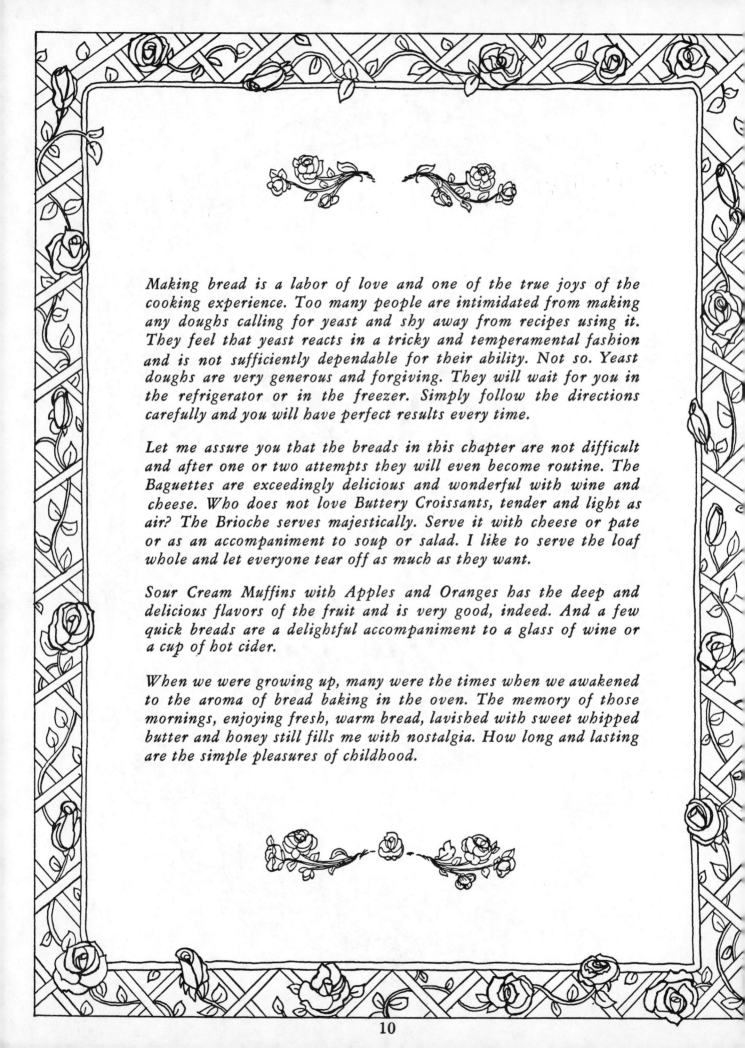

Making bread is a labor of love and one of the true joys of the cooking experience. Too many people are intimidated from making any doughs calling for yeast and shy away from recipes using it. They feel that yeast reacts in a tricky and temperamental fashion and is not sufficiently dependable for their ability. Not so. Yeast doughs are very generous and forgiving. They will wait for you in the refrigerator or in the freezer. Simply follow the directions carefully and you will have perfect results every time.

Let me assure you that the breads in this chapter are not difficult and after one or two attempts they will even become routine. The Baguettes are exceedingly delicious and wonderful with wine and cheese. Who does not love Buttery Croissants, tender and light as air? The Brioche serves majestically. Serve it with cheese or pate or as an accompaniment to soup or salad. I like to serve the loaf whole and let everyone tear off as much as they want.

Sour Cream Muffins with Apples and Oranges has the deep and delicious flavors of the fruit and is very good, indeed. And a few quick breads are a delightful accompaniment to a glass of wine or a cup of hot cider.

When we were growing up, many were the times when we awakened to the aroma of bread baking in the oven. The memory of those mornings, enjoying fresh, warm bread, lavished with sweet whipped butter and honey still fills me with nostalgia. How long and lasting are the simple pleasures of childhood.

Burgundian Cheese & Onion Bread
(Gougere au Fromage)

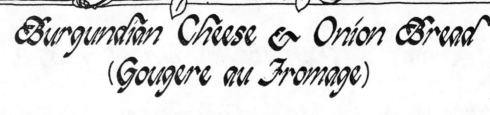

Whenever I serve this bread, it creates a great deal of spirit and excitement. Serve it with an herbed cheese, a delicate pate and a glass of wine and watch the happiness glow.

   1 cup flour
   1 tablespoon dried onion flakes

   1 cup milk
   4 tablespoons butter (1/2 stick)

   4 eggs, at room temperature
   2 teaspoons Dijon mustard
1/2 teaspoon salt

   1 cup grated Swiss cheese (1/4 pound)
   2 tablespoons grated Parmesan cheese

Place flour and onion flakes in the large bowl of an electric mixer.

In a saucepan, heat milk and butter until mixture comes to a boil. Pour boiling milk mixture into bowl with the flour and beat until the dough is smooth, about 2 minutes. Beat in the eggs, one at a time, beating well after each addition. Beat in the remaining ingredients.

Grease a 10-inch porcelain quiche baker. Spoon dough along the edge of the pan to form a 1 1/2-inch ring. Bake in a 400° oven for 15 minutes. Lower heat to 350° and continue baking for about 30 minutes or until Gougere is puffed and golden brown.

Serve warm with soup or salad or simply with a glass of wine. Serves 6.

Note: - *Gougere lovers rejoice. Notice that the batter does not need to be cooked in the saucepan before the eggs are added. This simplifies the Gougere considerably; yet it is every bit as delicious.*
   - *Batter can be made earlier in the day, spooned into the porcelain baker and refrigerated until ready to bake. Add a few minutes to baking time.*
   - *This pastry can be baked earlier in the day and heated before serving. But, it is best made at serving time.*

Chewy French Bread Sticks with Onions

Try this chewy delicious bread stick some evening soon. They are exceedingly easy to prepare and the dough is easily handled and does not need to rise.

1 1/2 cups lukewarm water
   2 teaspoons sugar
   1 envelope dry yeast

   4 cups flour
3/4 teaspoon salt

   1 egg, beaten
   dried onion flakes
   coarse salt

In large bowl of electric mixer, place water, sugar and yeast and allow mixture to rest for 5 minutes or until yeast is softened. Add flour and salt and beat until blended. Use a dough hook, or knead by hand until dough is smooth and soft, about 5 minutes. Do not let dough rise.

Divide dough into 16 pieces. Roll each piece of dough into a 1/4-inch thick rope and place on a greased cookie sheet. Brush tops with beaten egg and sprinkle top with dried onion flakes and coarse salt.

Bake in a 400° oven for about 15 minutes or until bread sticks are lightly browned. Yields 16 bread sticks.

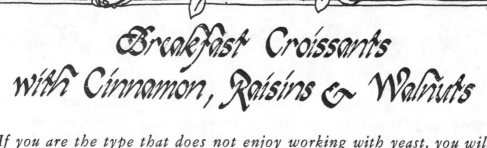

Breakfast Croissants with Cinnamon, Raisins & Walnuts

If you are the type that does not enjoy working with yeast, you will love this little treasure. The croissants look and taste as if they were made with yeast, but actually, the secret ingredient is cottage cheese. These lovely, delicate croissants are assembled in minutes and are especially good at breakfast or tea.

   1 cup cottage cheese
   3 ounces butter (3/4 stick)
   1 cup flour

1/2 cup finely chopped walnuts
1/2 cup sugar
1/2 cup finely chopped raisins
1/2 teaspoon cinnamon (or more to taste)

Beat together the cottage cheese and butter until the mixture is blended. Beat in the flour until the mixture is smooth, about 1 to 2 minutes.

Shape dough into a ball and sprinkle with a little flour to ease handling. Divide dough into thirds.

Roll each third out on a floured pastry cloth (use a stocking on your rolling pin, too), until circle measures about 10 inches.

Combine walnuts, sugar, raisins and cinnamon and toss until blended. Sprinkle 1/3 the walnut filling evenly over the dough. Cut dough into 8 triangular wedges. Roll each triangle from the wide end toward the center and curve into a crescent. Repeat with remaining dough.

Place croissants on a lightly buttered cookie sheet and bake at 350° about 30 to 35 minutes or until they are a deep golden brown. Remove from the pan and allow to cool on a brown paper bag. Yields 24 crescents.

Note: – Croissants freeze beautifully and are so nice to keep on hand. However, bake these on a day when there is no one around, or they will never make it to the freezer.

Easiest & Best French Bread (Baguettes)

After a good deal of experimenting, I have developed a way to make the best French bread — crisp, crusty and chewy — AND without your having to knead it (or even touch it, for that matter). I am thrilled to share this little treasure with you and I hope you use it often. The bread is simply delicious. You do need a heavy duty mixer and a 3-loaf Baguette pan and the rest is easy.

    1 package dry yeast
    1 teaspoon sugar
1/2 cup warm water (100° to 103°)

1 1/4 cups warm water (100° to 103°)
3 1/3 cups flour
1 1/2 teaspoons salt
    1 tablespoon oil
    1 egg, beaten

In a glass measuring cup, stir together yeast, sugar and 1/2 cup warm water. Allow to stand until foamy. This is called "proofing the yeast" and if it does not foam, yeast is not active and should be discarded.

In a large bowl of an electric mixer, place yeast mixture, additional water, flour and salt, and beat mixture for about 5 to 7 minutes or until dough is smooth and elastic. Dough will be very soft and sticky. Drizzle the oil evenly over the dough. Cover bowl with plastic wrap and then a towel and set it in a warm place (75° to 80°) until it is doubled in bulk. With a spatula, scrape dough down into the bowl, cover it as before and let it rise again until doubled.

Grease a 3-loaf Baguette pan, 8 1/2 x 17-inches. With a large kitchen spoon, scoop out 1/3 of the dough in each section and spread it out evenly. Brush tops with a little oil. Cover pan loosely with plastic wrap and allow dough to rise again until almost doubled. Remove plastic wrap, baste tops lightly with beaten egg and bake in a preheated 425° oven until tops are a beautiful golden brown and breads sound hollow when thumped, about 25 minutes. Remove breads from pan and cool on a rack. Yields 3 loaves.

Note: – At any point, dough can be refrigerated to hold back the rising. Remove from the refrigerator, and then continue the rising as indicated.
*   – Traditionally, an oven is steamed to get a golden crisp crust, but the egg works very well, and is a bit easier.*

14

Easiest & Best Buttery French Croissants

Now, at last, you can make these light, fluffy croissants without spending the usual laborious hours in the kitchen. These croissants are as light as air and the dough does not need to be folded or turned. In fact, follow the instructions carefully and you will practically not have to even touch the dough until you are ready to roll it out.

   1 package dry yeast
1/4 cup warm water (105°)
   2 teaspoons sugar

3/4 cup cold milk
   3 egg yolks

   4 cups flour
1/4 cup sugar
1/2 teaspoon salt

1 1/4 cups cold butter (2 1/2 sticks), cut into pieces

   1 egg beaten

In a glass measuring bowl, proof yeast, by stirring together yeast, water and sugar. Let stand for 10 minutes or so until yeast is dissolved and mixture starts to foam. Add milk and yolks and stir until nicely blended. Set aside.

In the large bowl of an electric mixer, place flour, sugar and salt. Add butter and beat until butter is the size of peas. Add yeast mixture and beat until blended. In the same bowl, gather dough into a ball, cover it with plastic wrap and a towel and place in the refrigerator overnight.

Cut dough into fourths. Working one fourth at a time, roll it out on a floured pastry cloth to about a 6-inch circle. Cut dough into 8 triangular wedges (like a pie). Roll out each triangle to 1/8-inch thickness. Roll it up from the wide side toward center. Shape into a crescent and place on a greased cookie sheet. Continue with remaining dough. Cover crescents lightly with wax paper and let rolls rise for about 1 hour. Brush them with beaten egg and bake at 350° for about 20 to 25 minutes or until tops are nicely browned. Yields 32 incredible croissants.

2~Minute Herb Bread with Onions & Cheese

    3 cups self-rising flour
    3 tablespoons sugar
    1 can (12 ounces) beer at room temperature
    2 tablespoons dried minced onions
1/2 cup grated Swiss cheese
1/4 cup grated Parmesan cheese
1/2 teaspoon thyme
1/2 teaspoon parsley

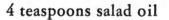

    4 teaspoons salad oil

In the large bowl of an electric mixer place first 8 ingredients and beat at low speed for 1 minute or until the mixture looks smooth and blended.

Oil two 4x8-inch foil loaf pans with 2 teaspoons oil, each. Pour batter evenly into each pan. Brush tops with some of the oil in the pans. Bake in a 350° oven for about 45 minutes or until top is golden brown and a cake tester inserted in center comes out clean. Cool in pans for 5 minutes and then remove from pans and finish cooling on a rack. Serve with sweet creamy butter. Yields 2 loaves.

Cottage Cheese Bread with Oranges, Raisins & Walnuts

1/4 cup butter, softened
1/3 cup sugar
    1 cup cottage cheese (can use lo-fat)
1/2 orange, grated
    1 egg

    1 cup flour
    1 teaspoon baking powder
1/4 teaspoon baking soda
1/8 teaspoon salt
1/2 cup golden raisins
1/2 cup chopped walnuts

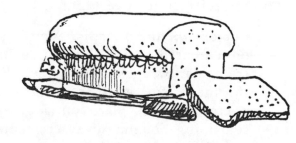

Beat together first 5 ingredients until blended. Stir in the remaining ingredients until just moistened. Do not overbeat. Pour mixture into a buttered 8x4-inch loaf pan and bake at 350° for 40 to 50 minutes or until it tests done. Incredibly delicious!

Brioche de Brillat Savarin

(Butter and Egg Bread)

This is my simplified version of the classic bread. It is an exceedingly delicate dough and serves majestically, crowned high and golden brown. Brioche needs little embellishment ... only lots of creamy, whipped sweet butter.

1/3 cup warm water (105° to 115°)
   3 packages active dry yeast
   3 teaspoons sugar

   3 eggs
1/4 cup sugar
   1 teaspoon vanilla
1/2 teaspoon salt

1/2 cup unsalted butter, melted and cooled
   3 cups flour, lightly packed

   melted butter

In a glass measuring cup, stir together warm water, yeast and sugar. Allow to stand until doubled in volume and bubbly. This is called "proofing the yeast" and if it does not foam, yeast is not active and should be discarded.

In a large mixer bowl, beat eggs, sugar, vanilla and salt. Add yeast mixture and beat until blended. Beat in melted butter and flour. If you have a dough hook, use it at this time. If not, then you must knead the dough until it is smooth and satiny, about 5 minutes. Shape dough into a ball and turn into a greased bowl. Cover with plastic wrap and let rise in a warm place (85°) until double in volume.

Punch dough down and shape it into a ball. Place in a 1 1/2-quart brioche pan or souffle dish that is lightly greased and floured. (Shape a ball on top by grasping a handful of dough and twisting it ... optional but traditional.) Cover and let rise again in a warm place until dough is doubled in volume. Remove plastic wrap.

Brush top with melted butter and bake in a 400° oven for 10 minutes. Reduce heat to 350° and continue baking for about 30 minutes or until top is a deep golden brown. A lovely crown will have formed. Allow to cool in baking dish on a rack.

Serve with creamy butter, cheese or pate, for a never to be forgotten treat.

Giant Popover with Cheese & Chives

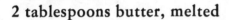

3 eggs
1 cup milk
1 cup flour
1/4 teaspoon salt
2 tablespoons dried chopped chives
1/4 cup grated Parmesan cheese

2 tablespoons butter, melted

Beat together the first six ingredients until mixture is blended. Do not overbeat. Let batter rest for 30 minutes.

Spread butter in a 12-inch round baker and pour in the batter. Bake in a 400° oven for about 30 minutes or until popover is puffed and golden. Serve at once.

Serve with sweet whipped butter. Excellent with soups or salads.

Note: – Batter can be made earlier in the day and refrigerated. However, bake just before serving or popover will deflate.

Orange Walnut Pumpkin Bread

This is one of my favorite breads. It is fragrant and delicious and slices beautifully. It is filled with orange and raisins and nuts and lots of spice and everything nice.

2 eggs
1/2 orange, grated. Remove any large pieces of membrane.
1/2 cup orange juice
1 1/8 cups sugar
1 cup canned pumpkin
1/4 cup butter, softened (1/2 stick)

2 cups flour
2 teaspoons baking powder
1/2 teaspoon baking soda
1/2 teaspoon salt
1 teaspoon cinnamon
2 teaspoons pumpkin pie spice

1 cup yellow raisins
1 cup chopped walnuts

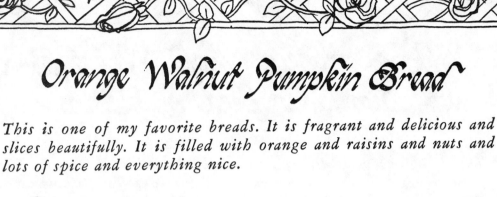

In the large bowl of an electric mixer, beat together first 6 ingredients until blended. Stir in the remaining ingredients by hand until flour is just moistened. Do not overmix. Pour batter into 4 greased baby loaf pans, 6 x 3 1/2 x 2 inches.

Bake in a 350° oven for about 40 to 45 minutes or until a cake tester inserted in center comes out clean. Remove from pans and cool on a rack. Serve "natural" or with a lovely orange glaze. Yields 4 loaves.

Orange Glaze

2 tablespoons orange juice
2 tablespoons grated orange peel
1 1/4 cups sifted powdered sugar

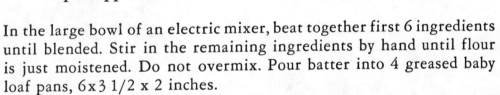

Combine all the ingredients until blended. Will yield enough glaze to top 4 baby loaves.

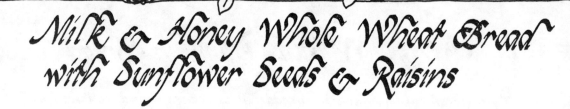

Milk & Honey Whole Wheat Bread with Sunflower Seeds & Raisins

This is an exceptionally easy bread that is filled with all kinds of good things that are considered "good for you," too. Whole wheat flour, oranges, honey, sunflower seeds and raisins all put together, produces a rather delicious loaf.

Liquid Mixture:
1 1/2 cups milk
   2 tablespoons lemon juice
  1/2 orange, grated. Remove any large pieces of membrane.
    1 egg, beaten
   2 tablespoons honey

Dry Mixture:
1 1/2 cups whole wheat flour
1 1/2 cups all-purpose flour
  3/4 cup brown sugar
   2 teaspoons baking powder
   1 teaspoon baking soda

1/2 cup toasted sunflower seeds
1/2 cup raisins

Place all the liquid ingredients in one bowl and stir until blended. Place all the dry ingredients into another bowl and toss to combine. Combine the two mixtures and stir until the dry ingredients are moistened. Do not leave lumpy and do not overmix. About 30 seconds of stirring should do it. Stir in the sunflower seeds and raisins.

Pour batter into a 1 1/2-quart souffle dish that has been greased and floured. Bake in a 350° oven for about 50 minutes or until the top is a lovely golden brown and a cake tester inserted in center comes out clean. Top will crack; this is normal. Serve with Sweet Whipped Butter and Honey. Yields one 7-inch round loaf.

Old~Fashioned Tea Bread with Walnuts & Raisins

1 egg
1 1/2 cups milk
2 tablespoons melted butter

3 cups flour
3 teaspoons baking powder
1/2 teaspoon salt
1 cup sugar

1 cup chopped walnuts
1/2 cup raisins

Beat together egg, milk and butter. Stir in the dry ingredients only until they are moistened. Stir in the nuts and raisins. Pour mixture into a 9x5x3-inch loaf pan that has been greased and floured.

Bake in a 350° oven for about 50 minutes to 1 hour or until a cake tester inserted in center comes out clean. Yields 1 loaf.

Date Bread with Orange & Walnuts

2 eggs
3/4 cup orange juice
4 tablespoons melted butter
1 teaspoon vanilla

1 3/4 cups flour
2 teaspoons baking powder
1/4 teaspoon salt
1/4 teaspoon baking soda
3/4 cup sugar

1 cup chopped dates
3/4 cup chopped walnuts

Beat together first 4 ingredients until blended. Add the dry ingredients all at once and stir until they are just moistened. Stir in the dates and nuts. Pour mixture into an 8x4x3-inch pan that has been greased and floured.

Bake in a 350° oven for about 50 minutes to 1 hour or until a cake tester inserted in center comes out clean. Cool in pan for 10 minutes and then remove pan and cool bread on rack. Yields 1 loaf.

Pumpkin Muffins
with Orange, Walnuts & Raisins

    1 1/4 cups flour
    1 1/4 cups sugar
        2 teaspoons baking powder
    1/4 teaspoon salt
    1 1/2 teaspoons pumpkin pie spice

        2 eggs
    1/2 cup butter, softened
        1 teaspoon vanilla
        1 cup sour cream
        1 cup canned pumpkin
    1/2 orange, grated. Remove any large pieces of membrane.

        1 cup chopped walnuts
        1 cup golden raisins

Combine flour, sugar, baking powder, salt and spice. Beat together eggs, butter, vanilla, sour cream, pumpkin and grated orange. Combine egg mixture and dry ingredients and stir only until blended. Stir in nuts and raisins.

Divide mixture between 24 paper-lined muffin cups. Bake in a 400° oven for 30 minutes or until a cake tester inserted in center comes out clean. Serve warm with sweet butter. Yields 24 medium muffins.

Sweet Whipped Butter & Honey

    1/2 cup butter, (1 stick)
    1/4 cup honey
        1 tablespoon frozen orange juice concentrate

Beat butter until light and fluffy. Beat in remaining ingredients until blended. Place butter into a pretty bowl and refrigerate until serving time. Remove from the refrigerator 10 minutes before serving. Yields 3/4 cup butter.

Sour Cream Muffins with Apples & Oranges

Want to start a legend at your house? Then try these delectable morsels some Sunday night, with honey-glazed chicken. Serve them warm with sweet whipped butter and listen to the musical m-m-m's with gladness.

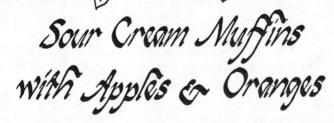

1/4 cup butter
1 cup sugar
2 eggs

3/4 cup sour cream
1 teaspoon vanilla

1 3/4 cups flour
2 teaspoons baking powder
pinch of salt

1 apple, peeled, cored and grated
1/2 orange, grated. Use peel, fruit and juice. Remove any large pieces of membrane.
cinnamon sugar

Beat butter and sugar until blended. Beat in eggs, sour cream and vanilla until blended.

Combine the flour, baking powder and salt and add to the egg mixture all at once. Stir by hand just until moistened. Do not beat or overmix. Leave a few lumps. Stir in the apples and orange just until mixed through.

Divide mixture between 18 paper-lined muffin cups (these will be about 2/3 full) and sprinkle top with 2 shakes of cinnamon sugar.

Bake in a 400° oven for 25 minutes or until a cake tester inserted in center comes out clean. Serve with creamy butter. Yields 18 muffins.

Note: – Muffins can be frozen.

If you are planning a backyard picnic or a barbecue, garlic breads are a perfect accompaniment to so many of the traditional alfresco dishes. There are an infinite variety of spreads so pick one that best compliments your meal.

French Bread with Garlic & Cheese

1 loaf crusty French bread, cut in half lengthwise
1 cup mayonnaise
2 cloves garlic, put through a press
3/4 cup grated Parmesan cheese
    paprika

Combine mayonnaise, garlic and grated cheese and spread mixture on cut sides of French bread. Sprinkle tops with paprika. Cut slices into bread about 2/3 through. Wrap each half in foil and heat in a 400° oven about 15 minutes or until heated through. Serves 6.

Herbed French Bread with Garlic & Cheese

1 loaf French bread, cut in half lengthwise
1/2 cup olive oil
2 cloves garlic, put through a press
1 tablespoon minced parsley
1 teaspoon Italian herb seasoning
1 cup grated Parmesan cheese
    paprika

Combine oil, garlic, parsley, Italian seasoning and brush mixture on cut sides of French bread. Cut slices into bread about 2/3 through. Sprinkle top with grated cheese and paprika. Broil for a few minutes until top is lightly browned and cheese is bubbly. Serves 6.

Hors D'Oeuvres & Small Entrees

Roulade Souffle with Creamed Crabmeat

Souffle Roll:

    4 tablespoons butter
1/2 cup flour
1 1/2 cups milk
1/2 cup cream
    1 teaspoon sugar

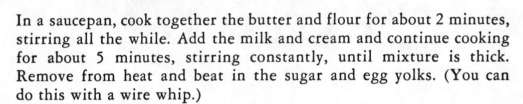

    4 egg yolks
4 egg whites, beaten stiff but not dry
1 tablespoon grated Parmesan cheese

In a saucepan, cook together the butter and flour for about 2 minutes, stirring all the while. Add the milk and cream and continue cooking for about 5 minutes, stirring constantly, until mixture is thick. Remove from heat and beat in the sugar and egg yolks. (You can do this with a wire whip.)

Gently fold in the beaten egg whites. Butter a 10x15-inch jellyroll pan. Line it with wax paper extended 2 inches longer on each end. Butter the wax paper. Spread batter evenly in prepared pan and bake it in a 350° oven for 35 to 40 minutes or until top is golden and souffle is set. Sprinkle top of souffle roll with the grated Parmesan cheese.

Invert pan onto overlapping strips of wax paper that are about 18 inches long. Carefully remove the baking paper. Spread top with Creamed Crabmeat Filling and carefully roll it up, lifting the wax paper to help you.

Place filled souffle on a lovely porcelain server, seam side down, and refrigerate. Garnish with lemon and green onion frills. Slice at the table and serve 10 or 12 as an hors d'oeuvre.

Creamed Crabmeat, Green Onions & Lemon

    1 package (8 ounces) cream cheese
1/3 cup chopped green onions
1/2 cup sour cream
    2 tablespoons lemon juice
1/2 pound crabmeat, picked over for bones and flaked

Beat cream cheese until light and fluffy. Stir in the remaining ingredients until blended.

Gateau Soufflé with Creamed Spinach, Bacon & Cheese

When you serve this incredible dish, get ready for applause and cries of "bravo." This delicate, light as air, soufflé gateau, is filled with the flavors of cream cheese, bacon, onions and cheese. It is sparkled with herbs and spice and "everything nice."

1 10 x 15-inch baked Souffle Roll

Spinach, Bacon and Cheese Filling:
2 packages (10 ounces, each) frozen chopped spinach, defrosted and drained dry
1/2 cup finely chopped green onions
2 packages (3 ounces, each) cream cheese with chives, softened
1/4 teaspoon poultry seasoning, or more to taste
    pinch of thyme
12 slices bacon, cooked crisp, drained and crumbled
1/2 cup grated Parmesan cheese
1/2 cup grated Swiss cheese
    salt and pepper to taste

Prepare Souffle Roll and invert on overlapping strips of wax paper. Carefully remove the baking paper and cut souffle into thirds, crosswise. Each third should measure about 5x10-inches.

Beat together the filling ingredients until nicely blended. Layer souffle and 1/2 the spinach mixture between each layer. Sprinkle top with a little grated Parmesan cheese. Place gateau on a lovely porcelain baker and heat in a 350° oven for about 15 to 20 minutes or until just heated through. Cut into slices and serve 6 as a small entree or for lunch.

Note: – Entire dish can be assembled 1 day earlier and stored in the refrigerator. Remove from the refrigerator about 30 minutes before serving and heat as described above.
– Garnish top with a thin layer of sour cream and sprinkle with a sprinkling of finely chopped green onions.

Liver Pate Mousse with Garlic & Herbs

This is a very unusual pate and quite different in taste and "spirit." You will find that, in spite of the fact that it can be prepared easily and quickly, it is still very delicious. Using the prepared Boursin, Rondelet or similar type Cream Cheese with Herbs and Garlic reduces preparation time.

1 pound chicken livers, cleaned. Remove any membranes
    or connective tissues.
2 shallots, chopped
1 apple, peeled, cored and grated
4 tablespoons butter

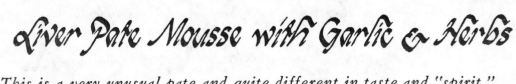

2 tablespoons Cognac

8 ounces Cream Cheese with Garlic and Herbs (see above)
    salt and pepper to taste

Saute livers, shallots and apple in butter until livers just lose their pinkness. Do not overcook. Heat Cognac in a brandy warmer, ignite and pour, carefully, over the livers. When the flames subside, place liver mixture in a processor or blender and puree until smooth. (If using a blender, you may have to add a little cream so that the blades do not jam.) Allow to cool a little.

Blend in the Cream Cheese with Garlic and Herbs and salt and pepper to taste, until mixture is thoroughly combined. Place pate in lovely ramekins or crocks. Brush tops with melted butter and refrigerate. Remove from the refrigerator about 15 minutes before serving. Serve with thin slices of French bread or a bland soda cracker.

Note: - Pate can be prepared 2 days before serving and stored in the refrigerator, tightly sealed with plastic wrap.
*   - Pate can be molded for a lovely effect. Line a 2-cup mold with plastic wrap. Place pate in mold and press in, to take the shape of the mold. Cover completely with plastic wrap. To unmold, remove plastic cover, invert on a serving dish, and remove plastic liner. Beautiful!*
*   - Do not freeze.*

Pate of Smoked Salmon with Chives & Dill

This lovely molded pate is always enjoyed by our friends. It is the essence of simplicity, can be prepared in advance and is really quite versatile. Serve it with crackers (I prefer a soda cracker) or black bread or miniature bagels.

    1 pound cream cheese
1/3 cup sour cream
1/4 pound smoked salmon, cut into 1-inch pieces
    1 tablespoon lemon juice or more to taste
1/8 cup chopped chives (or 1 tablespoon dried chives)
1/4 teaspoon dried dill weed

In a mixer or food processor, beat cream cheese and sour cream until light and fluffy. Add salmon and lemon juice and beat until salmon is nicely incorporated. Do not puree the salmon, but rather leave mixture flecked. Beat in chives and dill weed.

Lay a piece of plastic wrap (twice the length of the mold) into a lovely 1-quart mold (one without a hole in the center. This will enable you to remove the pate without any fuss at all.)

Place salmon in lined mold and press it down to conform to the shape of the design. Cover mold with the overlapping plastic wrap and refrigerate it until serving time.

To serve, remove overlapping plastic wrap, invert mold on a beautiful serving platter and carefully peel off the plastic wrap. Decorate platter with lots of parsley, cherry tomatoes and lemon slices. Serve with soda crackers or thin slices of black pumpernickel. Miniature bagels are also lovely. Yields about 3 cups pate.

*Note: - Entire dish can be prepared 1 day earlier and stored in the
          refrigerator.
        - Do not freeze.*

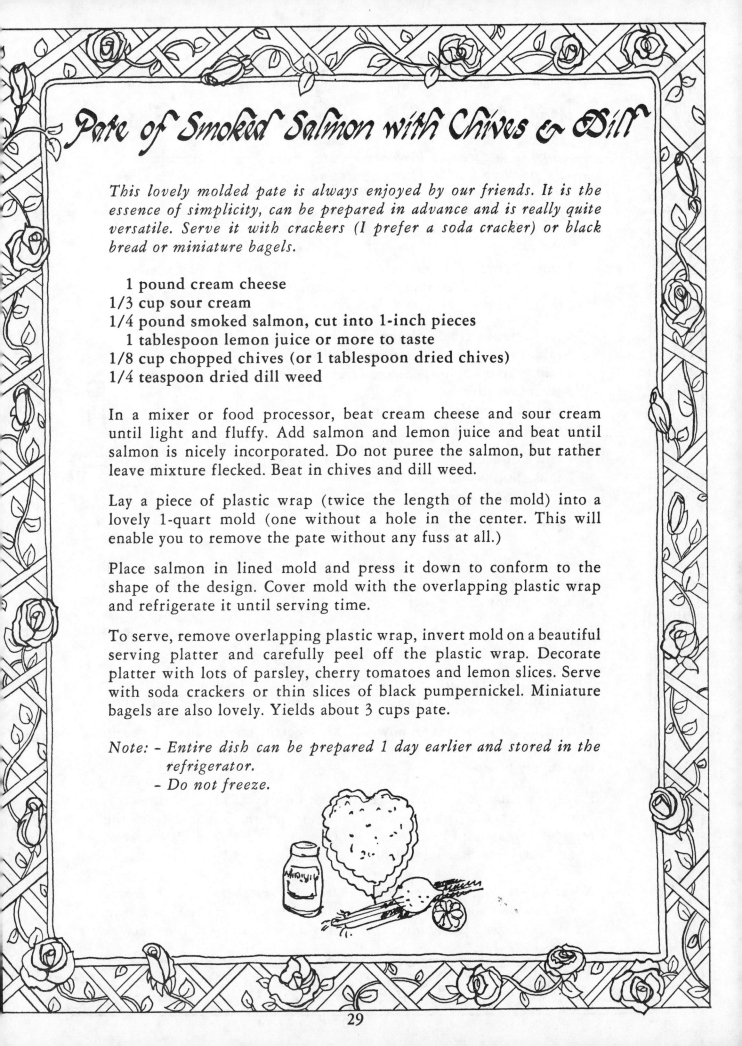

Pate Mousseline with Butter & Brandy

One of the differences between a pate and a pate mousseline is that a pate is sliced and a pate mousseline is spread. The mousseline is also very smooth and especially creamy with the addition of the whipped butter. This is an exceptionally delicious pate mousseline, sparkled as it is, with herbs and butter and brandy.

1 pound chicken livers, cleaned and cut into 1/2-inch pieces.
   Remove all connective membranes. Salt and pepper
   to taste.

4 tablespoons finely chopped onions
4 tablespoons finely chopped shallots
2/3 cup grated apple (peeled and cored) (about 1 1/2 apples)
1/4 teaspoon thyme
1/8 teaspoon poultry seasoning
1/4 cup (1/2 stick) butter

1/4 cup Cognac
   2 tablespoons sour cream
   2 tablespoons cream

3/4 cup (1 1/2 sticks) butter, softened

In a large skillet, saute together livers, onions, shallots, apples, and herbs in 1/4 cup butter. Saute until livers lose their pinkness and onions and apples are soft.

In a brandy warmer, heat the cognac, ignite it and carefully pour it over the liver mixture. Wait until the flames subside.

In a food processor or blender, puree the liver mixture with the sour cream and cream until the mixture is very smooth. Allow to cool.

Meanwhile, in the large bowl of an electric mixer, beat 3/4 cup butter until light and creamy. Add the pureed livers and beat until thoroughly blended.

Place pate mousseline in a large crock or in several smaller ramekins. Cover tightly with plastic wrap and refrigerate. Remove from the refrigerator about 15 minutes before serving. Serve with crackers, wafer-thin black bread or thinly sliced French bread.

Note: – Pate Mousseline can be frozen. In this case, I would recommend that you baste the top with melted butter to prevent darkening. Allow to defrost in the refrigerator overnight.

Country Beef & Pork Pate

(Pate de Campagne)

The difference between a pate and a meat loaf is panache — a dash of flair and style. Serve this with a glass of wine, some crusty French bread, several different mustards and those marvelous little pickles called cornichons. Keep a book of verse close by ... this is the stuff poetry is made of. Forget about the kids for this one. Pates are not for children. However, hopefully, they might enjoy this pate, for I have not used any livers.

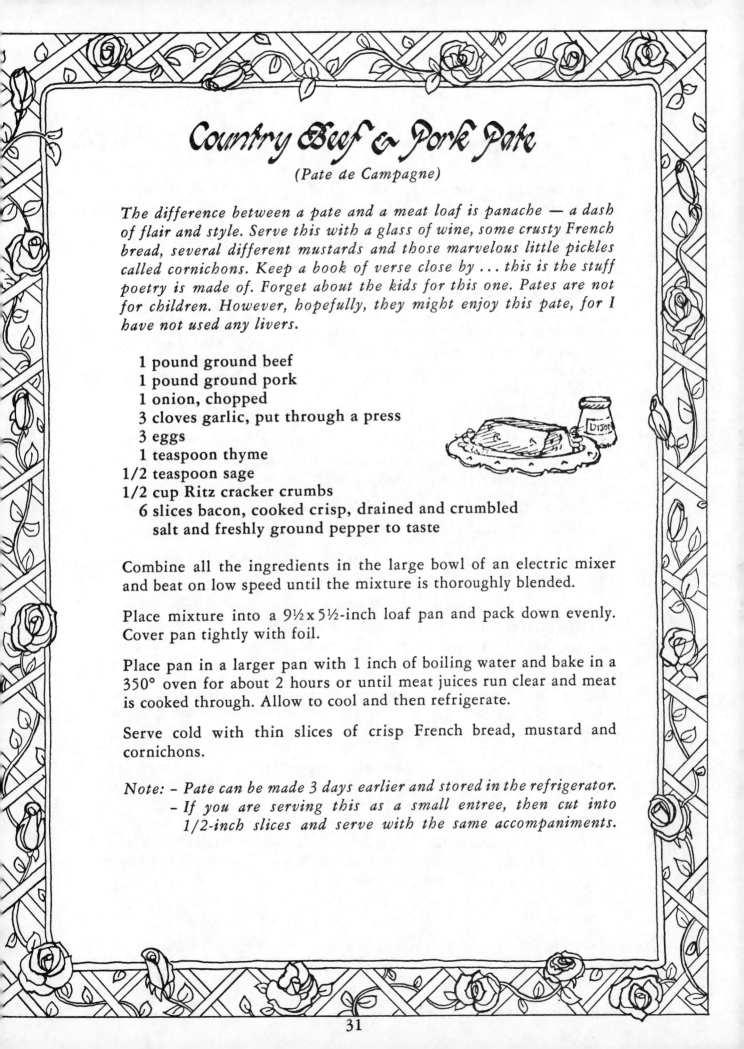

      1 pound ground beef
      1 pound ground pork
      1 onion, chopped
      3 cloves garlic, put through a press
      3 eggs
      1 teaspoon thyme
  1/2 teaspoon sage
  1/2 cup Ritz cracker crumbs
      6 slices bacon, cooked crisp, drained and crumbled
         salt and freshly ground pepper to taste

Combine all the ingredients in the large bowl of an electric mixer and beat on low speed until the mixture is thoroughly blended.

Place mixture into a 9½ x 5½-inch loaf pan and pack down evenly. Cover pan tightly with foil.

Place pan in a larger pan with 1 inch of boiling water and bake in a 350° oven for about 2 hours or until meat juices run clear and meat is cooked through. Allow to cool and then refrigerate.

Serve cold with thin slices of crisp French bread, mustard and cornichons.

Note: - Pate can be made 3 days earlier and stored in the refrigerator.
*   - If you are serving this as a small entree, then cut into 1/2-inch slices and serve with the same accompaniments.*

Pate Mousse with Chicken & Creme Fraiche

This exceedingly simple pate is incredibly light and cloud-like. It serves in elegant style and has a delicate and subtle taste.

3/4 pound boned chicken breasts, cut into 1-inch pieces
   2 tablespoons butter

   2 green onions, chopped
   2 shallots, chopped
   2 cloves garlic, chopped
      salt and white pepper to taste
   2 eggs
1/2 cup cream
1/2 cup sour cream

In a skillet, heat butter until sizzling hot, but not brown, and add chicken, onions, shallots, garlic and seasonings. Saute chicken for about 5 minutes or until cooked through. Do not overcook.

Place chicken mixture in a food processor bowl and process until chicken is a paste. Add eggs and blend.

Meanwhile, stir together cream and sour cream until blended. Add to processor bowl and blend.

Place mixture into an 8 x 4-inch buttered glass loaf pan and spread evenly. Cover with foil and place in a larger pan with 1-inch hot water. Bake in a 350° oven for about 55 minutes or until mousse is firm. Allow to cool.

Loosen sides, remove mousse on platter and refrigerate until ready to serve. Decorate top with Creme Fraiche with Green Onions. Serve with a delicate soda cracker.

Creme Fraiche with Lemon and Green Onions: Stir together 3 tablespoons cream, 3 tablespoons sour cream, 2 teaspoons lemon juice and 2 teaspoons chopped green onions until blended.

Note: – Pate Mousse can be prepared 1 day earlier and stored in the refrigerator. Spread top with Creme Fraiche with Lemon and Green Onions just before serving.

Chicken Pate Mousseline with Cream Cheese & Chives

        2 tablespoons butter
    3/4 pound boned chicken breasts, cut into 1-inch pieces
        3 shallots, chopped
        1 clove garlic, chopped
    1/4 teaspoon poultry seasoning
            pinch of thyme
            salt to taste

        2 packages (3 ounces, each) cream cheese with chives
    1/4 cup (1/2 stick) butter
        3 tablespoons chopped green onions
        1 tablespoon parsley

In a skillet, heat butter until sizzling hot, but not brown, and add chicken, shallots and seasonings. Saute chicken until it is cooked through, tossing and turning. Do not overcook. This should not take more than 5 minutes.

Place chicken mixture into processor bowl and blend until chicken is a paste. Allow to cool a little.

In a mixer, beat together cream cheese, butter, green onions and parsley until blended. Add chicken and continue beating until mixture is blended.

Line a 2-cup mold with plastic wrap. (Use a mold without a hole in the center.) Place pate in mold and press it down evenly. Cover mold with plastic wrap and refrigerate until firm. (It is very easy to unmold with the plastic liner.) Mask top with Lemon Cream.

Serve with a bland soda cracker. Yields 2 cups of pate.

Lemon Cream: Stir together 1/4 cup sour cream, 1 teaspoon lemon juice and 1 teaspoon green onions.

Note: - Pate can be prepared 2 days earlier and stored in the refrigerator. Mask with Lemon Cream just before serving.

Shrimp Butter with Lemon & Chives

1/2 pound cooked baby shrimp
1/2 pound cream cheese, at room temperature
  6 tablespoons butter, at room temperature
  4 tablespoons lemon juice

  2 tablespoons chopped chives
1/8 teaspoon dried dill weed

In a food processor or blender, blend together shrimp, cream cheese, butter, lemon juice until mixture is nicely blended. Don't puree the shrimp, but it should be finely chopped.

Stir in chives and dill until blended. Place shrimp butter into a pretty crock or bowl and refrigerate until serving time. Serve with a bland soda cracker or thinly sliced black bread or French bread.

Note: – Shrimp Butter can be prepared 1 day earlier and stored in the refrigerator until serving time.

Egg Butter with Sour Cream & Caviar

8 hard cooked eggs, shelled
8 tablespoons butter, at room temperature
1 tablespoon chopped chives
1 tablespoon mayonnaise
  salt to taste

1 cup sour cream
2 tablespoons lemon juice
4 tablespoons chopped chives or finely chopped
    green onions

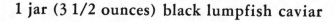

1 jar (3 1/2 ounces) black lumpfish caviar

In a blender or food processor combine eggs, butter, chives and mayonnaise and blend until mixture is nicely blended. Don't puree the eggs, but they should be finely chopped. Press mixture in a shallow glass serving bowl and spread evenly. Combine sour cream, lemon juice and chopped chives and spread over the eggs. Refrigerate until serving time. Just before serving, spoon the caviar decoratively over the sour cream. Do this carefully so as not to discolor the sour cream. Serve with crackers or thinly sliced rye bread.

Crabmeat Mousse Royale Mold with Lemon & Chives

Very delicate and delicious is this marvelous mousse that is literally fit for a king. Succulent crabmeat with sour cream, lemon, chives and a faint hint of Dijon mustard makes this dish an incredible hors d'oeuvre or small entree.

1 package (1 tablespoon) unflavored gelatin
1/4 cup cold water

2/3 cup mayonnaise, at room temperature
   4 tablespoons lemon juice
   2 green onions, finely chopped
   2 tablespoons finely chopped parsley
   4 tablespoons finely chopped chives
   2 teaspoons Dijon-style mustard
     salt and pepper to taste

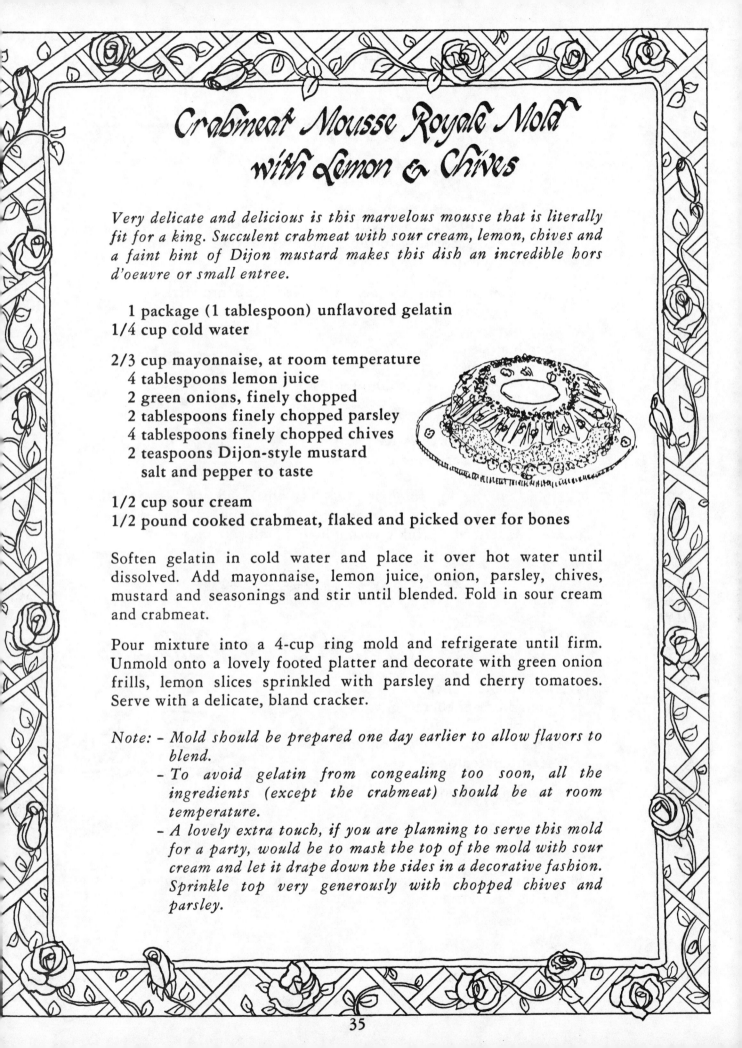

1/2 cup sour cream
1/2 pound cooked crabmeat, flaked and picked over for bones

Soften gelatin in cold water and place it over hot water until dissolved. Add mayonnaise, lemon juice, onion, parsley, chives, mustard and seasonings and stir until blended. Fold in sour cream and crabmeat.

Pour mixture into a 4-cup ring mold and refrigerate until firm. Unmold onto a lovely footed platter and decorate with green onion frills, lemon slices sprinkled with parsley and cherry tomatoes. Serve with a delicate, bland cracker.

Note: – Mold should be prepared one day earlier to allow flavors to blend.
*   – To avoid gelatin from congealing too soon, all the ingredients (except the crabmeat) should be at room temperature.*
*   – A lovely extra touch, if you are planning to serve this mold for a party, would be to mask the top of the mold with sour cream and let it drape down the sides in a decorative fashion. Sprinkle top very generously with chopped chives and parsley.*

Mushrooms & Artichokes Vinaigrette with Garlic & Dill

2 packages (10 ounces, each) frozen artichoke hearts,
    cooked according to the directions on the
    package until tender.

1 pound mushrooms, cleaned and dried. Cut into slices.
3 green onions, finely chopped
1/8 cup vinegar
1/4 cup lemon juice
1/2 cup salad oil
  2 cloves garlic, put through a press
1/4 teaspoon thyme
1/4 teaspoon dill
    salt and pepper to taste
1/4 cup grated Parmesan cheese

Combine all the ingredients in a glass bowl and stir. Cover bowl and refrigerate overnight. Remove vegetables with a slotted spoon to a bed of lettuce. Sprinkle with a little parsley. Serves 8.

Bleu Cheese Log with Toasted Almonds

1/2 pound Bleu Cheese
1/2 pound cream cheese
1/2 cup butter (1 stick)
  2 green onions, finely chopped
  1 teaspoon lemon juice

1/3 cup finely chopped toasted almonds

Allow ingredients to come to room temperature. Beat together all the ingredients, except the almonds, until mixture is blended.

Shape into a ball or a log and roll it in the chopped almonds. Wrap in plastic and refrigerate. Serve with a variety of crackers.

Mushrooms Stuffed with Crabmeat, Cheese & Chives

1 pound mushrooms, clean and remove stems. Brush
    mushrooms, inside and out, with melted butter.
1/2 pound crabmeat, pick over for bones
  3 packages (3 ounces, each) cream cheese with chives
1/2 cup grated Swiss cheese
1/3 cup garlic croutons, crushed into fine crumbs
  2 tablespoons finely chopped green onion

grated Parmesan cheese
paprika

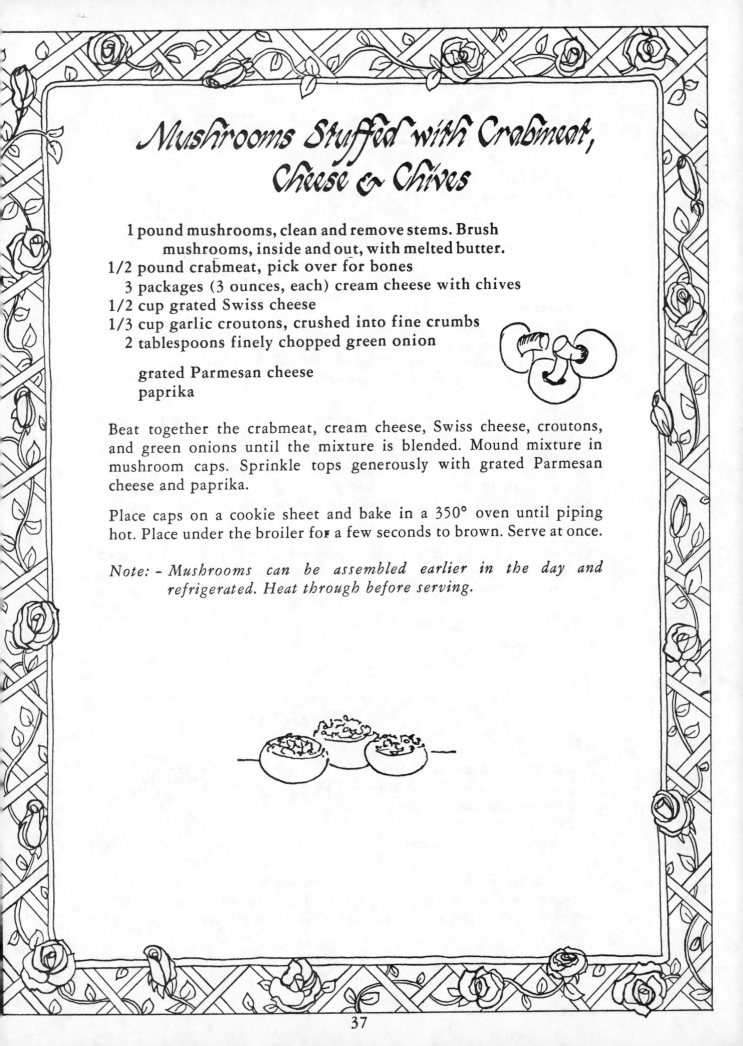

Beat together the crabmeat, cream cheese, Swiss cheese, croutons, and green onions until the mixture is blended. Mound mixture in mushroom caps. Sprinkle tops generously with grated Parmesan cheese and paprika.

Place caps on a cookie sheet and bake in a 350° oven until piping hot. Place under the broiler for a few seconds to brown. Serve at once.

Note: – Mushrooms can be assembled earlier in the day and refrigerated. Heat through before serving.

1 cup milk
4 tablespoons butter (1/2 stick)

1 cup flour
2 tablespoons chopped chives

4 eggs, at room temperature

1/2 teaspoon salt
1/8 teaspoon garlic powder
  4 tablespoons grated Parmesan cheese
  1 can (7 ounces) chopped clams, drained
      (reserve juice for another use)

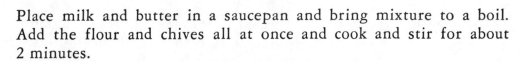

Place milk and butter in a saucepan and bring mixture to a boil. Add the flour and chives all at once and cook and stir for about 2 minutes.

Place dough in mixer bowl. Add eggs, one at a time, beating well after each addition. Beat in salt, garlic powder, cheese and clams until blended.

Drop batter by the spoonful into hot oil and fry until golden brown on both sides. Drain. Serve hot with Red Cocktail Sauce for dipping. Yields about 3 dozen small puffs.

Note: – Puffs can be prepared earlier in the day. Heat in a 375° oven until hot.

Red Cocktail Sauce

1/2 cup ketchup
1/2 cup chili sauce
  2 tablespoons prepared horseradish
  2 tablespoons lemon juice
  1 teaspoon chopped parsley
  1 teaspoon chopped chives

Combine all the ingredients and stir to blend. Place sauce in a glass serving bowl and refrigerate. Yields 1 1/4 cups sauce. Sauce can be prepared 1 or 2 days earlier and stored in the refrigerator.

Petite Ramekins with Cheese Souffle & Creamed Mushrooms & Herbs

Souffle Mixture:
  4 tablespoons butter
1/2 cup flour
  2 cups milk
  1 teaspoon sugar

  4 eggs
  1 cup grated Swiss cheese
    salt and pepper
    pinch of nutmeg

In a saucepan, cook together the butter and flour for about 3 minutes, stirring all the while. Add the milk and cook for about 5 minutes, stirring until mixture is thick. Remove from the heat and stir in sugar. Beat in eggs, one at a time, until thoroughly blended. Stir in cheese and seasonings.

Divide half the mixture between 8 ramekins that have been buttered. Divide the Creamed Mushroom and Herb Filling evenly between the ramekins. Cover the mushrooms with the remaining souffle mixture. Bake in a 400° oven for about 20 minutes or until top is golden brown and souffle have doubled in height. Serve at once. Serves 8.

Creamed Mushrooms & Herbs

  6 tablespoons butter
  1 onion, finely chopped
  1 pound mushrooms, thinly sliced
1/2 teaspoon thyme
1/4 teaspoon poultry seasoning
    salt and pepper to taste

  4 tablespoons flour
  1 cup cream
  1 cup sour cream

Saute onion and mushrooms in butter until onions are soft. Add seasonings and flour and cook for 3 minutes, stirring all the while. Add cream and sour cream and continue cooking and stirring until mixture has thickened.

Petite Cheddar Cheese Souffles in Ramekins

This is a lovely luncheon dish, light and very delicious. And this souffle is guaranteed not to make you nervous. There is no white sauce, no separating eggs, no beating the whites at the last minute. Just place all the ingredients in a blender or processor, let it run for about 1 minute and Voila! a beautiful souffle, light as air.

   5 eggs
   1 package (8 ounces) cream cheese
1/2 cup cream
1/4 pound Cheddar cheese, cut into cubes
1/2 cup grated Parmesan cheese
1/2 teaspoon curry powder
   salt and pepper to taste

Place eggs in blender container or processor bowl and blend for a few seconds. Now with the motor running, add the remaining ingredients in the order listed and blend for 10 seconds after the last addition.

Divide mixture evenly between 6 buttered ramekins and bake in a 375° oven for about 20 minutes or just until the center is set. Do not overbake. Serve at once. Serves 6.

Note: – Entire dish can be assembled earlier in the day and refrigerated. About 30 minutes before serving, remove from the refrigerator and let stand for 10 minutes. Then, bake as described above.

Piroshkis with Creamed Mushrooms & Herbs

Creamed Mushroom and Herb Filling:

4 tablespoons butter
1 large onion, finely chopped
1/2 pound mushrooms, finely chopped
2 teaspoons lemon juice
3 to 4 shakes garlic powder

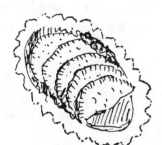

1/4 teaspoon poultry seasoning
1/8 teaspoon thyme flakes
　　salt and pepper to taste
2 tablespoons flour

1 cup sour cream
1/4 teaspoon dill weed

Saute onion in butter until onion is transparent. Add the mushrooms, lemon juice and garlic powder, and continue sauteing until mushrooms are tender and all the liquid is absorbed. Add seasonings and flour and cook and stir for 3 minutes. Add sour cream and dill and cook and stir for 2 minutes or until mixture is thickened and blended. Allow mixture to cool.

The Pastry:

1 package frozen patty shells, defrosted (6 shells)
1 egg, beaten
　　grated Parmesan cheese

On a floured pastry cloth, roll out each patty shell until dough is approximately 1/8-inch thick and dough measures about a 6-inch circle. Cut with a 2 3/4-inch cookie or biscuit cutter into 4 rounds. Roll out scrap to yield 1 more round. Continue with the remaining patty shells.

Place 1/2 teaspoon Mushroom Filling in center of each round, fold dough over and press edges down with the tines of a fork. Brush tops with beaten egg and sprinkle with grated cheese. Pierce tops with the tines of a fork.

Place piroshkis on a greased cookie sheet and bake at 400° for about 20 minutes. or until pastry is puffed and top is golden brown. Yields 30 piroshkis.

Petite Turnovers with Potatoes & Onions

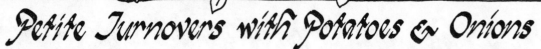

An excellent accompaniment to soup or salad and quite good for snacking, these delicious little pastries are a cross between the English Pastie and the Russian Piroges. Children seem to love these flaky "turnovers" and grownups do too.

Pastry:
  1 cup butter (2 sticks)
1/2 pound cream cheese
  2 cups flour
    pinch of salt

    beaten egg
    grated Parmesan cheese

In the large bowl of an electric mixer, cream together butter and cream cheese until blended. Add flour and salt and mix at low speed until the flour is incorporated and even. Place dough on floured waxed paper and sprinkle top with additional flour to make for easier handling. Shape into an 8-inch circle and wrap dough in the waxed paper and then foil. Refrigerate overnight.

Divide dough into four parts. Working one part at a time, roll it out on a floured pastry cloth until the dough is approximately 1/8-inch thick. Cut with a cookie or biscuit cutter into 2 3/4-inch rounds and accumulate scraps in the refrigerator to roll out at the end.

Place 1 teaspoon Potato Onion Filling on center of each round, moisten the edges and fold over. Press edges down with the tines of a fork. Brush tops with beaten egg and a dash of grated cheese.

Place turnovers on a buttered cookie sheet and bake at 350° for about 25 minutes or until tops are lightly browned. Yields about 50 turnovers.

Potato Onion Filling:
  2 large onions, finely chopped
1/4 cup butter
  2 cups mashed potatoes (can use instant mashed potatoes)
1/2 cup sour cream
  1 egg, beaten
    lots of salt and pepper

Saute onions in butter until onions are lightly browned. Mix in the remaining ingredients until blended. (Can be made earlier in the day and refrigerated.)

Stuffed Clams with Tomatoes & Onions & Cheese Crumbs

This is a delicious small entree, full of flavor and taste. It serves beautifully in clam shells and is very satisfying. It is an excellent beginning to a country French dinner and I hope you enjoy it.

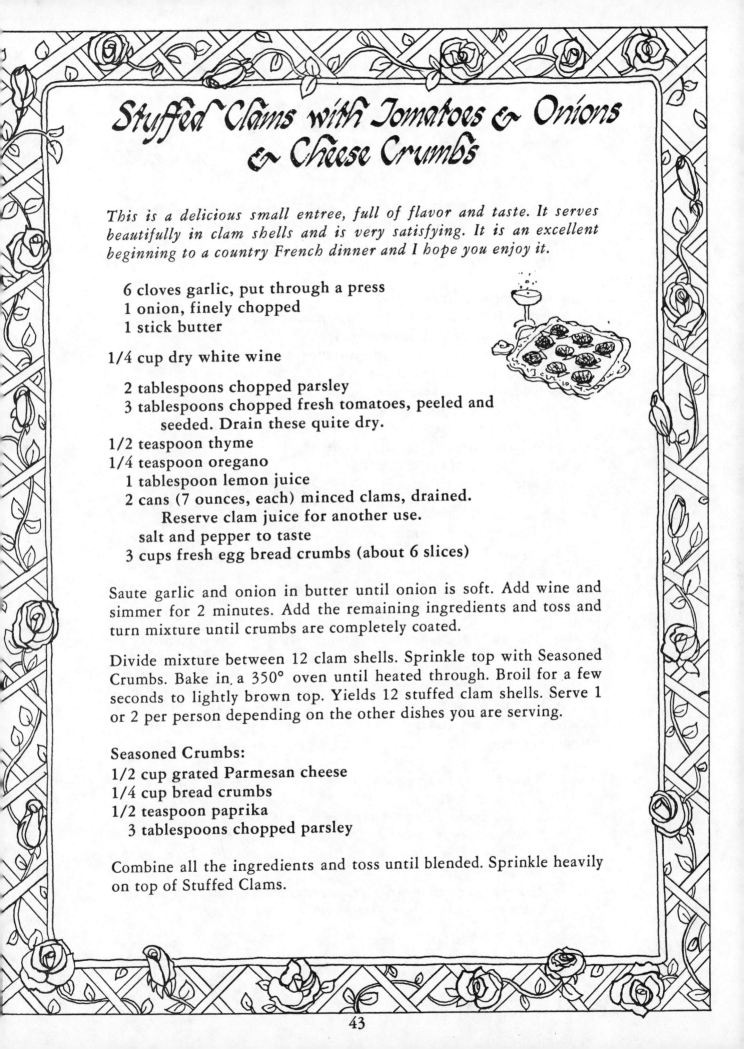

6 cloves garlic, put through a press
1 onion, finely chopped
1 stick butter

1/4 cup dry white wine

2 tablespoons chopped parsley
3 tablespoons chopped fresh tomatoes, peeled and
    seeded. Drain these quite dry.
1/2 teaspoon thyme
1/4 teaspoon oregano
1 tablespoon lemon juice
2 cans (7 ounces, each) minced clams, drained.
    Reserve clam juice for another use.
salt and pepper to taste
3 cups fresh egg bread crumbs (about 6 slices)

Saute garlic and onion in butter until onion is soft. Add wine and simmer for 2 minutes. Add the remaining ingredients and toss and turn mixture until crumbs are completely coated.

Divide mixture between 12 clam shells. Sprinkle top with Seasoned Crumbs. Bake in a 350° oven until heated through. Broil for a few seconds to lightly brown top. Yields 12 stuffed clam shells. Serve 1 or 2 per person depending on the other dishes you are serving.

Seasoned Crumbs:
1/2 cup grated Parmesan cheese
1/4 cup bread crumbs
1/2 teaspoon paprika
    3 tablespoons chopped parsley

Combine all the ingredients and toss until blended. Sprinkle heavily on top of Stuffed Clams.

Scallop Shells filled with Shrimp, Spinach & Cheese

You will probably never find an easier or more glamorous hors d'oeuvre or small entree. This whips together in seconds and when you serve it, the oohs and aahs will amaze you. They'll never guess how easy it all was . . . unless you tell.

1/2 pound cooked little bay shrimp
  1 package (10 ounces) frozen spinach, thawed and placed
      in a strainer and drained dry
  4 ounces cream cheese, at room temperature*
  2 tablespoons chopped chives
1/4 teaspoon poultry seasoning
  2 tablespoons chopped parsley
  1 egg, slightly beaten
  4 tablespoons grated Parmesan cheese
  6 tablespoons cracker crumbs
  salt and pepper to taste

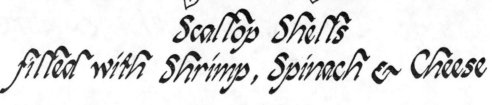

1/2 cup grated Parmesan cheese
1/2 cup Ritz cracker crumbs
  3 tablespoons melted butter

Stir together the first 10 ingredients until mixture is thoroughly blended.

Divide the filling between 6 scallop shells. Toss together the Parmesan, crumbs and butter and sprinkle tops with this mixture.

Place scallop shells on a cookie sheet and heat in a 350° oven until piping hot. You can broil the tops for a few seconds to brown, but watch carefully that you don't overdo it. Serves 6 as an hors d'oeuvre or small entree.

Note: – Entire recipe can be assembled earlier in the day and heated at time of serving.
    – Do not make a day earlier and do not freeze.
    – You can substitute 2 cans (7 ounces, each) of drained chopped clams for the shrimp. It is totally different but also, very good.
    * You can use the prepared cream cheese and chives and make this even easier. Omit the chopped chives.

Herbed Clams Filled
with Buttered Crumbs & Garlic

This is an incredibly easy and marvelous hors d'oeuvre. Served in individual clam shells makes it dramatic and enticing. Not the least of its virtues, it can be made a day earlier and can also be frozen.

1/2 cup (1 stick) butter
   6 cloves garlic, mashed or put through a press
   1 teaspoon Italian Herb Seasoning
   2 tablespoons chopped parsley (or 2 teaspoons parsley flakes)
   2 tablespoons dried onion flakes

   6 tablespoons dry white wine
   1 teaspoon paprika
1/4 cup grated Parmesan cheese
   1 tablespoon lemon juice

   3 cups fresh bread crumbs (about 6 slices fresh bread
      put into a blender or food processor)
   2 cans (7 ounces) chopped clams, drained; reserve clam juice

In a skillet, place first 5 ingredients and heat until butter is melted. Add the wine and cook mixture for about 2 minutes at a slow bubble. Wine will have evaporated. Add the remaining ingredients and turn and toss until the crumbs are well coated and mixture is blended. (You may have to add a little of the clam juice to bind the crumbs. Be sparing with this so that the crumbs do not get mushy. Fresh bread crumbs need less liquid than stale crumbs.)

Divide mixture between 12 medium clam shells. Sprinkle tops with a little paprika, parsley and a pinch of grated Parmesan. Heat in a 350° oven until piping hot. This will yield 12 stuffed shells. While one is adequate, they are so delicious that most people could easily handle 2, per serving.

Note: - If you freeze these, then allow them to defrost in the refrigerator overnight. Heat in a 350° oven until hot.
       - These can be made a day earlier and stored in the refrigerator.

Stuffed Clams with Spinach, Mushrooms & Herbed Sour Cream

Lovely, exciting and very delicious are these scallop shells filled with spinach, mushrooms, sour cream and herbs. The delicate sprinkling of cheese crumbs on top adds a delightful touch that I hope you enjoy.

2 packages frozen spinach (10 ounces, each) defrosted
    and drained and pressed dry

1/2 pound mushrooms, cleaned and sliced
1 onion, finely chopped
4 tablespoons butter

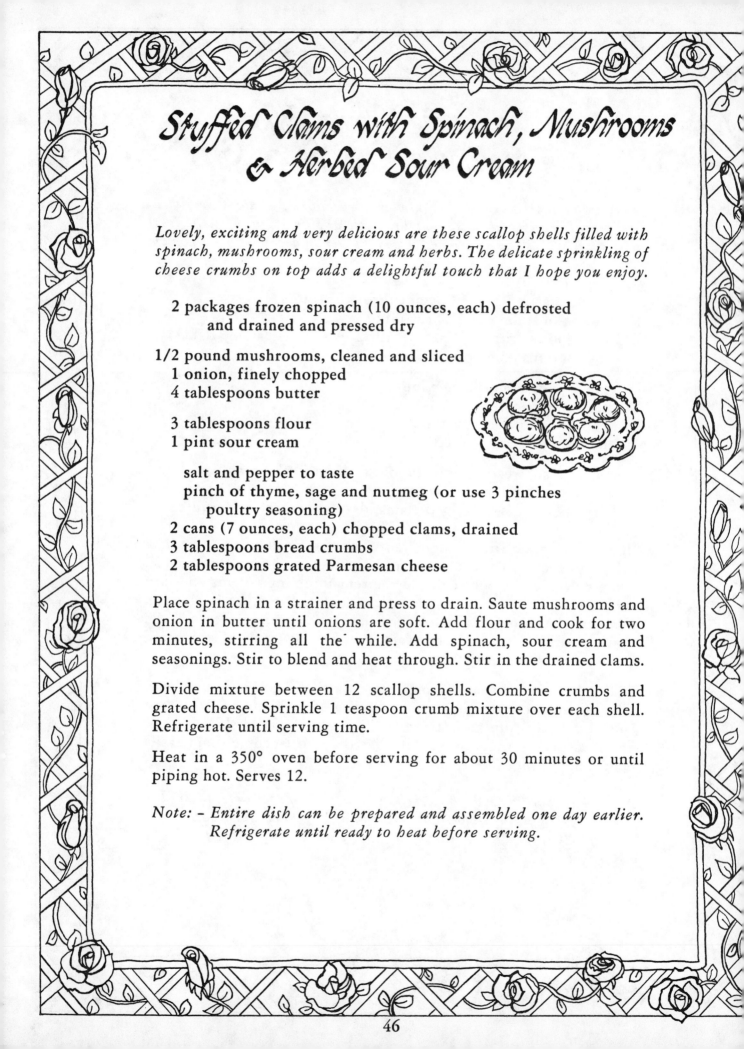

3 tablespoons flour
1 pint sour cream

salt and pepper to taste
pinch of thyme, sage and nutmeg (or use 3 pinches
    poultry seasoning)
2 cans (7 ounces, each) chopped clams, drained
3 tablespoons bread crumbs
2 tablespoons grated Parmesan cheese

Place spinach in a strainer and press to drain. Saute mushrooms and onion in butter until onions are soft. Add flour and cook for two minutes, stirring all the while. Add spinach, sour cream and seasonings. Stir to blend and heat through. Stir in the drained clams.

Divide mixture between 12 scallop shells. Combine crumbs and grated cheese. Sprinkle 1 teaspoon crumb mixture over each shell. Refrigerate until serving time.

Heat in a 350° oven before serving for about 30 minutes or until piping hot. Serves 12.

Note: – Entire dish can be prepared and assembled one day earlier. Refrigerate until ready to heat before serving.

Roulades of Mushrooms with Cream & Herbs

This is a very simple and interesting casing for hors d'oeuvres. By buttering the rolled bread slices, it forms a crisp and savory covering for an incredible number of fillings. And the finished product very much looks and tastes like it was encased in dough.

15 slices white bread. Cut away the crusts, and roll bread
      flat with a rolling pin. Brush tops with melted butter.

1/2 pound mushrooms, cleaned and thinly sliced
    1 tablespoon lemon juice
    2 tablespoons butter

    2 tablespoons flour
1/8 teaspoon poultry seasoning
    pinch of thyme
    salt and pepper to taste

3/4 cup sour cream
    melted butter

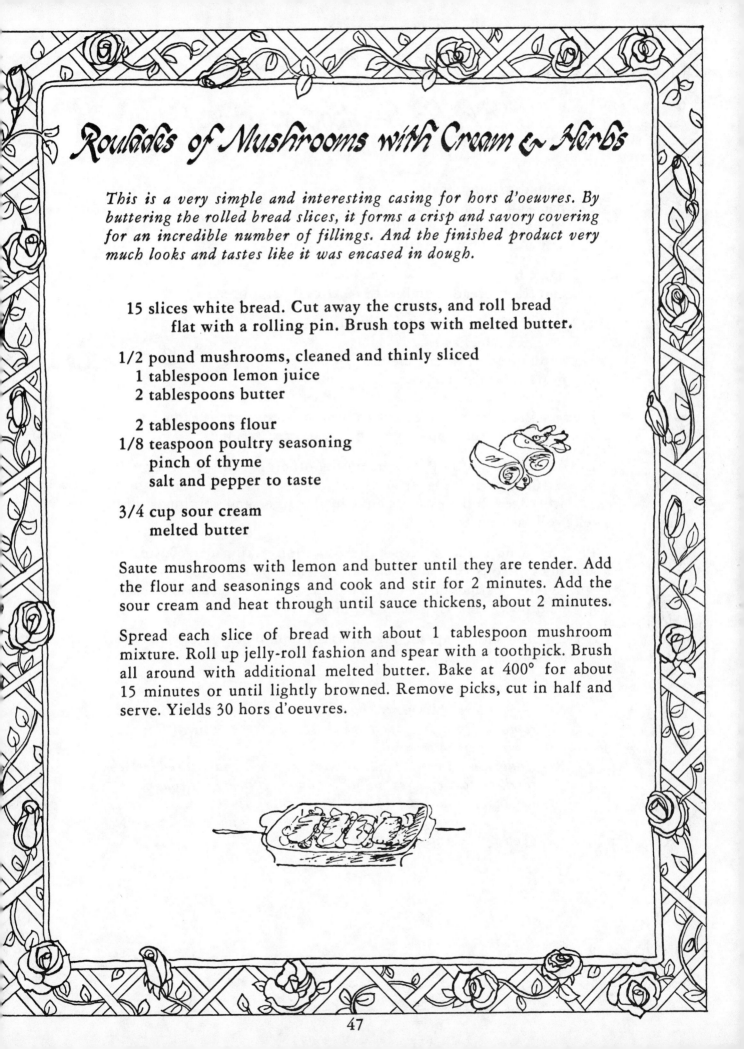

Saute mushrooms with lemon and butter until they are tender. Add the flour and seasonings and cook and stir for 2 minutes. Add the sour cream and heat through until sauce thickens, about 2 minutes.

Spread each slice of bread with about 1 tablespoon mushroom mixture. Roll up jelly-roll fashion and spear with a toothpick. Brush all around with additional melted butter. Bake at 400° for about 15 minutes or until lightly browned. Remove picks, cut in half and serve. Yields 30 hors d'oeuvres.

Phyllo Roulade de Boeuf

(Beef Roll in Phyllo Pastry)

1 pound ground beef
2/3 package dried onion soup
3 to 4 shakes garlic powder
   salt and pepper to taste

2 eggs, beaten
1/2 cup fresh bread crumbs (1 1/2 slices) (egg bread)

1/2 pound phyllo leaves (approx. 14 leaves,
     11 x 14-inches ea.)
1/2 cup butter, (1 stick) melted
   grated Parmesan cheese

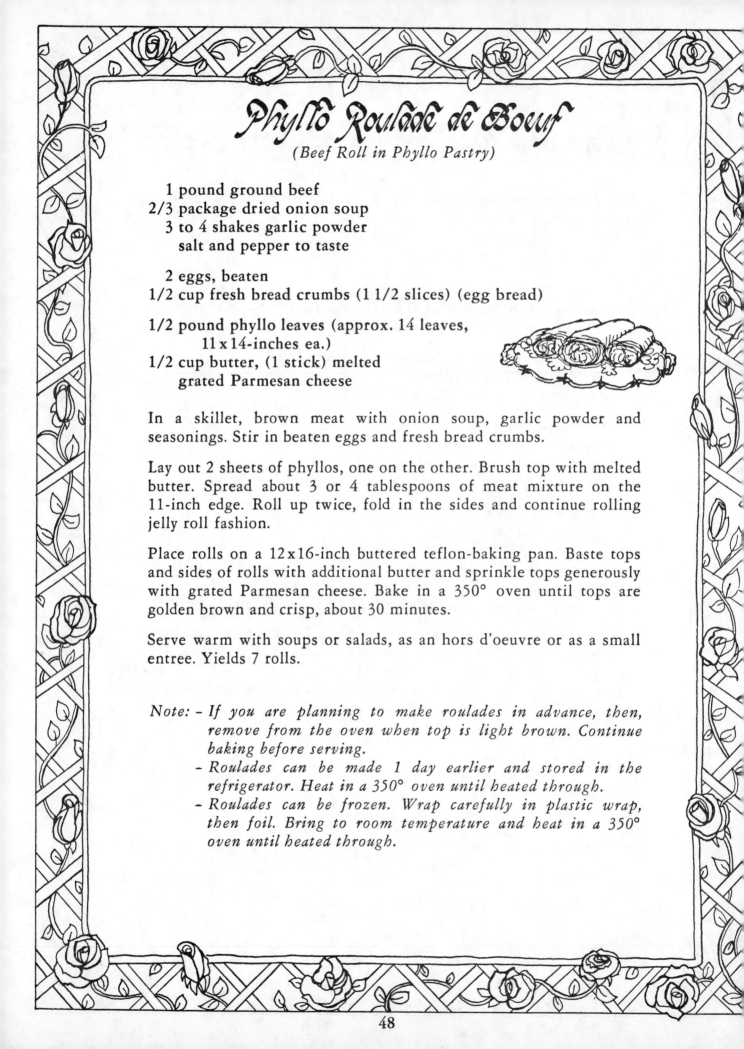

In a skillet, brown meat with onion soup, garlic powder and seasonings. Stir in beaten eggs and fresh bread crumbs.

Lay out 2 sheets of phyllos, one on the other. Brush top with melted butter. Spread about 3 or 4 tablespoons of meat mixture on the 11-inch edge. Roll up twice, fold in the sides and continue rolling jelly roll fashion.

Place rolls on a 12 x 16-inch buttered teflon-baking pan. Baste tops and sides of rolls with additional butter and sprinkle tops generously with grated Parmesan cheese. Bake in a 350° oven until tops are golden brown and crisp, about 30 minutes.

Serve warm with soups or salads, as an hors d'oeuvre or as a small entree. Yields 7 rolls.

Note: – If you are planning to make roulades in advance, then, remove from the oven when top is light brown. Continue baking before serving.
*   – Roulades can be made 1 day earlier and stored in the refrigerator. Heat in a 350° oven until heated through.*
*   – Roulades can be frozen. Wrap carefully in plastic wrap, then foil. Bring to room temperature and heat in a 350° oven until heated through.*

Follow the instructions for the preceding recipe and use these as alternate fillings. Each recipe will fill 1/2 pound of phyllo leaves. All instructions remain the same, including baking time.

Phyllo Roulade de Epinard
(Spinach and Cheese Filling)

1 package (10 ounces) frozen spinach, defrosted
    and drained
1 cup cottage cheese
4 ounces cream cheese
2 eggs
1/2 cup grated Parmesan cheese
1/2 cup fresh bread crumbs
2 tablespoons chopped chives
    salt and pepper to taste

Combine all the ingredients in a bowl and stir until blended.

Phyllo Roulade de Fromage
(Cheese Filling)

1 cup cottage cheese
4 ounces cream cheese
1/4 cup bread crumbs
1 egg
1/3 cup grated Parmesan cheese
pinch of salt

Combine all the ingredients in a bowl and stir until blended.

Note: – Phyllos, filled and baked with the above fillings, can be frozen. Follow the instructions for freezing in the previous recipe.

French Chicken Pie with Mushrooms & Herbs

This serves as a giant sunflower with puff pastry petals and a filling that is sparkled with sour cream and herbs.

1 package frozen patty shells, (6 shells), defrosted
1 tablespoon water
3 tablespoons grated Parmesan cheese

On a floured surface, stack 3 patty shells and roll them out to measure about 9-inches round. Place on a greased cookie sheet. Place Chicken with Mushrooms and Herbs on pastry, leaving a one-inch border of dough without filling.

Stack and roll remaining shells in the same manner. Place pastry over the first shell. Press edges down with your fingers and with your index finger, shape the edge into one-inch petals. Brush top with water, sprinkle with cheese and pierce with the tines of a fork.

Bake in a 400° oven for about 30 minutes or until pastry is puffed and a beautiful deep golden brown. Serve in wedges with Poached Apples in Orange Butter Glaze on the side. Serves 6.

Creamed Chicken with Mushrooms & Herbs

1/4 pound mushrooms, cleaned and sliced
  2 tablespoons butter
  2 tablespoons minced onion
1/4 teaspoon thyme flakes
    pinch of poultry seasoning

  2 cups cooked chicken, cut into small dice
1/3 cup Ritz Cracker crumbs
  1 cup sour cream
    salt and pepper to taste

Saute first 5 ingredients together until mushrooms are tender. Stir in the remaining ingredients until blended.

Note: – Entire dish can be assembled a day earlier and refrigerated, unbaked.

Creamed Chicken Gruyere Puffed Pastry Pie

Exciting, delicious and very easy is this lovely dish of flaky pastry filled with a delicate blend of chicken, sour cream and Gruyere cheese.

1 package frozen patty shells (6 shells), thawed
1 egg, beaten
2 tablespoons grated Parmesan cheese

On a floured surface, stack 3 patty shells and roll out to measure about 8 or 9-inches round. Place on a lightly greased cookie sheet. Brush edges with beaten egg. Place Chicken Gruyere Filling on pastry, leaving a one-inch border of dough without filling.

Stack and roll remaining shells in the same manner. Place pastry over the first shell. Press edges down with the tines of a fork to seal. Scallop edges for a lovely touch if you have the time. Brush top with beaten egg and pierce with a fork. Sprinkle top with grated Parmesan cheese.

Bake in a 400° oven for 25 or 30 minutes or until pastry is puffed and top is a rich golden brown. Serve in wedges with fresh fruit or buttered vegetables. Serves 6.

Chicken Gruyere Filling

2 cups cooked chicken, cut into small dice
1 cup sour cream
1 cup grated Gruyere or Swiss cheese
1/4 cup chopped chives (or 2 tablespoons dried chives)
1 tablespoon lemon juice
salt and pepper to taste
1/4 teaspoon thyme

Combine all the ingredients and toss until blended.

Note: – Entire dish can be assembled a day earlier and refrigerated, unbaked. Add 5 minutes to baking time.
– You can substitute leftover turkey for the chicken.

51

Zucchini & Mushroom Quiche with Onions & Cheese

1 pound zucchini, unpeeled and cut into
    1/8-inch thick slices
1/2 pound mushrooms, cleaned and sliced
2 onions, finely chopped
2 cloves garlic, put through a press
1/4 cup butter (1/2 stick)

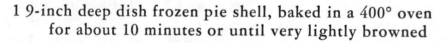

4 eggs
1 1/2 cups half and half
1 cup grated Swiss cheese
1/2 cup grated Parmesan cheese
salt and pepper to taste

1 9-inch deep dish frozen pie shell, baked in a 400° oven
    for about 10 minutes or until very lightly browned

Saute together first 5 ingredients until zucchini are tender and all of the liquid rendered has evaporated. Place mixture into prepared pie shell.

Beat together eggs, half and half, cheeses and seasonings until blended. Pour mixture into pie shell and distribute evenly.

Place quiche on a cookie sheet and bake in a 350° oven for 45 minutes or until custard is set and top is golden. Serves 6 as a small entree or for lunch.

Note: – This lovely quiche can be prepared in advance as follows. Shell can be baked and zucchini mixture cooked earlier in the day. Place zucchini mixture in shell and store in the refrigerator until ready to bake. Egg mixture can be beaten earlier in the day and stored in refrigerator. Just before ready to bake, pour egg mixture into the prepared shell and bake as directed above.

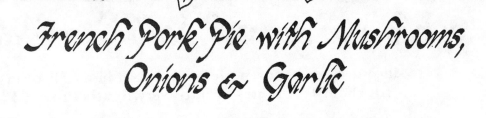

French Pork Pie with Mushrooms, Onions & Garlic

This is a delicious dish that is a hearty small entree and does well for lunch or supper. Serve it with warm poached fruit or a light salad. It can be baked earlier in the day and it can be frozen.

1 9-inch deep dish frozen pie shell, baked in a 400° oven
    for about 10 minutes or until very lightly browned

1 pound ground pork
1/2 pound mushrooms, cleaned and sliced
4 shallots, finely minced
1 large onion, finely chopped
2 cloves garlic, finely minced
2 tablespoons butter
   salt and pepper to taste

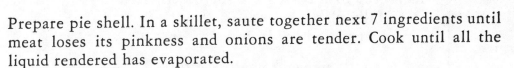

3 eggs
1 cup cream
1/2 cup grated Parmesan cheese
   salt and pepper to taste

Prepare pie shell. In a skillet, saute together next 7 ingredients until meat loses its pinkness and onions are tender. Cook until all the liquid rendered has evaporated.

Beat together eggs, cream, cheese and seasonings and stir in the meat mixture. Pour this into the prepared pie shell.

Place quiche on a cookie sheet and bake in a 350° oven for 45 minutes or until custard is set and top is golden. Serves 6 as a small entree or lunch.

Quiche with Spinach Soufflé & Cheese

1 9-inch deep dish frozen pie shell, baked in a 400° oven
for about 10 minutes or until very lightly browned

1 package (10 ounces) frozen chopped spinach, defrosted
1/2 cup cream cheese (4 ounces)
1/2 cup cream
2 eggs
1/3 cup fresh bread crumbs
1/2 cup grated Parmesan cheese
1/3 cup finely chopped green onions
pinch nutmeg
salt and pepper to taste

Prepare pie shell. Combine the remaining ingredients and beat until thoroughly blended.

Pour mixture into the prepared pie shell and place on a cookie sheet. Bake in a 350° oven for 45 minutes or until custard is set and top is golden. Serves 4 to 6.

French Tomato & Cheese Pie

1 9-inch deep dish frozen pie shell, defrosted.
Carefully place shell into a 10-inch
quiche pan and pat it down to fit.

1 can (1 pound) stewed tomatoes, drained
and finely chopped
1/4 pound mushrooms, thinly sliced
2 cups grated Swiss cheese (8 ounces)
1 tablespoon chopped parsley
1/4 teaspoon each basil and thyme
1/2 cup grated Parmesan cheese
anchovies, olives, onion rings or capers to taste

Bake pie shell in a 400° oven for about 10 minutes or until lightly browned. Combine the remaining ingredients (except the anchovies, etc.) and toss to mix well. Spread these evenly over the prepared shell. Place anchovies, olives (pitted), onion rings or capers to taste on top. Drizzle top with 2 teaspoons oil (optional, but very good).

Bake in a 350° oven until cheeses are melted and top is lightly browned, about 20 minutes. Serves 6.

Cottage Cheese Quiche with Eggplant & Swiss Cheese

1 9-inch deep dish frozen pie shell, baked in a 400° oven
    for about 10 minutes or until very lightly browned.

1 eggplant, peeled and cut into 1/4-inch thick slices
1 cup cottage cheese
1/2 cup cream cheese (4 ounces)
1 cup grated Swiss cheese
1/2 cup grated Parmesan cheese
3 eggs
1 cup cream
    salt and pepper to taste

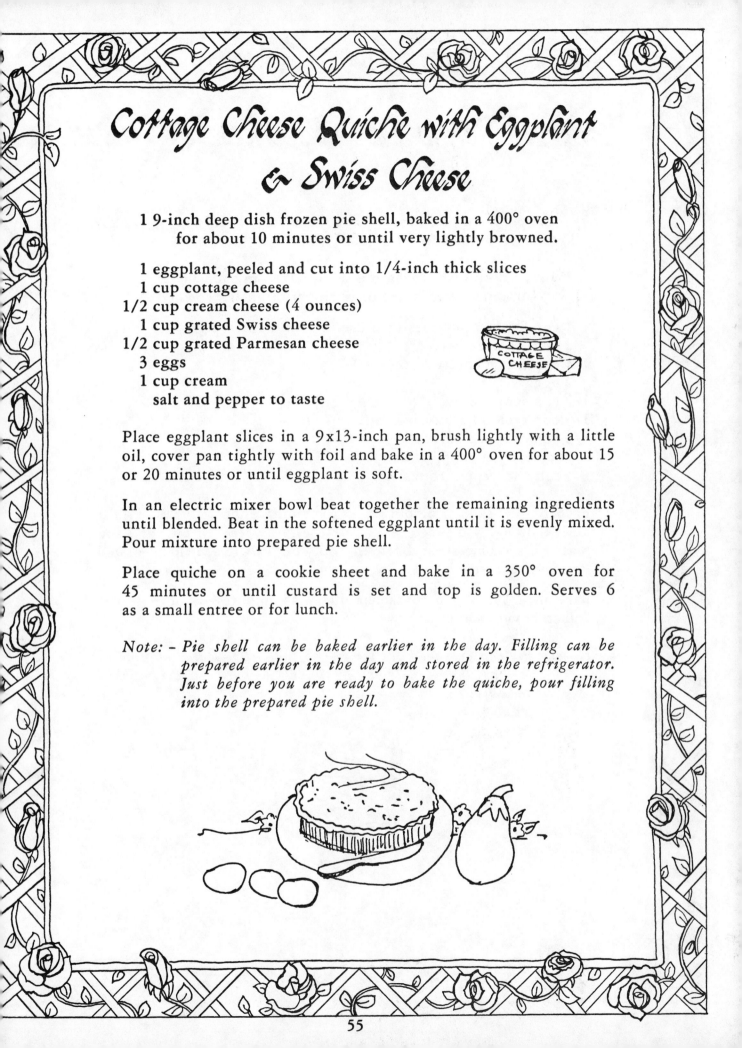

Place eggplant slices in a 9x13-inch pan, brush lightly with a little oil, cover pan tightly with foil and bake in a 400° oven for about 15 or 20 minutes or until eggplant is soft.

In an electric mixer bowl beat together the remaining ingredients until blended. Beat in the softened eggplant until it is evenly mixed. Pour mixture into prepared pie shell.

Place quiche on a cookie sheet and bake in a 350° oven for 45 minutes or until custard is set and top is golden. Serves 6 as a small entree or for lunch.

Note: – Pie shell can be baked earlier in the day. Filling can be prepared earlier in the day and stored in the refrigerator. Just before you are ready to bake the quiche, pour filling into the prepared pie shell.

French Potato Pie with Cheese & Chives

This simple little peasant dish is wholesome and very satisfying for a light lunch or supper.

    1 9-inch deep dish frozen pie shell, baked in a 400° oven
        for about 10 minutes or until very lightly browned

    1 cup mashed potatoes (can use instant mashed potatoes)
    2 cups cottage cheese
1/4 cup cream cheese (2 ounces)
    2 eggs
1/2 cup sour cream
1/3 cup grated Parmesan cheese
1/3 cup chopped chives
    1 tablespoon chopped parsley
      salt and pepper to taste

Prepare pie shell. Combine the remaining ingredients and beat until thoroughly blended. Pour mixture into prepared pie shell and place on a cookie sheet. Sprinkle top with a little additional grated Parmesan cheese.

Bake in a 350° oven for about 40 to 45 minutes or until top is golden brown. Serves 6.

Note: – Pie can be baked earlier in the day and reheated at time of serving. It is a little better, though, when it is freshly baked and served.

Casseroles

Chicken Casserole
with Mushrooms, Tomatoes & Saffron Rice

2 onions, chopped
2 cloves garlic, mashed
3 tablespoons butter
1/2 pound sliced mushrooms
1 cup rice

2 tomatoes, coarsely chopped
1 can (10½ ounces) chicken broth
1 jar (2 ounces) pimento strips
1/4 teaspoon saffron
salt and pepper to taste

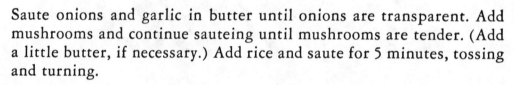

3 cups cooked chicken
1 package (10 ounces) frozen green peas

Saute onions and garlic in butter until onions are transparent. Add mushrooms and continue sauteing until mushrooms are tender. (Add a little butter, if necessary.) Add rice and saute for 5 minutes, tossing and turning.

Now add the remaining ingredients and stir until blended. Simmer mixture until rice is cooked and liquid is absorbed. Stir and serve hot. Serves 4.

Note: – *Entire casserole can be made earlier in the day and refrigerated. Reheat over low heat so that rice does not scorch.*
– *Do not freeze.*

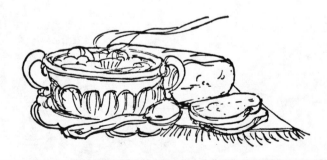

Country Cassoulet of Beef & Pork

(Casserole of Beans and Meat)

Preparing a cassoulet is usually a lengthy affair, requiring numerous pots and pans, a good deal of time and an incredible amount of cooking — all very discouraging details. Normally, the beans, poultry and meats are cooked separately and then combined and baked together in the oven. This simple cassoulet is my Mom's method of preparation — cooking all the ingredients together in one pan and losing nothing in the translation. There are no prescribed ingredients for a cassoulet, but it often contains duck or chicken, pork, beef, lamb and/or sausage in varying quantities.

1 pound Great Northern dried white beans, washed and
     picked over for any little pebbles or foreign matter
2 quarts water

3 tablespoons oil
1 pound beef chuck, cut into cubes
1 pound pork chops (and/or lamb chops)
2 onions, chopped
4 cloves garlic, put through a press

1 can (10 1/2 ounces) chicken broth
1 can (1 pound) stewed tomatoes, chopped
1 teaspoon Bovril, beef extract
1/4 teaspoon thyme flakes
    salt and pepper to taste

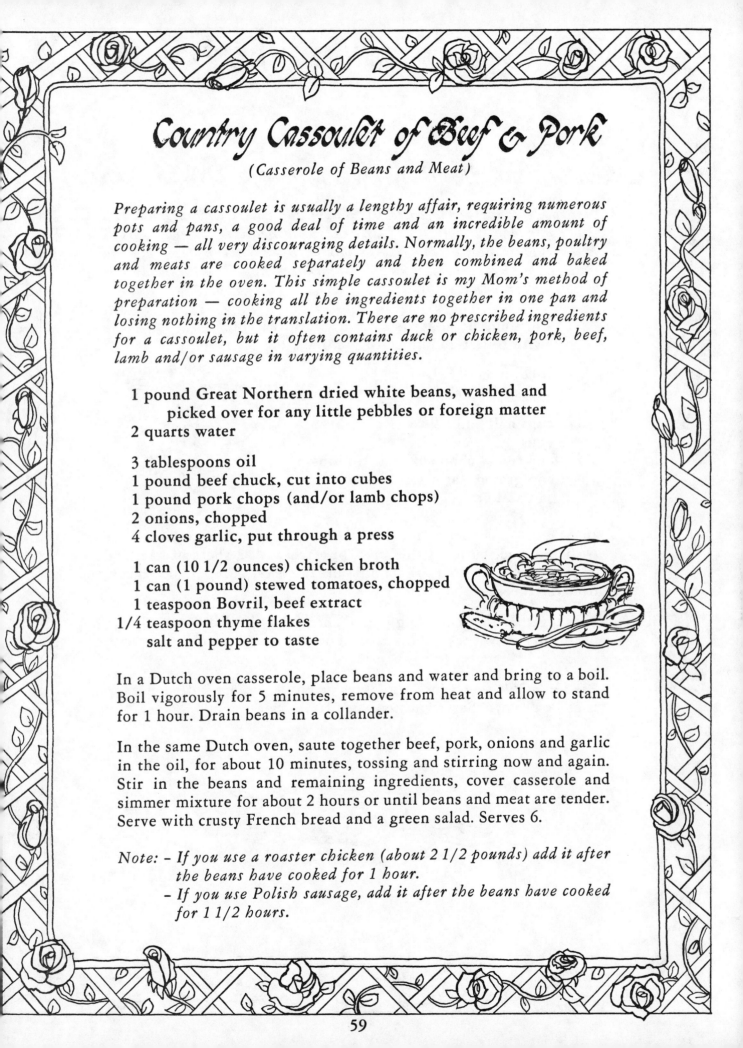

In a Dutch oven casserole, place beans and water and bring to a boil. Boil vigorously for 5 minutes, remove from heat and allow to stand for 1 hour. Drain beans in a collander.

In the same Dutch oven, saute together beef, pork, onions and garlic in the oil, for about 10 minutes, tossing and stirring now and again. Stir in the beans and remaining ingredients, cover casserole and simmer mixture for about 2 hours or until beans and meat are tender. Serve with crusty French bread and a green salad. Serves 6.

Note: - If you use a roaster chicken (about 2 1/2 pounds) add it after
      the beans have cooked for 1 hour.
    - If you use Polish sausage, add it after the beans have cooked
      for 1 1/2 hours.

Croque Monsieur with Ham & Swiss Cheese

A Croque Monsieur is basically a ham and Swiss cheese sandwich, dipped in egg or batter and grilled until cheese is melted. This is a lovely variation of the classic sandwich and it can be assembled earlier, popped into the oven 45 minutes before serving, and is excellent for a Sunday brunch.

12 slices egg bread, crusts removed. Spread bread
    with butter and mustard, on one side.

12 slices ham
12 slices Swiss cheese

1 1/2 cups half and half
  8 eggs
1/4 cup finely chopped green onions
1/2 cup grated Parmesan cheese
    salt and pepper to taste

In a 9x13-inch porcelain baker, that is nicely buttered, place 6 slices bread, buttered side up. Top each with 2 slices of ham and 2 slices of cheese. Place remaining bread slices, buttered side down, over the cheese.

Beat together the remaining ingredients until blended. Pour mixture over the sandwiches. Allow to rest in the refrigerator for several hours.

Bake in a 350° oven for 45 minutes or until eggs are puffed and top is golden brown. Serve with poached fruits. Serves 6.

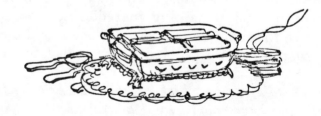

Eggplant with Tomato & Mozzarella

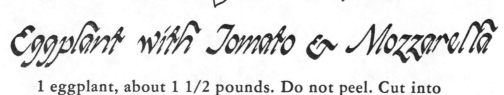

1 eggplant, about 1 1/2 pounds. Do not peel. Cut into
    1/4-inch slices

1/2 cup bread crumbs
1/2 cup grated Parmesan cheese
1/4 teaspoon garlic powder
    salt and pepper to taste

2 eggs, lightly beaten

1 cup grated Mozzarella cheese
1 cup grated Parmesan cheese
    Thick Meat Sauce

Combine bread crumbs, 1/2 cup Parmesan cheese, garlic powder and salt and pepper to taste. Dip eggplant slices in beaten egg and then in crumb mixture. Saute eggplant slices in hot oil until brown on both sides.

Now make two layers of the eggplant, Mozzarella, Parmesan and Thick Meat Sauce in a 9x13-inch pan.

Heat casserole in a 350° oven until it is piping hot and cheese is melted, about 20 minutes. Serves 4 or 5.

Thick Meat Sauce

2 tablespoons olive oil
2 cloves garlic, mashed
1 cup onions, chopped
1 pound lean ground beef

1 can (1 pound 12 ounces) Italian tomatoes, finely chopped
1 can (6 ounces) tomato paste
2 tablespoons sugar
1 teaspoon Italian Herb Seasoning
1 bay leaf
    salt and freshly ground pepper to taste

Saute garlic and onion in olive oil until onions are soft. Add meat and saute until meat loses its pinkness. Now add the remaining ingredients and simmer sauce uncovered, for about 20 to 30 minutes.

Noodles with Tomatoes & Cheese

1/2 pound medium noodles, cooked and drained
1/2 cup butter, melted

   1 pint cottage cheese
   1 package (8 ounces) cream cheese
   3 eggs
1/4 cup bread crumbs
   1 tablespoon chopped parsley
   1 teaspoon Italian Herb Seasoning
     pinch of thyme
     salt and pepper to taste
1/2 cup grated Parmesan cheese

Toss cooked noodles with butter in a 9 x 13-inch pan. Beat together the remaining ingredients and dot cheese mixture over the noodles. Toss again so that mixture is even. Pour Sweet Tomato Sauce over the top and again, toss it lightly to distribute sauce.

Bake in a 350° oven for about 45 minutes or until top of casserole is nicely browned. Cut into squares and serve warm. Serves 6 to 8.

Sweet Tomato Sauce

   1 can (1 pound 12 ounces) crushed tomatoes in tomato
      puree (Progresso Brand has an excellent one.)
1/8 teaspoon garlic powder
1 1/2 tablespoons dried onion flakes
   1 teaspoon Italian Herb Seasoning
   1 tablespoon oil
   1 tablespoon sugar
     salt and pepper to taste

Combine all the ingredients and simmer for 5 minutes. Yields about 3 cups sauce.

Note: – Entire dish can be assembled earlier in the day and stored in the refrigerator. Bake before serving.

Eggplant Casserole with Tomatoes, Garlic & Rice

(Ratatouille en Riz)

This is an extraordinary dish, exciting with the flavors of Provence and amazingly delicious. It is brimful of vegetables and garlic and herbs and all manner of "good things." Steaming the vegetables (instead of sauteing them in oil) will eliminate the use of about 1 cup of oil. In fact, I think the dish improves with this lighter treatment.

    1 small eggplant, peeled and cut into 1/4-inch slices
    4 zucchinis, unpeeled and cut into 1/2-inch slices
    1 tablespoon oil

    2 onions, chopped
    1 red pepper, seeds removed and cut into strips
    1 green pepper, seeds removed and cut into strips
    6 cloves garlic, put through a press

    2 cans, (1 pound, each) stewed tomatoes, drained
        and chopped
1/4 cup chopped parsley
1/4 teaspoon basil
1/4 teaspoon thyme
    salt and freshly ground pepper to taste

    3 cups cooked rice
1/4 cup grated Swiss cheese
1/4 cup grated Parmesan cheese

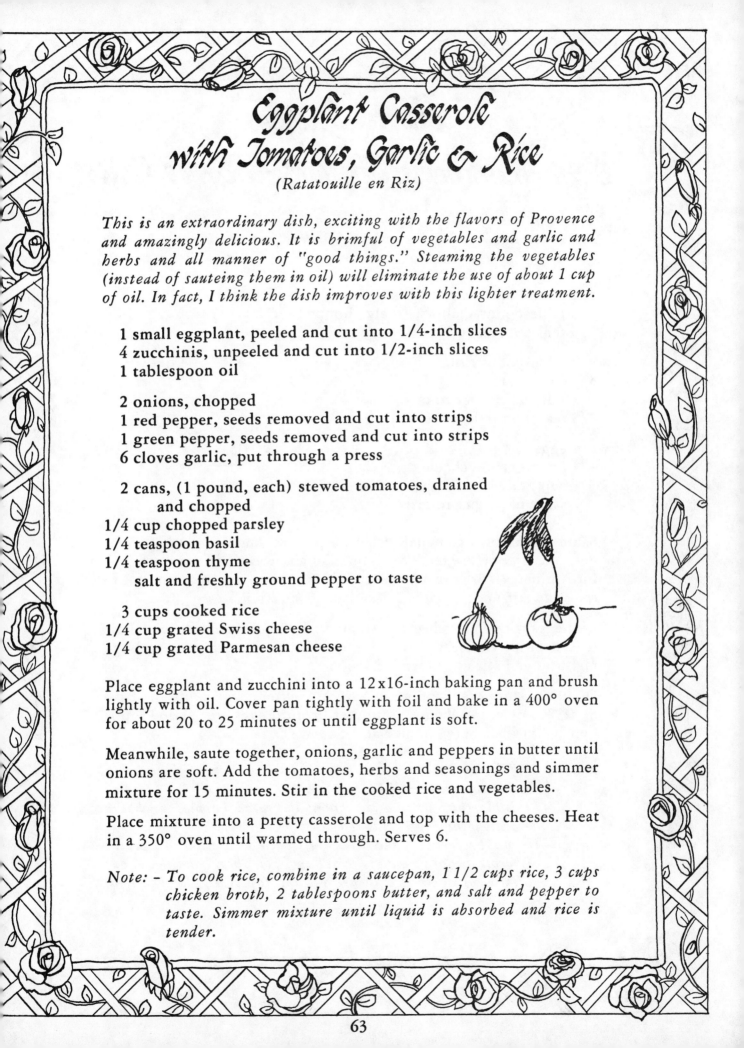

Place eggplant and zucchini into a 12x16-inch baking pan and brush lightly with oil. Cover pan tightly with foil and bake in a 400° oven for about 20 to 25 minutes or until eggplant is soft.

Meanwhile, saute together, onions, garlic and peppers in butter until onions are soft. Add the tomatoes, herbs and seasonings and simmer mixture for 15 minutes. Stir in the cooked rice and vegetables.

Place mixture into a pretty casserole and top with the cheeses. Heat in a 350° oven until warmed through. Serves 6.

Note: – To cook rice, combine in a saucepan, 1 1/2 cups rice, 3 cups chicken broth, 2 tablespoons butter, and salt and pepper to taste. Simmer mixture until liquid is absorbed and rice is tender.

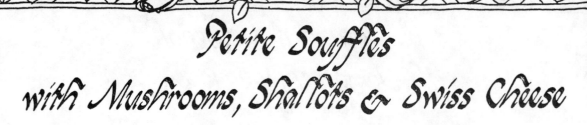

Petite Soufflés
with Mushrooms, Shallots & Swiss Cheese

*This very lovely souffle is an excellent choice for a luncheon dish.
Mushrooms, sauteed in butter with shallots, and sparkled with herbs
and cream is a grand combination with the delicate Swiss cheese.*

1/2 pound mushrooms, thinly sliced
  2 tablespoons shallots, finely chopped
  4 tablespoons butter

  2 tablespoons flour
3/4 cup cream
  salt and pepper to taste
1/8 teaspoon poultry seasoning

  6 eggs
1/2 pound cream cheese
  1 cup grated Swiss cheese
  salt and pepper to taste

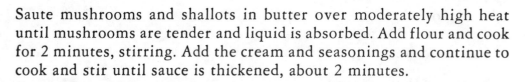

Saute mushrooms and shallots in butter over moderately high heat
until mushrooms are tender and liquid is absorbed. Add flour and cook
for 2 minutes, stirring. Add the cream and seasonings and continue to
cook and stir until sauce is thickened, about 2 minutes.

Beat eggs with cream cheese until mixture is thoroughly blended. Beat
in the Swiss cheese and seasonings. Combine mushroom and egg
mixtures and stir until blended.

Divide mixture evenly between 6 lightly buttered ramekins and bake
in a 375° oven for about 20 minutes or until eggs are set and top is
lightly browned. Serve immediately. Serves 6.

*Note: - Souffle can be assembled several hours earlier and stored in
      the refrigerator until baking time.*
*   - Sprinkle tops with a teaspoon of grated Parmesan cheese
      before baking for a textured crust.*
*   - If you prefer to bake the souffle in a shallow porcelain
      casserole (approximately 9 x 11 inches), then bake for about
      30 minutes or until eggs are set and top is a golden brown.*

2~Minute Spinach Souffle with Imperial Cheese Sauce

This lovely souffle takes minutes to assemble and is every bit as good as the original. It is a delicate and beautiful luncheon dish and a grand accompaniment to dinner. As if all this were not enough, imagine, it can also be assembled earlier in the day and baked before serving.

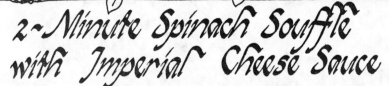

- 5 eggs
- 1 package (8 ounces) cream cheese
- 1 cup cream
- 1/2 cup grated Parmesan cheese
- 1 whole green onion (without the whiskers)
- 1/8 teaspoon nutmeg
    - salt and pepper to taste

- 1/2 package (about 1/2 cup) frozen chopped spinach, defrosted and drained
- 4 slices bacon, cooked crisp and crumbled

Place first 7 ingredients in a blender or food processor and blend for 2 minutes. Add spinach and blend for 2 seconds. Stir in the bacon.

Place mixture into a buttered and lightly floured 1 1/2-quart souffle dish and bake in a 375° oven for about 45 minutes or until top is golden and center is still a little soft. Serve at once with a spoonful of Imperial Cheese Sauce. Serves 6.

Imperial Cheese Sauce

- 2 tablespoons butter
- 2 tablespoons flour

- 1 cup half and half
- 1/2 cup sour cream

- 2 tablespoons chopped chives
    - salt and pepper to taste
- 3/4 cup grated Swiss cheese
- 1/4 cup grated Parmesan cheese

Cook butter and flour for 2 minutes, stirring. Add half and half and sour cream and cook and stir until sauce is thickened. Add the remaining ingredients and cook over low heat until cheese is melted. Serve at once. Delicious!

Herbed Noodles
with Cheese, Lemon & Green Onions

When you are thinking of serving a grand noodle dish for a buffet or informal dinner, this is a good one to consider. It presents beautifully with a cheese-crisped top sprinkled with parsley and green onions. The faint hint of lemon and herbs, combined with the melted cheeses, is simply delicious.

1 package (12 ounces) green (spinach) noodles, cooked
    until tender and drained. Toss cooked noodles in
    1 stick melted butter.

1 pound Ricotta cheese
1 package (6 ounces) Mozzarella cheese, grated
1 cup grated Parmesan cheese
3 eggs
1/2 cup finely chopped green onion
1/4 cup finely chopped parsley
  1 or 2 cloves garlic put through a press
1/2 teaspoon Italian Herb Seasoning
  3 tablespoons lemon juice
    salt and pepper to taste

In a 9 x 13-inch pan, toss the melted butter with the cooked noodles. Beat together the remaining ingredients until thoroughly blended. Pour mixture on the noodles and toss and turn until the cheese mixture and the noodles are blended.

Bake in a 350° oven for about 50 minutes or until top is golden and casserole is puffed and set. Sprinkle top with additional onions and parsley and a little lemon juice. Serves 8.

Note: – Entire casserole can be assembled earlier in the day and baked before serving.

– This casserole is so satisfying that it can be served as a main dish if you are planning a vegetarian dinner. A lovely addition in this case would be to add 1 package (10 ounces) frozen chopped spinach, drained, to the cheese mixture. Adjust seasonings and bake as described above.

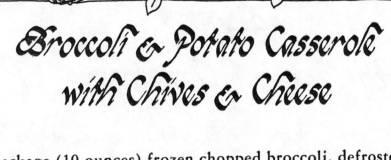

Broccoli & Potato Casserole with Chives & Cheese

1 package (10 ounces) frozen chopped broccoli, defrosted
1 can (1 pound) sliced boiled potatoes, chopped
3 eggs, beaten
3/4 cup cream
1 cup grated Swiss cheese
1/2 cup grated Parmesan cheese
3 tablespoons chopped chives
2 tablespoons chopped parsley
1 cup cottage cheese
1/2 cup fresh bread crumbs
salt and pepper to taste

Combine all the ingredients in a bowl and stir until thoroughly mixed. Place mixture into a heavily buttered 9x13-inch pan and spread evenly. Drizzle top with a little melted butter.

Bake in a 350° oven for about 50 minutes or until top is golden brown. Cut into squares and serve warm. Serves 6.

Note: – If you use a porcelain baker, then this casserole can be baked and served in the same dish.
– Dish can be baked earlier in the day and heated before serving.

Noodle Casserole with Zucchini, Tomatoes & Cheese

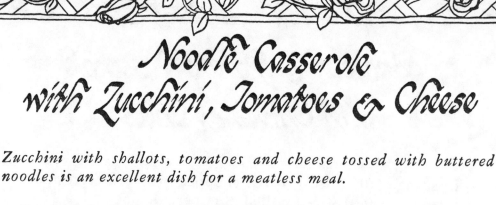

Zucchini with shallots, tomatoes and cheese tossed with buttered noodles is an excellent dish for a meatless meal.

1 pound Italian zucchini, grated. Sprinkle with 1/2 teaspoon salt and allow to drain in a strainer. Press dry.
1 onion, chopped
3 cloves garlic, put through a press
2 shallots, minced
4 tablespoons olive oil

1 can (1 pound) stewed tomatoes, drained and finely chopped. Reserve juice for another use.

1 cup grated Swiss cheese
1/2 cup grated Parmesan cheese
salt and pepper to taste

1 package (8 ounces) medium egg noodles, cooked, drained and tossed in 4 tablespoons melted butter

Saute first 5 ingredients together until zucchini and onions are tender. Add the chopped tomatoes and simmer mixture for 10 minutes or until sauce is thick but not soupy.

Toss the cooked noodles with the cheeses until blended. Toss noodles with the sauce. Place in a lovely porcelain baker and heat in a 350° oven until heated through. Serves 4 as a main course or 6 as a side dish.

Note: – Entire casserole can be assembled earlier in the day and refrigerated. Bring to room temperature before heating. Heat in a 350° oven until heated through.

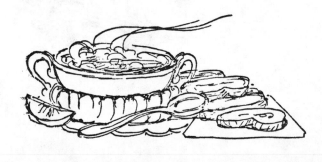

Creamed Spinach with Mushrooms & Onions in Cheese Sauce

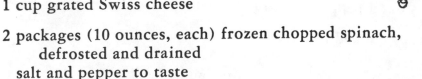

This is a lovely dish to serve on a buffet. You'll find no wrinkled noses with this spinach dish.

1 onion, chopped
1/2 pound mushrooms, cleaned and sliced
4 tablespoons butter
2 tablespoons flour

1 cup cream
1 cup sour cream
1 cup grated Swiss cheese

2 packages (10 ounces, each) frozen chopped spinach,
    defrosted and drained
salt and pepper to taste
nutmeg

Saute onion and mushrooms in butter until onions are soft. Stir in flour and cook for 2 to 3 minutes, stirring all the while. Add cream and sour cream and cook, stirring until sauce thickens. Stir in the Swiss cheese.

Add half the cheese sauce to the drained spinach and spread in an oval porcelain baker. Top spinach with the remaining cheese sauce. Sprinkle top with a dash of nutmeg.

Heat in a 350° oven until heated through, about 30 minutes. Serves 6 to 8.

Note: – Entire dish can be assembled earlier in the day and refrigerated. Heat before serving as described above.

Zucchini Casserole with Tomatoes, Cheese & Rice

1 clove garlic
1 pound zucchini, scrubbed. Do not peel.
1/2 pound mushrooms, cleaned and sliced
    4 tablespoons butter

    2 tomatoes, seeded and chopped
    3 green onions, chopped

    2 eggs
1/2 cup sour cream
    1 cup grated Swiss cheese
    salt and pepper to taste

    3 cups cooked rice

Saute together, garlic, zucchini and mushrooms in butter until vegetables are soft. Place zucchini in a large bowl. Add tomatoes and green onions to zucchini.

Beat together eggs, sour cream, Swiss cheese, salt and pepper. Combine all the ingredients in a bowl and stir until nicely blended.

Place mixture in a porcelain baker and bake in a 350° oven for 45 minutes or until eggs are set and casserole is heated through. Serves 6.

Note: – Entire casserole can be assembled earlier in the day (several hours before baking) and stored in the refrigerator.
      – Do not freeze.

Herbed Zucchini Mold with Cheese, Onions & Garlic

(Timbale de Courgettes Gratinees)

1 pound zucchini, sliced. Not necessary to peel.
1 large onion, chopped
2 cloves garlic, put through a press
4 tablespoons butter

3 cups cottage cheese
1 cup grated Parmesan cheese
3/4 cup breadcrumbs
1/2 teaspoon Italian Herb Seasoning

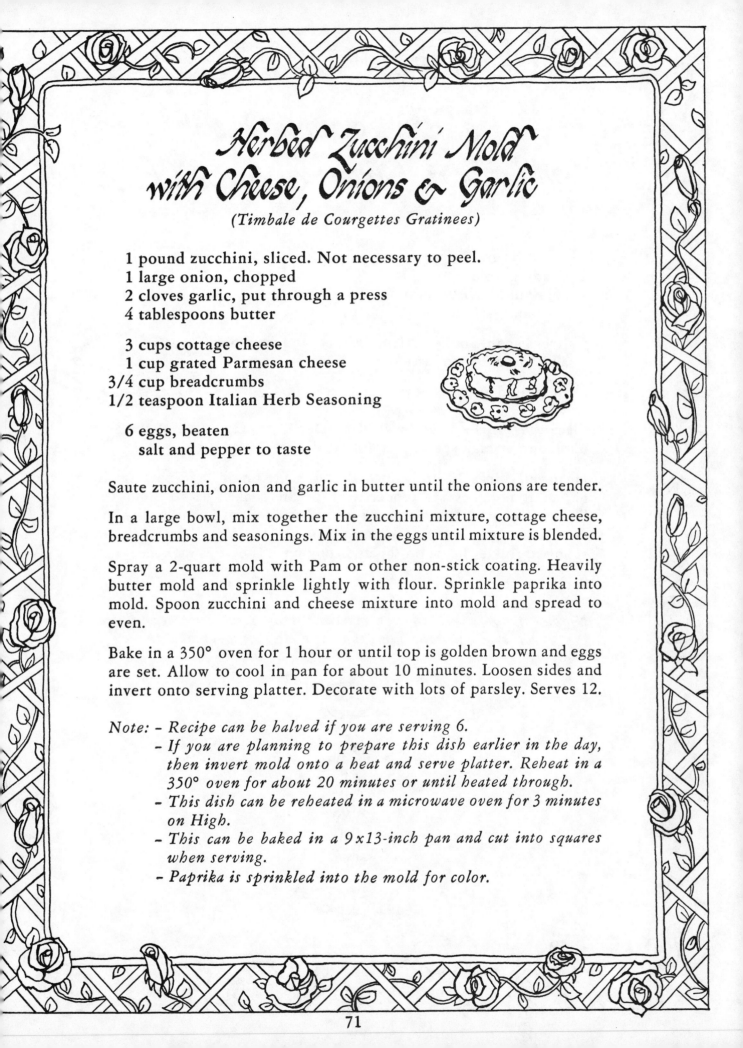

6 eggs, beaten
salt and pepper to taste

Saute zucchini, onion and garlic in butter until the onions are tender.

In a large bowl, mix together the zucchini mixture, cottage cheese, breadcrumbs and seasonings. Mix in the eggs until mixture is blended.

Spray a 2-quart mold with Pam or other non-stick coating. Heavily butter mold and sprinkle lightly with flour. Sprinkle paprika into mold. Spoon zucchini and cheese mixture into mold and spread to even.

Bake in a 350° oven for 1 hour or until top is golden brown and eggs are set. Allow to cool in pan for about 10 minutes. Loosen sides and invert onto serving platter. Decorate with lots of parsley. Serves 12.

Note: – *Recipe can be halved if you are serving 6.*
– *If you are planning to prepare this dish earlier in the day, then invert mold onto a heat and serve platter. Reheat in a 350° oven for about 20 minutes or until heated through.*
– *This dish can be reheated in a microwave oven for 3 minutes on High.*
– *This can be baked in a 9 x 13-inch pan and cut into squares when serving.*
– *Paprika is sprinkled into the mold for color.*

Fluffy Country Omelet
with Bacon, Onions & Swiss Cheese

6 eggs

1 onion, finely chopped
1 potato, grated
4 tablespoons oil (cannot substitute butter
    or margarine)

6 slices bacon, cooked crisp, drained and crumbled
  salt and pepper to taste

1 cup grated Swiss cheese

Place eggs in the large bowl of an electric mixer and beat for 3 or 4 minutes at high speed.

Meanwhile, in a 10 or 12-inch skillet, saute onions and potatoes in oil, until potatoes are tender. Stir in the cooked bacon. Pour the beaten eggs over the onion mixture and stir and turn gently, allowing uncooked egg to run to the bottom. When top is still soft, but not runny, sprinkle cheese on top and cook until cheese is melted.

Serve omelet open. Serves 3 or 4.

Note: – If you use butter or margarine, eggs will not stay fluffy.
*   – It is very important that you do not overcook the eggs.*

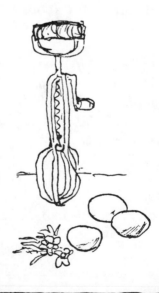

HELPFUL KITCHEN TIPS
TO SAVE YOU TIME AND MONEY!

BUTTERMILK SUBSTITUTE — One tablespoon of vinegar or lemon juice in a measuring cup and add enough whole milk to bring the liquid up to the 1 cup line. Let stand for 5 minutes.

KEEP BROWN SUGAR SOFT — Store in a coffee can with snap-on lid.

GET THE MOST FOR YOUR MEAT DOLLAR — Roast your meat between 300°F. and 325°F.; it will shrink less and be more tender. Don't salt roast beef or steak until it is three-quarters cooked. It will retain its juices better if seasoned this way.

INCREASE SHELF LIFE OF VEGETABLES — All vegetables with tops, such as Carrots, Beets, etc., should have the greenery removed before storing.

Pancakes

Few foods have the grace and style of crepes. These noble little pancakes are so incredibly versatile, it is a pity there are still a few who are afraid to tackle them.

Let me assure you, that underneath their delicate and dainty appearance, lies a staunch and sturdy character. They are really not as fragile as they appear.

When you serve crepes, mealtimes can never be boring for crepe dishes range from a triumph of simplicity to dishes of regal splendor. Crepes can be served for breakfast, lunch or dinner and for any course during the meal. They can be rolled, folded or stacked with an amazing variety of fillings.

And, to add to their numerous virtues, and best of all, crepe dishes are a grand choice for entertaining, for so many of them can be prepared in advance. This allows for just a quick trip to the kitchen to start reheating, eliminating any last-minute worries and jitters.

Read the instructions carefully and once you have mastered the technique (which is not difficult) you will prepare these majestic little pancakes often.

You will notice that there are two important changes in the technique of making crepes. First, the resting period (to relax the gluten in the flour) has been eliminated. Very often I have omitted this step and differences in the results were imperceptible. Secondly, no more need to grease the pan after the first crepe. The butter has been added to the batter and that eliminates another pitfall, of improperly greasing the pan.

CREPES — GENERAL ADVICE

1. Crepe batters can be made in a mixer or a blender. You can use a rotary beater or a wire whip.

2. Batter can be allowed to rest for 1 hour (optional).

3. The success of your crepes will very much be determined by the quality pan you are using. It is essential that you use a fine quality pan, about 6 to 8 inches wide. It should have rounded sides. If you are a beginner to crepes, I would recommend that you use a good-quality Teflon-coated pan. It is very easy to use and almost assures you of success. It eliminates the problems of crepes sticking to the pan or being difficult to turn. Furthermore, Teflon-coated pans usually have a heat-resistant handle which is very helpful when you are working quickly, tilting and turning.

4. Unfilled crepes may be stored and frozen between layers of waxed paper.

CREPES — TECHNIQUE

1. Crepes are made over moderately high heat. Heat pan and butter it with a napkin or paper towel. Wipe off any excess butter. Pan should be very hot, but butter should not brown.

2. Lift pan off heat. With the other hand, pour about 1/8 cup of batter into the pan. Quickly tilt and turn the pan, so that the bottom is completely covered with batter. Pour out any excess batter.

3. Place pan back on the heat and continue cooking the crepe for about 45 seconds or until top is dry. Turn and cook other side for about 15 seconds. Remove crepe onto a platter.

4. Heat pan and start again from Step 2. (Batter recipes that follow contain extra butter. This eliminates greasing the pan after each crepe.

THE CRUCIAL POINT IS THAT THE PAN MUST BE HOT WHEN THE BATTER IS POURED. PAN MUST THEN BE TILTED AND TURNED IMMEDIATELY TO COVER THE BOTTOM WITH A THIN LAYER OF BATTER.

Basic French Crepes

1 cup flour
1 cup milk
4 eggs
4 tablespoons melted butter
  pinch of salt

In a bowl, with a rotary beater, beat together all the ingredients until blended. Proceed to make crepes as directed under CREPES, TECHNIQUE. Yields 16 7-inch crepes.

Crepes with Sour Cream & Herbs

1 cup flour
1 cup milk
1/2 cup sour cream
3 eggs
1 teaspoon chopped parsley
1 tablespoon chopped chives
4 tablespoons melted butter
  pinch of salt

In an electric mixer, combine all the ingredients and beat until the mixture is blended. Proceed to make crepes as directed under CREPES, TECHNIQUE. Yields 16 7-inch crepes.

Crepes with Onions & Dill

1 cup flour
1/2 cup milk
1/2 cup water
  4 eggs
1/8 teaspoon onion powder
1/4 teaspoon dill weed
  4 tablespoons melted butter
    pinch of salt

In a blender container, place all the ingredients and blend for 30 seconds or until mixture is nicely mixed. Proceed to make crepes as directed under CREPES, TECHNIQUE. Yields 16 7-inch crepes.

Crepes with Cheese & Chives

> 1 cup flour
> 1 1/2 cups milk
> 3 eggs
> 1/4 cup grated Parmesan cheese
> 2 tablespoons chopped chives
> 4 tablespoons melted butter

In a blender container, place all the ingredients and blend for 30 seconds or until mixture is nicely mixed. Proceed to make crepes as directed under CREPES, TECHNIQUE. Yields 16 7-inch crepes.

Basic Dessert Crepes

> 1 cup flour
> 1 1/4 cups milk
> 3 eggs
> 2 tablespoons sugar
> 1 tablespoon finely grated orange peel
> 3 tablespoons melted butter
> pinch of salt

In an electric mixer, combine all the ingredients and beat until the mixture is blended. Proceed to make crepes as directed under CREPES, TECHNIQUE. Yields 16 7-inch crepes.

Grand Marnier Dessert Crepes

> 1 cup flour
> 1 cup milk
> 2 tablespoons sugar
> 2 tablespoons Grand Marnier Liqueur
> 3 eggs
> 4 tablespoons melted butter
> pinch of salt

In an electric mixer, combine all the ingredients and beat until the mixture is blended. Proceed to make crepes as directed under CREPES, TECHNIQUE. Yields 16 7-inch crepes.

French Orange Dessert Crepes

1 cup flour
1 1/4 cups milk
3 eggs
2 tablespoons sugar
1 tablespoon finely grated orange peel
3 tablespoons melted butter
  pinch of salt

In a bowl, with a rotary beater, beat together all the ingredients until blended. Proceed to make crepes as directed under CREPES, TECHNIQUE. Yields 16 7-inch crepes.

Chocolate Crepes with Creme de Cacao

1 cup milk
1 cup flour
4 eggs
2 tablespoons Creme de Cacao Liqueur
2 tablespoons Nestle's Quik or sweetened chocolate mix
4 tablespoons melted butter
  pinch of salt

In an electric mixer, combine all the ingredients and beat until the mixture is blended. Proceed to make crepes as directed under CREPES, TECHNIQUE. Yields 16 7-inch crepes.

French Crepes with Nuts & Brandy

1 cup flour
1 cup milk
4 eggs
4 tablespoons melted butter
1/4 cup ground walnuts, pecans or almonds
2 tablespoons sugar
1 tablespoon brandy
  pinch of salt

In a blender container, place all the ingredients and blend for 30 seconds or until mixture is nicely mixed. Proceed to make crepes as directed under CREPES, TECHNIQUE. Yields 16 7-inch crepes.

Crepes with Chicken, Raisins, Almonds & Instant Sauce Hollandaise

16 7-inch Basic French Crepes

1 tablespoon butter
1 clove garlic, finely minced

1/4 cup cream
2 packages (3 ounces, each) cream cheese with chives
1 tablespoon lemon juice
1 egg yolk

2 tablespoons chopped raisins
3 tablespoons chopped almonds
2 cups cooked chicken, diced
salt to taste

Saute garlic in butter for 2 minutes just to soften. Beat together cream, cream cheese, lemon juice and egg yolk until blended. Beat in garlic, raisins, almonds and cooked chicken.

Place 2 tablespoons chicken mixture on each crepe and roll it up jellyroll fashion. Place crepes, seam side down, in a buttered porcelain baker. Heat in a 350° oven until heated through.

Serve with a spoonful of warm Instant Sauce Hollandaise on the top. Sprinkle a few chopped chives over all. Serves 8.

Note: – These are lovely served in individual oval au gratin bakers.
– Crepes can be filled earlier in the day and stored in the refrigerator.

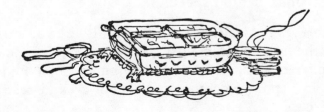

Instant Sauce Hollandaise

        3 egg yolks
1 1/2 tablespoons lemon juice
        pinch of salt and white pepper

    3/4 cup butter (1 1/2 sticks)

Place egg yolks, lemon juice, salt and pepper in a blender container and blend for 10 seconds at high speed.

Heat butter until it is sizzling hot and bubbly, but be careful not to brown it. Add the hot, sizzling butter very, very slowly and in a steady stream, while the blender continues running at high speed. When the butter is completely incorporated, sauce is ready. Yields about 1 cup sauce.

Instant Sauce Bernaise

        3 egg yolks
1 1/2 tablespoons lemon juice
        pinch of salt and white pepper
    1 tablespoon tarragon vinegar
    2 teaspoons chopped parsley
    2 tablespoons chopped green onions
1/4 teaspoon dried tarragon or to taste

    3/4 cup butter

Place all the ingredients, except the butter, in the blender container. Blend for 10 seconds at high speed.

Heat butter until it is sizzling hot and bubbly, but be careful not to brown it. Add the hot, sizzling butter, very slowly, in a steady stream, while the blender continues running at high speed. When the butter is completely incorporated, sauce will be thick and ready to serve. Yields about 1 cup.

Crepes with Shrimp, Cheese & Chives with Instant Sauce Bernaise

16 7-inch Crepes with Cheese and Chives

2 tablespoons butter
2 cloves garlic, finely minced
4 shallots, finely minced
4 tablespoons chopped chives

1 tablespoon flour

1 cup sour cream
1/4 cup white wine
1/2 teaspoon Dijon mustard

1/2 pound cooked baby shrimp
1 hard cooked egg, coarsely chopped
1 cup grated Swiss cheese
1/4 cup grated Parmesan cheese
salt and pepper to taste

In a skillet, saute garlic, shallots and chives in butter until the shallots are wilted. Add flour and cook for 2 minutes, turning and stirring.

Add cream, wine and mustard and cook until sauce thickens. Stir in the remaining ingredients. Place about 2 tablespoons filling on each crepe and roll it up jellyroll fashion. Place crepes, seam side down, in a buttered porcelain baker. Heat in a 350° oven until heated through.

Serve with a spoonful of Instant Sauce Bearnaise on the top. Serves 8.

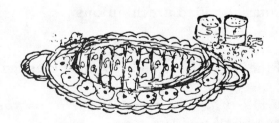

Crepes Florentine with Instant Cheese & Chive Sauce

16 7-inch Crepes with Sour Cream and Herbs

1 package (10 ounces) frozen chopped spinach,
    defrosted and drained
2 packages (3 ounces, each) cream cheese and chives
1 cup cottage cheese
2 eggs
1/2 cup grated Parmesan cheese
1/3 cup chopped green onion
1/3 cup fresh bread crumbs
    pinch of nutmeg
    salt and pepper to taste

Combine all the ingredients, except the crepes, and mix until blended. Place about 2 tablespoons filling on each crepe and roll them up. Place seam side down and in one layer in a buttered casserole. Spoon Instant Cheese and Chive Sauce over the top and heat casserole in a 350° oven until heated through and cheese sauce is melted.

Run under the broiler for a few seconds to brown. Serves 8 for lunch or 5 for dinner.

Instant Cheese & Chive Sauce

1 cup grated Swiss cheese
1 cup sour cream
1/4 cup grated Parmesan cheese
1 tablespoon lemon juice
2 tablespoons chopped green onions
    pinch of salt

Combine all the ingredients and stir until blended.

Note: – Entire dish can be prepared earlier in the day. Spoon sauce on top just before heating.

Crepes Provencal with Eggplant, Tomatoes & Cheese

16 7-inch Basic French Crepes

1 small eggplant, peeled and cut into 1/4-inch thick slices
4 zucchini, scrubbed and cut into 1/4-inch thick slices

2 tablespoons oil
1 large onion, finely chopped
1/2 green pepper, chopped
2 cloves garlic, finely minced
1 can (1 pound) stewed tomatoes, drained and chopped
1 can (8 ounces) tomato sauce
1 tablespoon sugar
1/2 teaspoon basil
1/4 teaspoon thyme
1 tablespoon chopped parsley
salt and pepper to taste

Place eggplant and zucchini in a 9x13-inch baking pan and drizzle lightly with oil. Cover pan tightly with foil and bake in a 400° oven for about 20 minutes or until eggplant is soft. Chop the eggplant and zucchini.

Meanwhile, cook together the remaining ingredients and simmer mixture for 20 minutes or until sauce thickens. Stir in the eggplant and zucchini.

Place 2 tablespoons of filling on one side of each crepe. Starting from that side, roll it up, and place it in a greased porcelain baker, seam side down. Sprinkle top with the remaining filling and

2 cups grated Swiss cheese
1/2 cup grated Parmesan cheese

Bake in a 350° oven until crepes are piping hot and cheese is melted. Serves 8.

Note: – Entire dish can be assembled earlier in the day and stored in the refrigerator. 30 minutes before serving, heat in a 350° oven until heated through.

Crepes with Crabmeat in Creamed Mushroom & Wine Sauce

16 7-inch Crepes with Onion and Dill

1/2 pound mushrooms, cleaned and sliced
  2 cloves garlic, finely minced
  2 shallots, finely minced
  3 tablespoons butter

  2 tablespoons flour

  1 cup cream
1/3 cup dry white wine

1/2 pound cooked crabmeat, flaked and
     picked over for bones
  1 cup grated Swiss cheese
1/4 cup grated Parmesan cheese
  1 jar (6 ounces) marinated artichoke hearts,
     drained and chopped
1/4 teaspoon dill weed
    salt and pepper to taste

Saute mushrooms, garlic and shallots in butter until mushrooms are tender. Add flour and cook and stir for 2 minutes. Stir in the cream and wine and continue cooking and stirring until sauce thickens. Stir in the remaining ingredients.

Place about 2 tablespoons filling on each crepe and roll it up jellyroll fashion. Place them seam side down in a buttered porcelain baker. Brush tops with Lemon Butter Wash.

Heat in a 350° oven for about 15 or 20 minutes or until heated through. Serves 8.

Lemon Butter Wash

1/4 cup butter (1/2 stick), melted
  1 tablespoon lemon juice
  2 tablespoons grated Parmesan cheese

Combine the ingredients and stir until blended.

Layered Crepe Gateau with Brandied Apples & Caramel Pecans

There are few desserts you could make that are more delicious and more memorable than this glorious combination of caramelized apples, brandy and pecans. Not the least of its virtues, it can be made a day earlier, served warm or cool, and is very easy to prepare.

4 apples, peeled, cored and grated
1/2 cup butter
1/2 cup sugar
1/2 cup orange juice
  1 tablespoon grated orange peel
  1 teaspoon grated lemon peel
  2 tablespoons brandy

1/2 cup apricot jam

3/4 cup chopped toasted pecans

7 7-inch French Orange Dessert Crepes

In a saucepan, cook together first 7 ingredients until apples are soft and sauce is a pale golden caramel. Remove apples to a bowl, with a slotted spoon, and stir in the apricot jam.

To the caramel in the pan, stir in the chopped pecans.

In a 1 1/2-quart souffle dish, layer the crepes and the apple mixture, starting and ending with the crepes. Pour caramel and pecans over the crepes. Cut into wedges and serve warm or at room temperature with a spoonful of the caramel and pecans over all. Serves 6 to 8.

Gateau of Chocolate Crepes with Chocolate Sour Cream Frosting

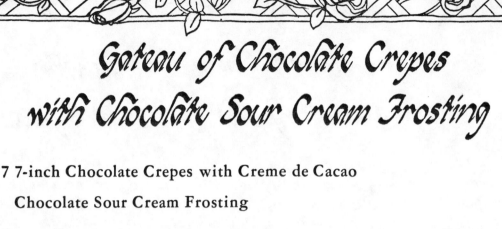

7 7-inch Chocolate Crepes with Creme de Cacao

Chocolate Sour Cream Frosting

Place 1 crepe on a serving platter and spread top evenly with about 1 tablespoon Chocolate Sour Cream Frosting. Continue layering the crepes and frosting until all the crepes are stacked.

Spread remaining frosting thinly on the tops and sides. Refrigerate until serving time. Frosting does not harden but remains beautifully soft. Serves 6.

Chocolate Sour Cream Frosting

1 cup (6 ounces) semi-sweet chocolate chips
1 cup sour cream
1 tablespoon Creme de Cacao Liqueur

In the top of a double boiler, over hot, not boiling water, melt the chocolate chips. Now, stir in the sour cream, 2 tablespoons at a time, until the mixture is nicely blended. Stir in the liqueur. Yields about 1 3/4 cup frosting.

Royal Crepes Suzette with Grand Marnier Almond Butter Sauce

There are so many recipes for Crepes Suzette available, that I thought I would take a few liberties with this classic dish. The Orange Butter has been substituted with an incredible Grand Marnier Sauce and the almonds, while not traditional, add a certain zest to this majestic dessert.

16 7-inch Grand Marnier Dessert Crepes

Grand Marnier Almond Butter

1/4 cup Cognac

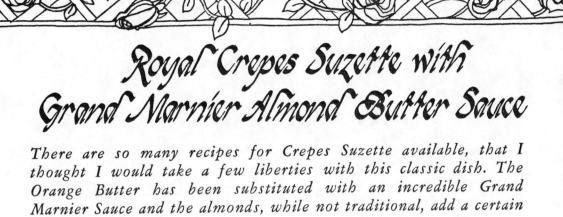

Baste crepes on both sides with Grand Marnier Almond Butter Sauce. Fold crepes in half, then half again. Arrange on a chafing dish, overlapping in rows or in a circle. Pour remaining hot sauce over the top.

Heat the Cognac, ignite it and carefully pour over the crepes. When the flames subside, serve the crepes and spoon a little sauce over the top. Serves 8.

Grand Marnier Almond Butter Sauce

    1 cup butter
3/4 cup sugar
    1 cup orange juice
    3 tablespoons grated orange, remove any
        large pieces of membrane
    2 to 3 tablespoons Grand Marnier Liqueur
    1 teaspoon lemon juice
1/3 cup finely chopped toasted slivered almonds

Combine first 6 ingredients and simmer mixture for 8 minutes or until it becomes syrupy. Stir in almonds. Yields about 3 cups sauce.

Note: – Crepes can be made several days earlier and stored between sheets of wax paper in the refrigerator.
– Sauce can be prepared earlier in the day and reheated at time of serving.

Cottage Cheese Pancakes with Orange Applesauce & Cinnamon

1 cup cottage cheese
3/4 cup flour
3 eggs
4 tablespoons sugar
3 tablespoons milk
4 tablespoons melted butter
1/2 teaspoon vanilla

Combine all the ingredients in a mixing bowl and beat with a fork until they are combined. Do not overmix.

Drop 1/4 cup batter on a lightly greased preheated griddle. When bottom of pancake is golden brown and top is bubbly, turn and brown the other side.

Serve warm with a dollup of sour cream and strawberries in syrup. Also very good with Orange Applesauce with Cinnamon. Yields 12 pancakes.

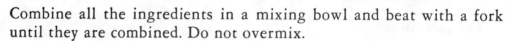

Orange Applesauce & Cinnamon

1 jar (1 pound) applesauce
3 ounces (1/2 can) frozen orange juice concentrate.
    Defrost but do not dilute.
cinnamon

Stir together applesauce and orange juice. Place mixture in a glass bowl and sprinkle cinnamon to taste on top.

Soups

&

Garnitures

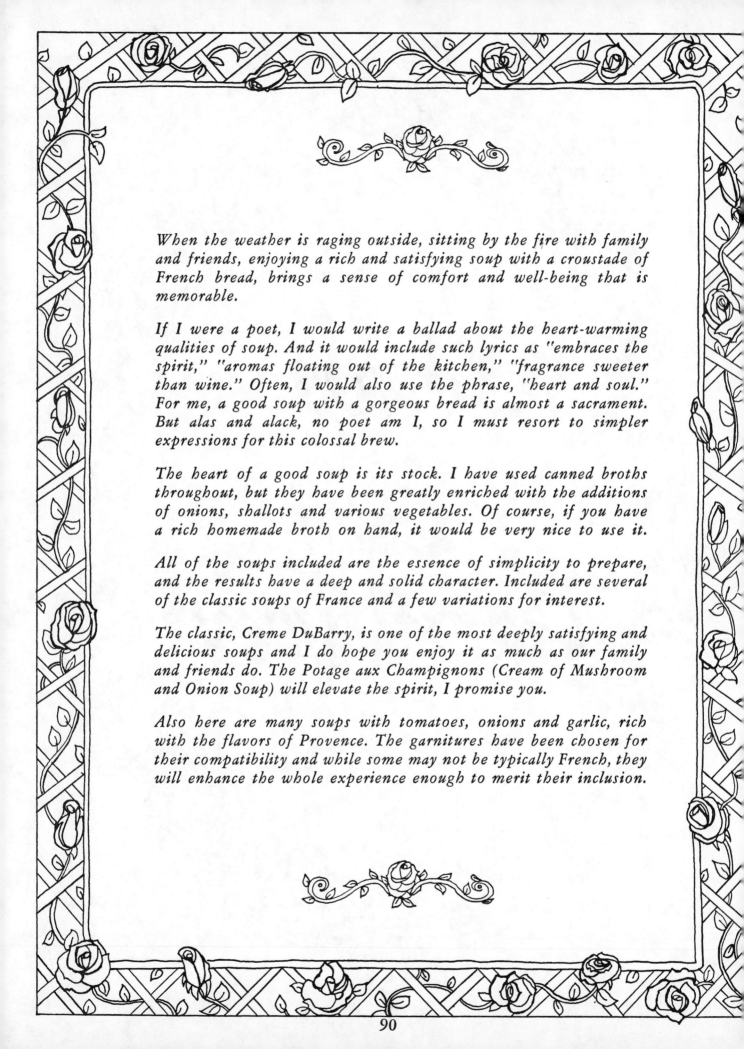

When the weather is raging outside, sitting by the fire with family and friends, enjoying a rich and satisfying soup with a croustade of French bread, brings a sense of comfort and well-being that is memorable.

If I were a poet, I would write a ballad about the heart-warming qualities of soup. And it would include such lyrics as "embraces the spirit," "aromas floating out of the kitchen," "fragrance sweeter than wine." Often, I would also use the phrase, "heart and soul." For me, a good soup with a gorgeous bread is almost a sacrament. But alas and alack, no poet am I, so I must resort to simpler expressions for this colossal brew.

The heart of a good soup is its stock. I have used canned broths throughout, but they have been greatly enriched with the additions of onions, shallots and various vegetables. Of course, if you have a rich homemade broth on hand, it would be very nice to use it.

All of the soups included are the essence of simplicity to prepare, and the results have a deep and solid character. Included are several of the classic soups of France and a few variations for interest.

The classic, Creme DuBarry, is one of the most deeply satisfying and delicious soups and I do hope you enjoy it as much as our family and friends do. The Potage aux Champignons (Cream of Mushroom and Onion Soup) will elevate the spirit, I promise you.

Also here are many soups with tomatoes, onions and garlic, rich with the flavors of Provence. The garnitures have been chosen for their compatibility and while some may not be typically French, they will enhance the whole experience enough to merit their inclusion.

Creme Du Barry
An Elegant Cream of Cauliflower Soup

As many times as I have prepared this soup, someone always remarks that it is the best soup they have ever tasted. It is one of my very favorites, as well. When you consider its utter simplicity in preparation and the incredible results, I hope you enjoy this often.

1 cup cream
1 cup sour cream

2 packages (10 ounces, each) frozen cauliflower, defrosted
2 onions, chopped
2 shallots, minced (about 2 heaping tablespoons)
2 cloves garlic, minced
2 tablespoons lemon juice
1/4 cup butter (1/2 stick)

3 cans (10 1/2 ounces, each) chicken broth
    salt and white pepper to taste

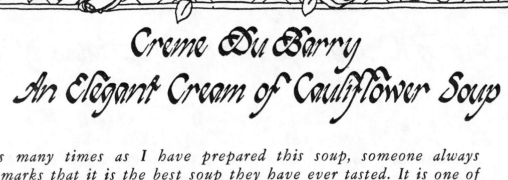

1 tablespoon minced parsley
2 tablespoons minced chives
1/4 teaspoon dill weed

In a glass bowl, stir together the cream and sour cream and set aside.

In a Dutch oven, saute together cauliflower, onion, shallots and garlic in lemon juice and butter until onions and cauliflower are soft. Do not allow the vegetables to brown. In a processor or in a blender in batches, puree cauliflower mixture with some of the broth.

Pour blended soup back into the Dutch oven and add the remaining chicken broth, seasonings and herbs. Simmer soup for a few minutes. Add the cream mixture and stir until it is blended. Heat through and serve with a sprinkling of chives and dill. Serves 6.

Note: – Entire soup can be prepared 1 day earlier with the exception of adding the creams. Heat the soup, stir in the creams and heat through.
– Piroshkis with Herbed Mushrooms are an incredible accompaniment.

French Onion Soup with Croustades of Cheese

(Soupe a L'Oignon Gratineed)

The essence of a good onion soup is made when the onions are cooked very slowly in butter ... the longer, the better. What you are actually doing, is sweating or melting the onions and releasing their intense flavor. As far as ingredients go, there is very little that varies one onion soup recipe from another. The distinguishing factor is usually in technique. The onions, when sauteed very, very slowly, will turn a rich brown color and become limp. There should be no evidence of the edges becoming crisp or fried.

6 onions, medium-sized, remove skins and whiskers.
    Slice onions in half lengthwise and cut them
    into 1/8-inch slices.
1 clove garlic, put through a press
2 shallots, finely chopped
2 teaspoons honey
4 tablespoons butter (1/2 stick)

4 tablespoons dry white wine

2 tablespoons flour

2 cans (10 1/2 ounces, each) beef broth
1 can (10 1/2 ounces) chicken broth
1 cup water
    salt and pepper to taste

6 slices French bread, toasted
1 1/2 cups grated Swiss or Gruyere cheese
6 tablespoons grated Parmesan cheese

6 slices Swiss or Gruyere cheese

In a 4-quart saucepan, saute onions, garlic and shallots with honey and butter, over low heat, until onions are golden and soft. Add wine and cook until it has evaporated. Add flour and cook for 3 minutes, stirring and turning. Add broths, water and seasonings and heat through, stirring now and again.

Place 6 oven-proof soup bowls on a cookie sheet. Place 1 slice French bread, 1/4 cup grated Gruyere, 1 tablespoon grated Parmesan, and soup in each bowl. Heat in a 350° oven for about 20 minutes. Place 1 slice of Gruyere over each bowl and continue baking until cheese is melted. Serve at once. Serves 6.

Potage aux Champignons et L'Oignons

(Cream of Mushroom and Onion Soup)

This incredibly delicious soup will elevate a simple occasion into a party. Deeply rich and fragrant, makes it particularly satisfying.

    1 pound mushrooms, cleaned and thinly sliced
    2 tablespoons lemon juice
    4 shallots, finely chopped
    2 large onions, finely chopped
    3 cloves garlic, put through a press
1/2 teaspoon sugar
1/2 teaspoon thyme
1/8 teaspoon poultry seasoning
    6 tablespoons butter (3/4 stick)

1/4 cup dry white wine

    3 tablespoons flour

    3 cans (10 1/2 ounces, each) chicken broth
    2 cups cream
    salt and pepper to taste

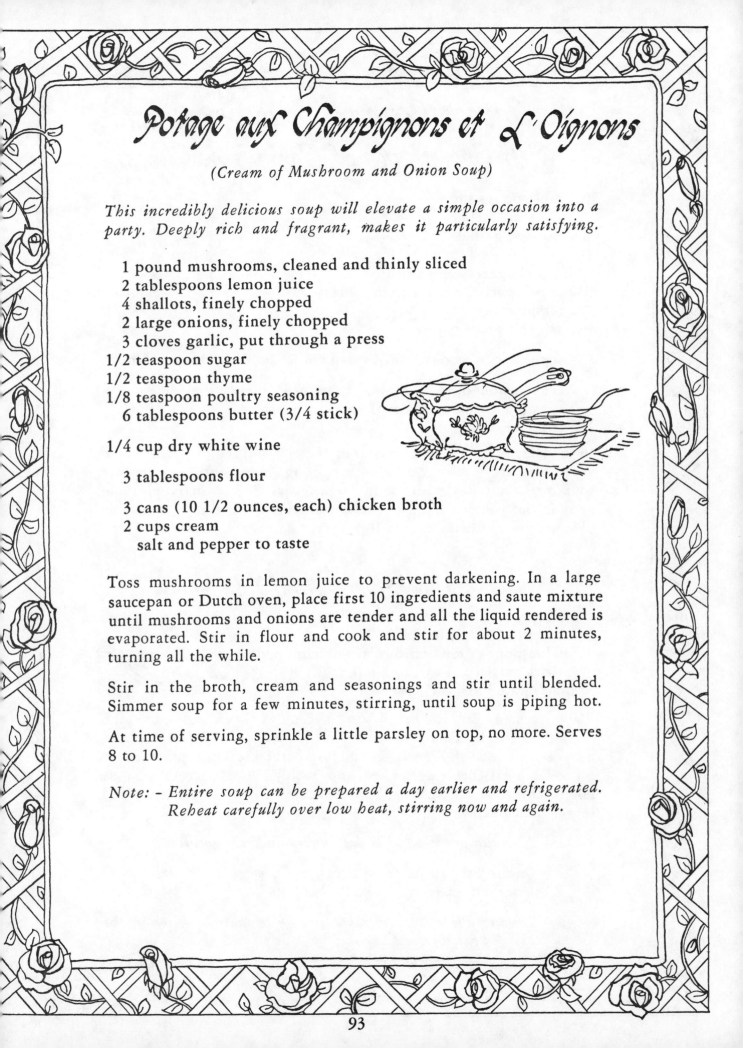

Toss mushrooms in lemon juice to prevent darkening. In a large saucepan or Dutch oven, place first 10 ingredients and saute mixture until mushrooms and onions are tender and all the liquid rendered is evaporated. Stir in flour and cook and stir for about 2 minutes, turning all the while.

Stir in the broth, cream and seasonings and stir until blended. Simmer soup for a few minutes, stirring, until soup is piping hot.

At time of serving, sprinkle a little parsley on top, no more. Serves 8 to 10.

Note: - Entire soup can be prepared a day earlier and refrigerated. Reheat carefully over low heat, stirring now and again.

French Country Soup Provencal with Croustades of Tomato & Cheese

4 tablespoons butter
2 onions, finely chopped
2 carrots, grated
1/4 cup finely chopped celery
1/4 cup chopped green onions
2 cloves garlic, put through a press
1/2 teaspoon thyme
salt and pepper to taste

4 slices bacon, cooked until crisp and crumbled. Discard fat.

2 cans (1 pound, each) stewed tomatoes, finely chopped
2 cans (10 1/2 ounces, each) chicken broth
1/3 cup rice, raw

In a Dutch oven, saute together first 8 ingredients until the vegetables are tender. Add the remaining ingredients and simmer soup for 30 minutes, with the lid slightly ajar. Soup is marvelous just as it is, but you can add a touch of glamour by floating a Croustade of Tomato and Cheese on the top. Serves 6.

Croustades of Tomato & Cheese

6 slices French bread, toasted
1 tomato, finely chopped
3 tablespoons green onions, finely chopped
1 clove garlic, put through a press
3/4 cup grated Swiss cheese

Place toasted French bread on a cookie sheet. Combine the remaining ingredients and stir until blended. Divide mixture between 6 slices of French bread. Just before serving, place under a broiler until cheese is melted and bubbly. Watch carefully so as not to burn. With a spatula, slip 1 slice of bread on each soup and serve. Delicious!

Note: – Soup can be prepared a day earlier and refrigerated.

– Croustades can be toasted earlier in week and stored in an airtight container.

– Tomato and cheese mixture can be prepared earlier in the day and refrigerated.

Spinach & Mushroom Soup with Buttered Herbed Crisps

This is a very delicious soup that is also quite easy to prepare. It is filled with homey goodness and the Buttered Herbed Crisps adds a touch of glamour. Serve it with a dollup of sour cream and a sprinkling of chives, and all's well in the world.

   1 onion, chopped
1/2 pound mushrooms, cleaned and thinly sliced
1/4 cup butter (1/2 stick)
    pinch of thyme

   2 tablespoons chopped parsley
   2 cans (10 1/2 ounces, each) chicken broth
   4 tablespoons chopped chives

   1 package (10 ounces) frozen chopped spinach, defrosted
   1 cup cream
    salt and pepper to taste

In a saucepan, over a medium-high heat and uncovered, saute together onions and mushrooms in butter until onions are soft. Add thyme, parsley, chicken broth and chives and stir to combine. Add spinach and cook for 5 minutes. Add cream and seasonings and heat through.

Serve hot with a dollup of sour cream and a sprinkling of chives. Buttered Herbed Crisps is an especially delicious accompaniment. Serves 4 to 6.

Note: – Entire dish can be prepared earlier in the day and refrigerated. Reheat over low heat, stirring.

Buttered Herbed Crisps

   6 slices fresh white bread, remove crusts
   6 tablespoons melted butter
   1 tablespoon minced parsley
   1 tablespoon minced chives
1/4 teaspoon thyme flakes

With a rolling pin, roll each slice of bread flat. Combine butter and herbs. Brush bread with butter mixture and place on a cookie sheet. Bake in a 350° oven, basting bread and turning until bread is crisp on both sides. Cut bread into triangles or other decorative shape.

Spinach Soup with Rice & Mushrooms

A robust soup with a sturdy heart and solid character.

2 large onions, finely minced
2 shallots, minced
2 cloves garlic, minced
2 tablespoons butter
2 tablespoons olive oil

1/2 pound mushrooms, sliced

1 package (10 ounces) frozen chopped spinach
1 cup cooked rice (or 1/3 cup raw rice)
3 cans (10 1/2 ounces, each) chicken broth, undiluted
2 tablespoons lemon juice, or to taste

salt and pepper to taste

Combine first 5 ingredients and in a skillet, saute them until the onions are soft. Add the mushrooms and continue sauteing until the mushrooms are tender and the liquid is absorbed.

Transfer mixture to a saucepan, and add the remaining ingredients. Simmer soup for 20 minutes. (If using raw rice, add another 5 or 10 minutes.) Serve with Petite Cottage Cheese Muffins and creamy whipped butter. Serves 4 to 6.

Note: – *If you have 1 quart of homemade chicken stock on hand, it would be very nice, indeed.*
– *Soup can be made earlier in the day and refrigerated. Reheat at time of serving.*

Petite Cottage Cheese Muffins

1 cup small curd cottage cheese
2 tablespoons sour cream
1 tablespoon oil
1 teaspoon sugar
2 eggs, beaten
1/2 cup Bisquick, prepared biscuit mix
1 teaspoon dried chives

Combine all the ingredients and mix until blended. Butter 24 teflon-coated hors d'oeuvre-size muffin molds and fill 1/2 full with batter. Bake in a 350° oven for 25 minutes or until muffins are puffed and golden brown. Yields 24 muffins.

Country French Vegetable Soup with Onions & Cheese

There is probably no easier soup anywhere; yet the results will really amaze you. This soup is hearty and hardy and will do very well on a night that you are planning a light dinner.

2 cans (10 1/2 ounces, each) chicken broth
2 cans water
1 teaspoon chicken stock base
2 tablespoons butter
2 cloves garlic, put through a press
   pinch of thyme
   salt and pepper to taste

1 can (1 pound) stewed tomatoes, chopped
1 package (10 ounces) cut green beans
1 cup chopped onions (you can use the frozen
   chopped onions)
2 potatoes, peeled and grated

1 1/2 cups grated Swiss cheese

In a large saucepan (about 3 to 4 quarts), combine all the ingredients, except the Swiss cheese. Bring soup to a boil, lower heat, and simmer soup, partially covered, until the vegetables are tender, about 40 to 50 minutes. Soup can be made ahead to this point.

When ready to serve, bring soup to a boil. Remove from heat and stir in the cheese. Serve at once with Toast Points with Garlic and Cheese. Serves 6.

Buttered Toast Points with Garlic & Cheese

6 slices black bread, crusts removed. Flatten each slice
   with a rolling pin. Toast lightly.
6 teaspoons butter
   garlic powder
4 tablespoons grated Parmesan cheese

Spread butter on each slice of bread. Sprinkle with garlic powder to taste. Place cheese on a flat plate and dip buttered side of toast on the cheese to coat it nicely. Broil bread for a few seconds until cheese is bubbly and lightly browned.

Easiest & Best Lentil Soup

1 pound lentils, rinsed in a strainer
2 cans (10 1/2 ounces, each) beef broth
4 cups water
2 cups chopped onions
3 carrots, thinly sliced
  salt and pepper to taste
1 package onion soup

Place all the ingredients in a Dutch oven, cover and simmer soup for 1 1/2 hours or until lentils are tender. This produces an exceedingly thick and hearty soup and it couldn't be easier. Serve it with thin slices of Apple Bread and sweet butter. Serves 6 to 8.

Cinnamon Apple Bread with Raisins & Walnuts

2 eggs
1 cup sugar
1/2 cup oil
1 teaspoon vanilla

1 1/2 cups flour
1 teaspoon baking powder
1/2 teaspoon baking soda
1/8 teaspoon salt
2 teaspoons cinnamon

1 cup grated apples
1/2 cup raisins
1/2 cup walnuts

Beat together eggs, sugar, oil and vanilla until thoroughly blended, about 1 minute. Stir in flour, baking powder, soda, salt and cinnamon until blended. Stir in apples, raisins and walnuts. Pour mixture into a 9x5x3-inch loaf pan that has been greased and floured. Bake in a 350° oven for about 50 minutes to 1 hour or until a cake tester inserted in center comes out clean.

Cool in pan for 10 minutes; then remove pan and cool on rack. Yields 1 loaf.

Tomato Vegetable Soup with Cheese & Herbs

This lovely soup is practically a meal in itself. It is rich and robust and very exciting . . . just a marvelous winter soup. Please use 8-ounce souffle dishes or porcelain bowls that can go into the oven for the simplest way of serving this soup.

      2 large onions, chopped
      1 stalk celery, scraped and sliced
      1 small carrot, thinly sliced
      1 clove garlic, put through a press
      4 tablespoons (1/2 stick) butter
1/2 teaspoon thyme flakes
      1 teaspoon parsley flakes
         salt and pepper to taste

      1 can (16 ounces) stewed tomatoes, finely chopped
      2 cans (10 1/2 ounces, each) chicken broth
1/3 cup raw rice
      2 teaspoons sugar

Saute first 8 ingredients together until the vegetables are tender. Puree the vegetables in a blender or food processor, using some of the broth, if necessary, to allow blades to turn freely.

In a saucepan, place the pureed vegetables with the remaining ingredients and simmer mixture for about 20 minutes or until the rice is tender. Divide soup between 6 soup bowls that can go into the oven. Place bowls on a cookie pan (to facilitate removing from the oven). When ready to heat soup, place a Croustade of Cheese on top and heat in a 350° oven until piping hot. Broil tops for a few seconds to lightly brown. Serves 6 very fortunate people.

Croustades of Cheese with Herbs

6 slices white bread. Cut a round from each with a 2 1/2-inch
      biscuit or cookie cutter. Brush each with melted butter
      and crisp in a 350° oven.
4 ounces Swiss cheese, grated (about 1 cup)
4 tablespoons sour cream
2 tablespoons chopped chives
1 tablespoon chopped parsley

Combine Swiss cheese, sour cream, chives and parsley and mix until even. Spread mixture on top of each bread round. If preparing earlier in the day, refrigerate.

Potage of Tomatoes & Clams

1 can (1 pound) stewed tomatoes, finely chopped
1 can (8 ounces) tomato sauce
1 cup tomato juice
1 cup clam juice
2 tablespoons oil
1 teaspoon sugar
1 onion, finely chopped
1 clove garlic, mashed
1/2 teaspoon thyme flakes
    pinch of tumeric
2 tablespoons chopped parsley
    salt and pepper to taste

Combine all the ingredients in a large saucepan and simmer mixture for 30 minutes. Add

2 cups half and half
2 cans (7 ounces, each) chopped clams

and heat through. Serve with some crusty French bread and sweet butter. Serves 6.

Note: - Soup base can be made one or two days earlier. Reheat soup, add the cream and the clams and continue heating until soup is piping hot.
*   - Float 1 teaspoon of sour cream on soup when serving, as a delicious optional.*
*   - Serve the soup with Croustades of French Bread with Cheese and Voila! you have a party.*

Croustades of French Bread with Cheese

6 slices French bread, lightly toasted

4 tablespoons mayonnaise
6 tablespoons grated Swiss cheese
1 clove garlic, put through a press
1 tablespoon lemon juice

Combine mayonnaise, cheese, garlic and lemon juice. Spread mixture evenly between the 6 slices of bread. When ready to serve, broil bread for a few seconds or until top is lightly browned and bubbly.

Note: - Bread can be assembled earlier in the day and placed in pan. Cover well with plastic wrap. Remove plastic before broiling.

Potage of Cabbage & Tomatoes Provence Style

2 pounds chuck flanken-style ribs, meaty and lean
    (sometimes called short ribs)
1 small head of cabbage (about 1 1/2 pounds), grated or
    coarsely chopped
1 cup sauerkraut
1 can (1 pound) stewed tomatoes, finely chopped
3 cans (10 1/2 ounces, each) chicken broth
1 can (10 1/2 ounces) beef broth
1 teaspoon Bovril, meat extract base
3 onions, chopped
2 cloves garlic, put through a press
1 carrot, finely grated

2 tablespoons lemon juice
2 tablespoons sugar

salt and pepper to taste

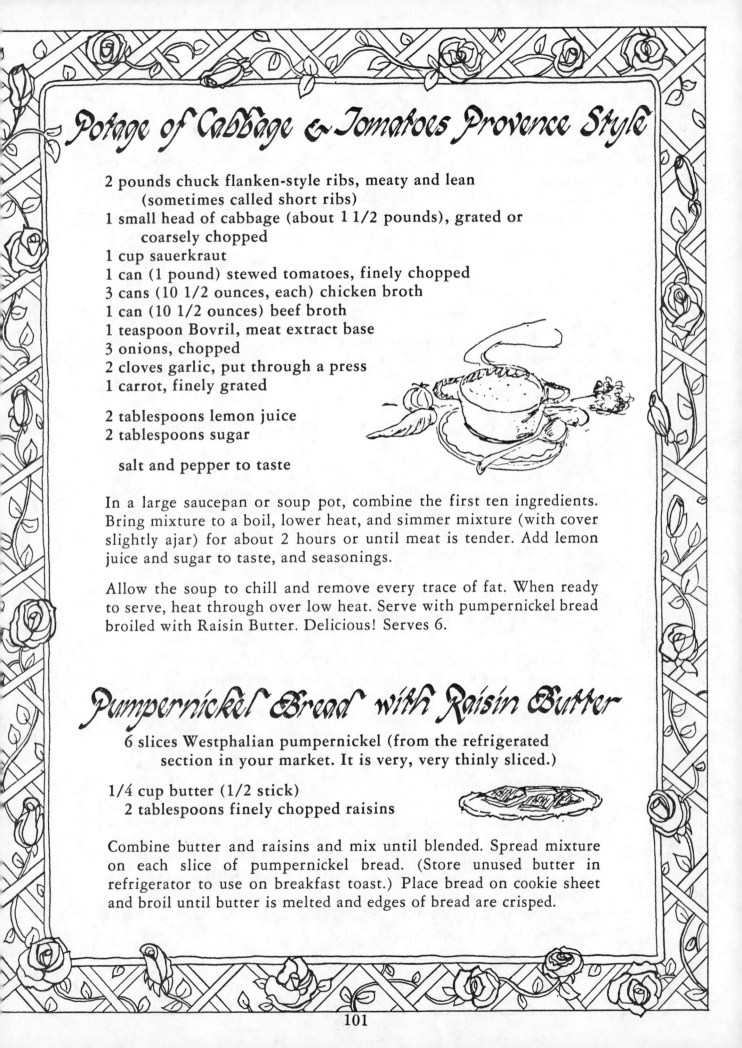

In a large saucepan or soup pot, combine the first ten ingredients. Bring mixture to a boil, lower heat, and simmer mixture (with cover slightly ajar) for about 2 hours or until meat is tender. Add lemon juice and sugar to taste, and seasonings.

Allow the soup to chill and remove every trace of fat. When ready to serve, heat through over low heat. Serve with pumpernickel bread broiled with Raisin Butter. Delicious! Serves 6.

Pumpernickel Bread with Raisin Butter

6 slices Westphalian pumpernickel (from the refrigerated
    section in your market. It is very, very thinly sliced.)

1/4 cup butter (1/2 stick)
2 tablespoons finely chopped raisins

Combine butter and raisins and mix until blended. Spread mixture on each slice of pumpernickel bread. (Store unused butter in refrigerator to use on breakfast toast.) Place bread on cookie sheet and broil until butter is melted and edges of bread are crisped.

Cream of Potato & Onion Soup

This is a fascinating soup because it is made with instant mash potato flakes. It can be prepared quickly and does not at all appear as a "jiffy" dish. If you have the time to prepare 1 cup of mashed potatoes from scratch, that is very good, too.

1 large onion, minced
2 cloves garlic, put through a press
2 shallots, minced
2 tablespoons butter

2 cans (10 1/2 ounces, each) chicken broth
3 tablespoons chopped chives
2 tablespoons chopped parsley
   salt and pepper to taste

1 cup instant mash potato flakes (use straight from the box)

1 cup sour cream

In a saucepan, saute onion, garlic and shallots in butter until onion is soft. Add the broth, chives, parsely and seasonings, and bring mixture to a simmer. Stir in the potato flakes and simmer for 10 minutes. Stir in the sour cream and heat through. Serve with Croustades of Cheese as a delightful accompaniment. Serves 4 or 5.

Croustades of Cheese

6 slices egg bread. Cut away the crusts and roll bread flat
   with a rolling pin. Brush tops with melted butter.
6 teaspoons grated Parmesan cheese
6 teaspoons chopped chives
6 slices Swiss cheese, at room temperature

melted butter
grated Parmesan cheese

Sprinkle 1 teaspoon grated Parmesan cheese on buttered side of each slice of bread. Sprinkle each with chives and top with 1 slice of Swiss cheese. Roll up jelly-roll fashion and spear with a toothpick to fasten. Brush all around with additional melted butter and sprinkle lightly with grated Parmesan cheese. Bake at 400° for about 15 minutes or until lightly browned and cheese is melted. Remove picks and serve with soups or salads.

Cold Puree of Asparagus Soup with Crispettes of Cheese

2 packages (10 ounces, each) frozen asparagus, cooked
    according to the directions on the package.
    Cut off the tips and set aside.

1 onion, finely chopped
2 shallots, finely chopped
2 cloves garlic, put through a press
4 tablespoons butter (1/2 stick)

2 cans (10 1/2 ounces, each) chicken broth
1 cup half and half
1 cup sour cream
    salt and pepper to taste

Saute onion, shallots and garlic in butter until onions are soft, but not browned. In a processor or a blender, place asparagus spears and onion mixture and process until it is pureed. You may need a little broth, if you are using a blender, so that the blades do not jam.

In a saucepan, place pureed vegetables and chicken broth and heat through. Add cream and sour cream, and stir until blended. Taste for salt and pepper and heat through, but do not boil. Refrigerate soup until serving time. When serving, float asparagus tips on top and serve with Crispettes of Cheese. Serves 6.

Crispettes of Cheese

6 slices good quality white bread, crusts removed
4 tablespoons melted butter
4 tablespoons grated Parmesan cheese
3 teaspoons chopped chives

With a rolling pin, flatten bread slices. Place on a cookie sheet and baste with butter. Bake in a 350° oven until bread crispens, basting with butter every few minutes. You may need a little more butter. Sprinkle top with cheese and chives and return to oven until cheese is bubbly. Allow to cool and store in an airtight container until serving time. Can be made earlier in the day. Serve Crispettes at room temperature. Makes 6 slices, and serves 6.

Easiest & Best Vichyssoise ~ Leek Soup

This delicately flavored soup is a classic. Traditionally served cold as Vichyssoise, *it is also excellent served hot as* Potage aux Poireaux. *Hot or cold, it is delicious and satisfying. And to top it all, it is easy to prepare.*

1 pound leeks, use the white part and as much of the tender
      green. Slice it thinly. Wash away any trace of sand.
1 pound potatoes, peeled and sliced
2 tablespoons butter
2 cans (10 1/2 ounces, each) chicken broth
2 cans water
  salt to taste

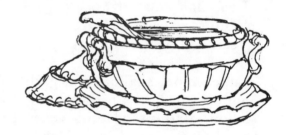

1/2 cup cream
1/2 cup sour cream
  2 tablespoons chopped parsley
  2 tablespoons chopped chives
  1 tablespoon lemon juice

In a large saucepan (about 3 to 4 quarts), combine leeks, potatoes, butter, chicken broth, water and salt to taste. Bring mixture to a boil, lower heat and simmer soup with the cover slightly ajar for about 50 minutes or until the vegetables are soft.

Meanwhile, combine cream, sour cream, parsley, chives and lemon juice and stir until blended. Leave the cream mixture at room temperature while the soup is simmering. It should thicken nicely.

When the vegetables are cooked soft, puree them in a blender or processor until they are finely chopped and smooth but not liquefied like baby food. In other words, leave a little texture and bite.

Add the cream mixture and stir until blended. Serve either hot or cold. Sprinkle top with a few additional chopped chives. If soup is too thick, add extra broth. Serves 6.

Note: – You can substitute 1 pound of yellow onions for the leeks. Soup will have a somewhat different character but will also be quite good.
*   – Entire dish can be made 1 day earlier and stored in the refrigerator. Reheat over low heat, stirring occasionally.*

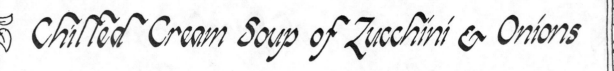

Chilled Cream Soup of Zucchini & Onions

A delicate blend of zucchini, onions, herbs in a savory combination of sour cream and buttermilk, makes this delicious cold soup a delight for lunch. Served with Burgundian Cheese Pastry "makes it the stuff poetry is made of."

1 1/2 pounds zucchini, scrubbed and sliced. **Do not peel.**
  2 large onions, chopped
  2 cloves garlic, mashed
1/2 teaspoon sugar
1/2 teaspoon dill weed
  4 tablespoons butter

  1 can (10 1/2 ounces) chicken broth
  1 cup sour cream (or 1 1/2 cups)
  1 cup buttermilk (or 1 1/2 cups)

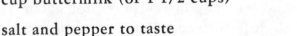

  salt and pepper to taste

In a large skillet, saute together the first 6 ingredients until the onions are soft and the zucchini is tender. Do this over low heat; vegetables should be soft. Place the zucchini mixture into a processor or blender and puree the mixture until it is smooth. (If you use a blender, you may need a little broth so that the blades run freely.)

Pour pureed soup base into a saucepan and stir in the remaining ingredients until thoroughly blended. (If soup is too thick, add a little more sour cream and buttermilk.)

Pour soup in a lovely bowl and sprinkle top with additional dill weed to taste. Refrigerate until well chilled. Serve cold in pretty glass bowls with a dollup of sour cream and a light sprinkling of dill weed. Serves 6 to 8.

Note: - Soup can be made 1 day earlier and stored in the refrigerator.

  - Soup is very good served warm.

Cold Fresh Peach Soup with Strawberries & Cream

   3 cups peach nectar
3/4 cup orange juice
    pinch of cinnamon

   6 peaches, peeled and pitted

1/2 cup cream
1/2 cup sour cream
  1 package (10 ounces) frozen strawberries
    in syrup, defrosted

Combine peach nectar, orange juice and cinnamon in a saucepan and bring to a simmer. Cook peaches in the juices for about 5 minutes or until peaches are slightly softened. Puree peaches in a blender or food processor. Return peaches to saucepan.

Stir in the remaining ingredients until blended. Pour soup into a pretty glass bowl and refrigerate until serving time. Serve with date nut bread and cream cheese. Serves 6.

Note: – Soup can be prepared earlier in the day and stored in the refrigerator. Do not prepare a day earlier.

Salads
&
Dressings

Asparagus in Herbed Vinaigrette

2 packages (10 ounces, each) frozen asparagus, cooked
   until tender and drained. Chill.

1 cup oil (can use 1/2 olive oil)
1/4 cup lemon juice
2 teaspoons Dijon-style mustard
1 clove garlic, put through a press
2 tablespoons minced parsley
2 tablespoons chopped chives
1/2 teaspoon dried thyme flakes
1 teaspoon sugar
   salt and pepper to taste

Lay cooked asparagus flat in a shallow dish.

Combine the remaining ingredients in a glass jar with a tight-fitting lid and shake until blended. Pour about 1/4 cup dressing (or more to taste) over the asparagus. Refrigerate overnight to allow flavors to blend. Store unused dressing in the refrigerator.

Yields about 1 1/2 cups dressing.

Green Pea & Tomato Salad Francaise

A wonderful change of pace salad that is rich and flavorful and exceedingly delicious.

2 packages (10 ounces, each) frozen peas, cooked in
      1/4 cup water until tender and drained. Chill.
2 medium tomatoes, coarsely chopped
1/2 cup mayonnaise
1/2 cup sour cream
3 green onions, finely chopped
6 strips bacon, cooked crisp, drained and crumbled
3 tablespoons lemon juice
   salt and pepper to taste

Combine all the ingredients and stir to blend. Refrigerate until serving time. Serves 8.

Note: - *May be prepared one day earlier and stored in the refrigerator.*
      - *If you prefer, you may substitute 1/2 thinly sliced onion for the green onions.*

Salade a la Nicoise with Lemon Garlic

This is a sort of happy medium in preparing this exceptionally delicious salad. For as many times as I have ordered this salad, in Nice and along the southern coast of France, not twice has it ever been served the same. Actually, you have a good deal of latitude. Include those vegetables which make you the happiest (although green beans are most often included.)

1 1/2 pounds potatoes, cooked, peeled and sliced
   1 can (1 pound) whole green beans, drained
   2 tomatoes, sliced
   3 slices red onions, separated into rings
   1 can (7 ounces) tuna fish, drained
   8 black olives
   2 hard-cooked eggs, peeled and quartered
   1 can (2 ounces) flat anchovies in oil, drained

     lettuce leaves to line platter

Combine potatoes, green beans, tomatoes and red onions in a bowl and drizzle with 1/2 Lemon Garlic Dressing. Allow to marinate in the refrigerator for several hours.

To serve, line a platter with lettuce leaves. Arrange attractively the tuna, olives, eggs, anchovies and marinated vegetables. Drizzle a little dressing over all and pass the remaining dressing at the table. Serves 4 to 6.

Lemon Garlic Dressing

3/4 cup oil
   6 tablespoons lemon juice
   2 tablespoons red wine vinegar
1/3 cup finely chopped green onions
   2 tablespoons chopped parsley
   1 clove garlic, put through a press
     salt and pepper to taste
   1 teaspoon Dijon-style mustard (optional)

Combine all the ingredients in a jar with a tight-fitting lid and shake vigorously to blend. Store in the refrigerator until ready to use. Yields about 1 1/4 cups dressing.

Green Pea Salad with Garlic & Dill Dressing

1 package (10 ounces) frozen green peas, cooked
    until tender but not too soft

Garlic and Dill Dressing:
4 tablespoons red wine vinegar
2 tablespoons water
1 tablespoon sugar
5 ounces oil
1/8 teaspoon garlic powder
2 tablespoons chopped parsley
2 tablespoons chopped chives
2 tablespoons grated Parmesan cheese
1/2 teaspoon dill weed
    salt and pepper to taste

Place cooked peas in a bowl. Combine dressing ingredients in a glass jar with a tight-fitting lid and shake until blended. Pour dressing to taste over the peas and store unused dressing in the refrigerator. Allow peas to marinate in the dressing for at least 4 hours in the refrigerator. Overnight is good, too. Serve as an accompaniment to quiches, and the like. This is an interesting cold vegetable. Serves 4 or 5.

Cauliflower, Tomato & Onion Salad in Lemon Cream Dressing

2 packages (10 ounces, each) frozen cauliflower
3 tomatoes, cut into thin wedges
3 green onions, finely chopped
2 tablespoons chopped parsley
    salt and pepper to taste

3/4 cup cream
    3 tablespoons lemon juice
    1 tablespoon vinegar
1/4 cup oil
1/8 teaspoon garlic powder
    1 teaspoon sugar

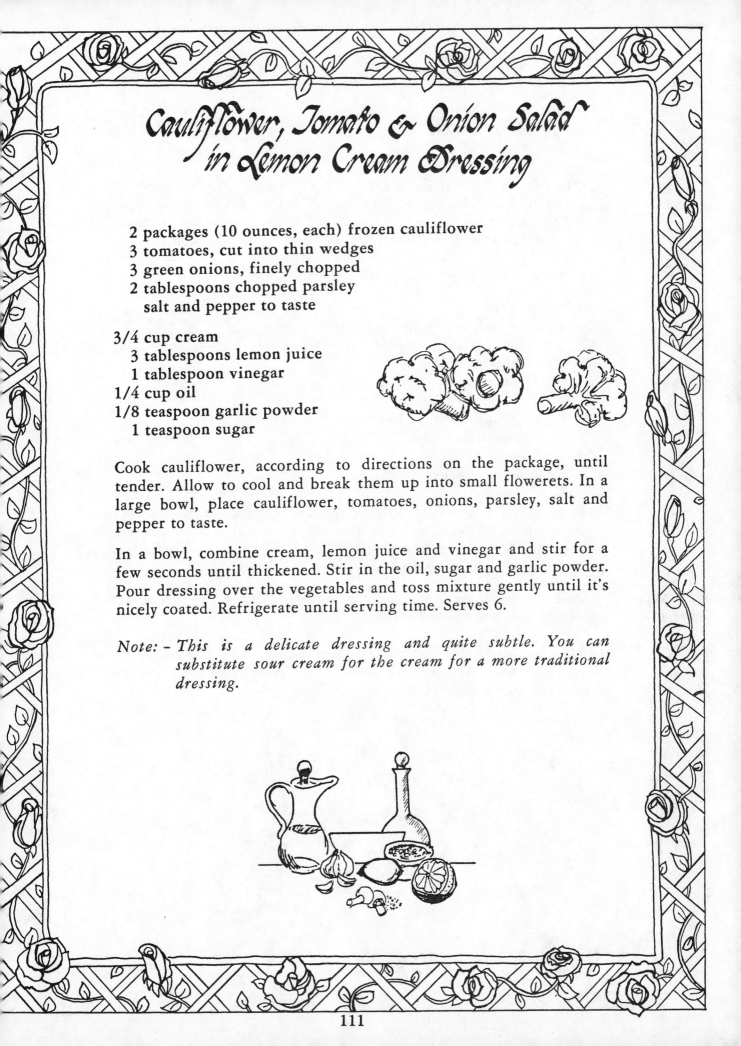

Cook cauliflower, according to directions on the package, until tender. Allow to cool and break them up into small flowerets. In a large bowl, place cauliflower, tomatoes, onions, parsley, salt and pepper to taste.

In a bowl, combine cream, lemon juice and vinegar and stir for a few seconds until thickened. Stir in the oil, sugar and garlic powder. Pour dressing over the vegetables and toss mixture gently until it's nicely coated. Refrigerate until serving time. Serves 6.

Note: – This is a delicate dressing and quite subtle. You can substitute sour cream for the cream for a more traditional dressing.

Green Beans Vinaigrette with Herbs

The best Green Bean Salad I have ever eaten was in a little restaurant in Paris. I still delight in the memory. It was served quite simply on a little plate without a trace of garnish. However, one taste, and it became the stuff that dreams are made of. This is how it tasted.

1 can (16 ounces) whole green beans

1/2 cup oil
 1 teaspoon Dijon-style mustard
 1 tablespoon wine vinegar
 2 tablespoons lemon juice
 1 shallot, minced
 1 green onion, minced
 1 tablespoon chopped parsley (or 1 teaspoon dried
  parsley flakes)
1/4 teaspoon thyme
 salt and pepper to taste

Place green beans in a bowl. Combine the remaining ingredients in a glass jar with a screw-top lid and shake vigorously. Pour dressing over green beans and toss to coat. Any unused dressing can be stored in the refrigerator.

Allow to marinate in refrigerator overnight. Serve on a bed of lettuce or as a cold vegetable. Serves 4.

Note: – Salad can be prepared 2 days earlier and stored, covered, in the refrigerator. Toss every so often to coat the green beans with the dressing.

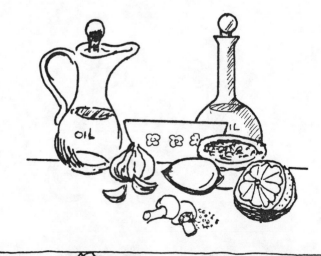

Mushroom, Tomato, Bacon Salad in Lemon Garlic Dressing

Lemon Garlic Dressing:

1/4 cup oil
   2 tablespoons lemon juice
   1 clove garlic, cut in fourths
   1 teaspoon Dijon-style mustard
   1 tablespoon finely chopped parsley
   1 tablespoon finely chopped chives
   salt and freshly ground pepper to taste

Salad:

1/2 pound mushrooms, cleaned and sliced
   2 tomatoes, peeled, seeded and chopped. Allow to drain.
   6 slices bacon, cooked crisp, drained and crumbled
   1 green onion, finely chopped

Combine first seven ingredients in a glass jar with a screw-top lid and shake vigorously. Refrigerate until ready to use.

Place mushrooms, tomatoes, bacon and green onion in a bowl. Pour dressing over the salad (remove the garlic) and toss until mushrooms are well coated. Serve soon after tossing. Within an hour is acceptable, although I prefer to serve this salad at once. Serve on a bed of lettuce with a few grinds of fresh pepper. Serves 4.

Note: – If you clean and slice the mushrooms earlier in the day, then toss them in a little lemon juice so that they do not darken.

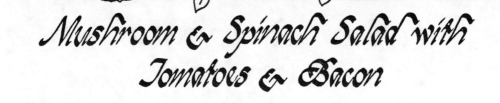

Mushroom & Spinach Salad with Tomatoes & Bacon

2 tomatoes, thinly sliced
1/2 pound mushrooms, cleaned and sliced
1 1/2 pounds fresh spinach. Wash 3 or 4 times to remove every
trace of sand. Cut off stems and tear into pieces.
8 slices bacon, cooked crisp, drained and crumbled
4 green onions, chopped
2 hard cooked eggs, chopped

Place all the ingredients in a bowl and toss to combine. Refrigerate until serving time.

When ready to serve, pour dressing over the salad, and toss until everything is nicely coated. Do not pour too much dressing, but enough to film the salad. Serve at once. Serves 4 for a luncheon salad or 6 as an accompaniment to dinner.

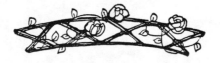

Spinach Salad Dressing

1 cup oil
1/4 cup red wine vinegar
1 clove garlic, put through a press
1/4 teaspoon basil
1 teaspoon sugar
1 teaspoon Dijon-mustard
salt and freshly ground pepper to taste

Combine all the ingredients in a jar with a tight-fitting lid and shake vigorously until mixture is blended. Yields 1 1/4 cups dressing.

Note: - You can add 1 cup garlic croutons and toss these at serving time.

French Potato Salad Vinaigrette

In France, potato salad is most often served in a vinegar and oil dressing rather than with mayonnaise. This lovely salad flecked with green and red can be served either at room temperature or chilled.

2 pounds potatoes

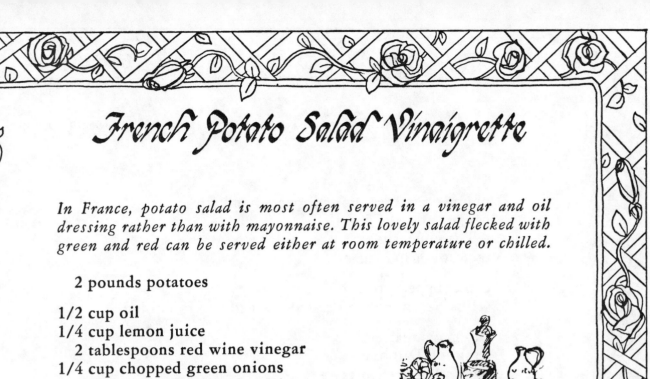

1/2 cup oil
1/4 cup lemon juice
   2 tablespoons red wine vinegar
1/4 cup chopped green onions
   2 tablespoons chopped parsley
   1 jar (2 ounces) pimento strips, drained
   1 clove garlic, put through a press
1/2 teaspoon sugar
   salt and freshly ground pepper to taste

Cook the potatoes, unpeeled, in boiling water, until they are tender. Run them under cold water, peel and slice them.

Combine the remaining ingredients in a glass jar with a tight-fitting lid and shake vigorously. Pour dressing over the potatoes and toss to blend. Refrigerate several hours or overnight. Serve chilled or at room temperature. Serves 6.

Potato Salad with Eggs & Onions

2 pounds potatoes, boiled, peeled and sliced
1 carrot, grated
2 tablespoons sugar
3 tablespoons vinegar

1/2 cup chopped green onions
6 strips bacon, cooked crisp, drained and crumbled

1 cup mayonnaise
1 teaspoon Dijon mustard
salt and pepper to taste
3 hard cooked eggs, chopped

Combine potatoes, carrots, sugar and vinegar and toss until blended. Allow to rest for 10 minutes.

Add the remaining ingredients and toss mixture until blended.

Place salad in a bowl, cover and refrigerate for several hours or overnight. Serves 6.

Potato Salad au Creme Fraiche

1/2 cup sour cream
1/2 cup cream
  3 tablespoons lemon juice
  2 tablespoons chopped green onion or chives
  2 tablespoons chopped parsley

  2 pounds potatoes, boiled, peeled and sliced
  1 carrot, grated
  1 tablespoon sugar
  1 tablespoon vinegar
    salt and pepper to taste

Combine sour cream, cream, lemon juice, onions and parsley and stir until mixture is well combined. Allow to rest at room temperature until thickened (about 20 minutes) and refrigerate.

Cook the potatoes, unpeeled, in boiling water, until they are tender. Run them under cold water, peel and slice them.

In a large bowl, place potatoes, carrot, sugar, vinegar, salt and pepper and toss until mixture is nicely combined. Allow mixture to rest for 10 minutes. Now add the cream mixture and toss and turn until potatoes are evenly coated. Refrigerate for several hours. Overnight is better. Serves 4 to 6.

Salad with Vegetables, Bacon & Cheese with Lemon Herb Dressing

The Salad:

    1 large head Iceberg lettuce
    2 tomatoes, chopped
    4 green onions, chopped
1/2 pound bacon, cooked crisp, drained and crumbled
    1 cup grated Swiss cheese

    1 cup garlic croutons

Combine all the ingredients (except the croutons, which will be added at the end) and toss to blend. Place in refrigerator until serving time.

Pour Lemon Herb Dressing over the salad and toss until everything is nicely coated. Use only enough dressing to film the salad without making puddles on the bottom of the bowl. Serve at once. Serves 4.

Lemon Herb Dressing

1/2 cup oil
1/4 cup lemon juice
    1 tablespoon chopped chives
    1 tablespoon chopped parsley
1/4 teaspoon oregano flakes
    1 egg, beaten
1/3 cup grated Parmesan cheese
1/8 teaspoon garlic powder
    salt and freshly ground pepper to taste

Combine all the ingredients in a jar with a tight-fitting lid and shake vigorously until mixture is nicely blended.

Fish & Shellfish

Scallops in White Wine Cream Sauce
(Coquilles Saint Jacques)

1 1/2 pounds scallops, cut into slices 1/4-inch thick.
    Wash and remove every trace of sand.
  1 clove garlic (put through a press, optional)
  4 tablespoons butter
    salt and pepper to taste

1/2 pound mushrooms, cleaned and sliced
  4 shallots, finely chopped
  4 tablespoons butter
  2 tablespoons lemon juice

  3 tablespoons flour
  1 cup cream
1/2 cup sour cream
1/4 teaspoon thyme flakes

  Cheese Topping

In a skillet, saute scallops and garlic in butter for about 5 minutes, turning, or until scallops lose their transparency and become opaque. Season with salt and pepper and remove scallops with a slotted spoon. (Garlic is not traditional, but I like it in this dish.)

In the same skillet, saute mushrooms and shallots in butter and lemon juice until mushrooms are tender. Add in the flour and cook for 3 minutes, stirring. Add cream, sour cream and thyme flakes and cook and stir until sauce is thickened. Stir in the cooked scallops.

Spoon mixture into 8 individual buttered scallop shells and sprinkle tops with 2 tablespoons Cheese Topping. Heat in a 350° oven until heated through and cheese is melted. Brown tops for a few seconds under the broiler. Serves 8.

Cheese & Chive Topping

3/4 cup grated Swiss cheese
1/4 cup grated Parmesan cheese
  1 teaspoon chopped parsley
  2 teaspoons chopped chives

Combine all the ingredients in a jar with a screw-top lid and shake until blended.

Bouillabaisse a la Provencal with Croustades of Garlic Butter

Sonnets and odes could not describe the soul-satisfying qualities of this Mediterranean fish chowder. There are many and varying opinions as to which fish to use, but this soup base works very well with most fish and shellfish available in your area. I have simplified the preparation by simmering all the ingredients together, omitting initial sauteing. The results are an incredible chowder that will surely delight family and friends. Please don't think for a moment that this is difficult. Actually, there are a lot of ingredients, but preparation is the essence of simplicity.

Soup Base:
    1 cup onions, finely chopped
1/2 cup leeks, sliced. Use only the white part.
        Leeks are traditional but 1 cup chopped green
        onions can be substituted.
    4 tablespoons olive oil
    2 cans (1 pound, each) stewed tomatoes, finely chopped
    6 tablespoons tomato paste
    1 cup dry white wine
    1 can (7 ounces) minced clams
    2 cups clam juice
    1 tablespoon minced garlic
    1 teaspoon sugar
1/4 cup minced parsley
1/2 teaspoon thyme flakes
1/4 teaspoon basil
1/4 teaspoon saffron
1/4 teaspoon tumeric
1/2 teaspoon red pepper flakes
    salt and pepper to taste

In a Dutch oven, combine all the ingredients and simmer mixture for 30 minutes, uncovered. Bring soup to a rolling boil and add:

2 pounds of assorted filleted fish or shellfish, cut into 1 or 2-inch slices. Include halibut, red snapper, flounder, cod, perch, haddock or sole. Clams, scallops, crab and lobster are also very good additions and add a great deal of excitement to this dish.

Keep soup at a rolling boil for about 10 minutes or until the fish becomes opaque. Do not overcook. Serve in deep soup bowls with a Croustade with Garlic Butter on top. Serves 6.

Note: – If you use shrimp, make certain that the black veins are removed. Crab and lobster should be well scrubbed and cut into pieces. All clams that do not open should be discarded.

– Soup base can be made earlier in the day and refrigerated. Bring soup to a rolling boil and then add the fish.

CROUSTADES WITH GARLIC BUTTER: In a skillet heat together 2 tablespoons butter, 1 tablespoon olive oil and 3 cloves garlic, mashed. When it is sizzling hot, quickly saute 6 slices of French bread in it until golden brown.

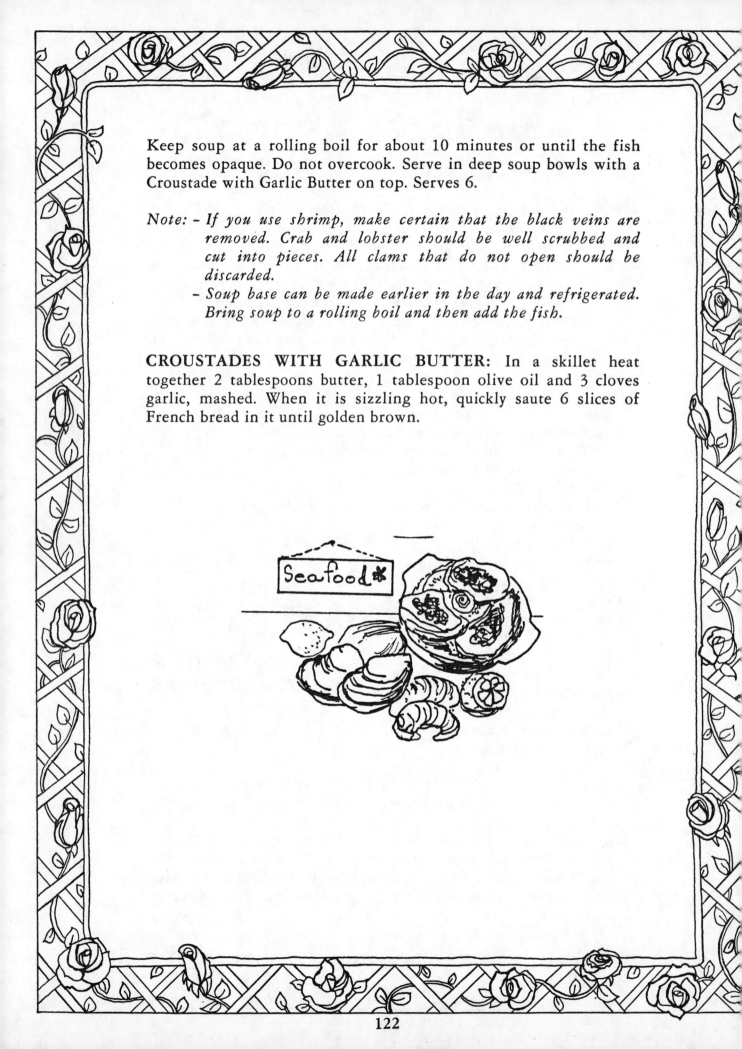

The Best Bouillabaisse Americaine

This recipe first appeared in "The Love of Eating," but it is so good I had to include it in my French book. While it seems lengthy, preparation is actually very simple. This is an excellent dish to serve on an evening when family and friends are dining together. It does wonders for the soul and spirit. Traditionally made with many varieties of fish and shellfish, this dish is also incredibly delicious with only 1 kind of fish.

1/4 cup oil
  1 cup chopped onions
  3 cloves garlic, finely minced
  1 can (1 pound) stewed tomatoes, chopped
  1 can (7 ounces) minced clams
  2 cups tomato juice
  3 cups clam juice
  1 tablespoon dried parsley flakes
1/4 teaspoon basil
  1 teaspoon thyme flakes
  2 teaspoons sugar
  pinch of saffron
  pinch of tumeric
  salt and pepper to taste
  2 pounds of perch, flounder or halibut fillets (or 2 pounds
      of assorted fish or shellfish, including cod, snapper,
      haddock, sole, scallops, clams, crab or lobster)

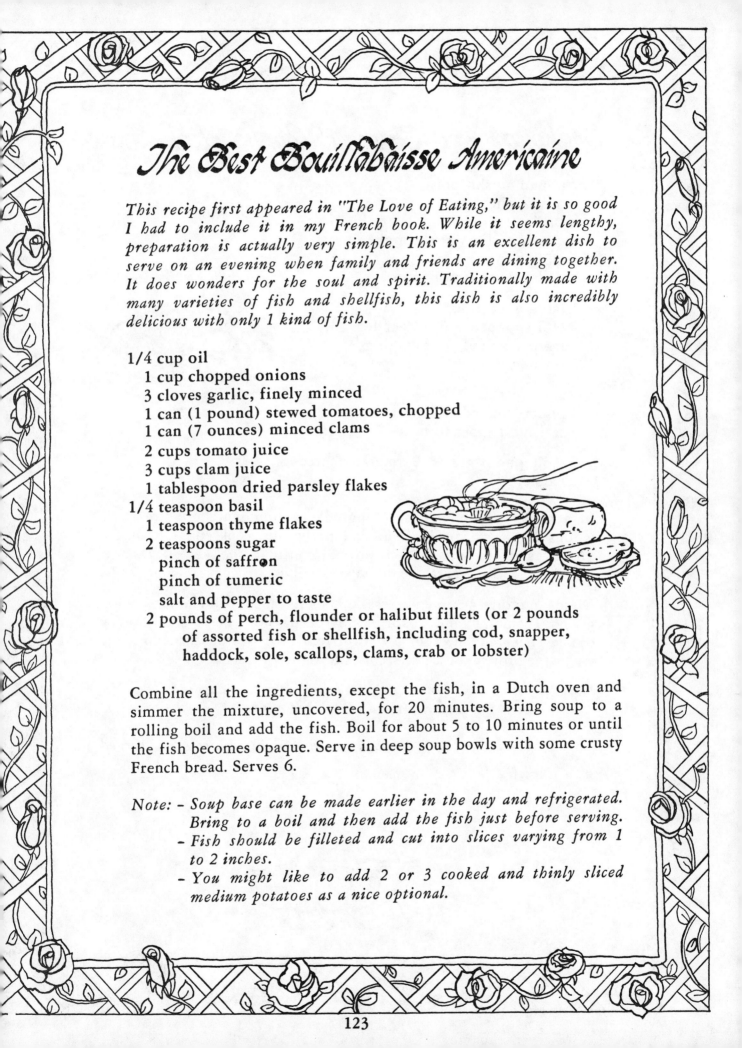

Combine all the ingredients, except the fish, in a Dutch oven and simmer the mixture, uncovered, for 20 minutes. Bring soup to a rolling boil and add the fish. Boil for about 5 to 10 minutes or until the fish becomes opaque. Serve in deep soup bowls with some crusty French bread. Serves 6.

Note: – *Soup base can be made earlier in the day and refrigerated. Bring to a boil and then add the fish just before serving.*
     – *Fish should be filleted and cut into slices varying from 1 to 2 inches.*
     – *You might like to add 2 or 3 cooked and thinly sliced medium potatoes as a nice optional.*

Crabmeat in a Creamed Garlic Herb Sauce

1/2 pound mushrooms
1 onion, chopped
4 shallots, chopped
4 cloves garlic, put through a press
4 tablespoons butter
2 tablespoons lemon juice

1 tablespoon flour
2 tablespoons chopped parsley
1/4 teaspoon poultry seasoning
1/8 teaspoon thyme flakes

1 cup cream
1 pound cooked crabmeat
salt and pepper to taste

6 tablespoons grated Parmesan cheese
parsley

In a skillet, combine first 6 ingredients and saute mixture until onions are soft. Stir in flour and herbs and cook for 2 minutes, turning and stirring. Add cream and continue cooking until sauce is thickened. Stir in crabmeat and seasonings.

Divide mixture between 6 scallop shells and sprinkle tops with grated Parmesan and a sprinkling of parsley. Place shells on a cookie sheet and heat in a 350° oven until heated through. Run under the broiler for a few seconds to lightly brown. Serves 6.

Note: – Entire dish can be prepared earlier in the day and stored in the refrigerator. Heat as described above.

– Entire dish can be baked in a porcelain casserole and served at the table.

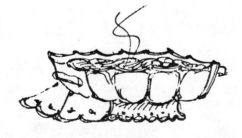

Crabmeat & Shrimp with Mushrooms, Garlic & Cheese

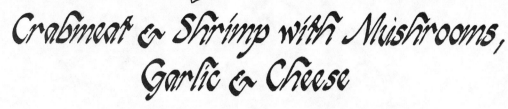

1/2 pound cooked crabmeat, picked over for bones
    and shredded
1/4 pound cooked baby shrimp

1/2 pound mushrooms, sliced
    1 tablespoon lemon juice
    2 cloves garlic, finely minced
    2 shallots, finely minced
    4 tablespoons butter

1/2 cup sour cream
    1 egg, beaten
    1 cup grated Swiss cheese
1/4 cup grated Parmesan cheese

    Seasoned Bread Crumbs

Place crabmeat and shrimp in one layer in a 10-inch oval au gratin baker. Toss mushrooms with lemon juice and saute them with the shallots and garlic in the butter until the mushrooms are tender. Sprinkle mushroom mixture over the shellfish.

Stir together sour cream, egg, Swiss cheese and grated Parmesan and spread evenly over the mushroom layer. Sprinkle top with Seasoned Bread Crumbs. Bake in a 350° oven for about 12 to 15 minutes or until the cheese is melted. Run under the broiler for a few seconds to lightly brown. Serves 6 as a small entree or 4 for lunch.

Seasoned Bread Crumbs: Cook together 1/3 cup bread crumbs, 1/3 cup grated Parmesan cheese, 1 clove mashed garlic, and 4 tablespoons melted butter until mixture is blended.

Imperial Creamed Crabmeat with Buttered Cheese Crumbs

This dish presents magnificently and for all its excitement, it is exceedingly simple to prepare. When you serve it, everyone will think you spent hours in the kitchen and no one will ever guess that you simply stirred a few ingredients together ... unless you tell.

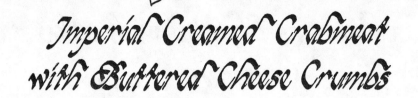

2 tablespoons lemon juice
1 pound cooked crabmeat, picked over for bones
    and flaked
4 ounces cream cheese
1/2 cup cream
3 green onions, finely chopped
1/4 teaspoon dill weed
    salt and pepper to taste
1/4 cup grated Parmesan cheese

4 tablespoons fresh bread crumbs
4 tablespoons grated Parmesan cheese
2 tablespoons melted butter

Combine first 8 ingredients and stir until blended. Divide mixture between 6 scallop shells.

Combine crumbs, cheese and melted butter and toss until blended. Sprinkle mixture over the shells. Bake in a 350° oven until heated through, about 15 minutes. Run under the broiler for a few seconds to lightly brown. Serves 6.

Note: – Entire dish can be baked in a porcelain casserole and served at the table.

Salmon & Mushrooms in Champagne Lemon Butter

6 slices salmon, about 1-inch thick

6 tablespoons butter
1/4 pound mushrooms, thinly sliced
3 tablespoons lemon juice
3/4 cup champagne
3 tablespoons chopped chives
salt to taste

In pan you will cook salmon, melt the butter. Stir in the next 5 ingredients. Place salmon in one layer in pan and baste thoroughly with the champagne mixture.

Cover pan and cook at a simmer for about 30 minutes or until salmon flakes easily with a fork. Place salmon and mushrooms on a lovely platter. Cook sauce over high heat until it is reduced to 1/3. Spoon sauce over the salmon.

Serve with Dilled Cucumber Sauce on the side. Serves 6.

Dilled Cucumber Sauce

1 cup sour cream
1/4 cup finely minced green onions
2 tablespoons lemon juice
1 tablespoon vinegar
1/2 teaspoon dill weed
1 teaspoon sugar
salt and white pepper to taste

1 cucumber, cut in half lengthwise. With a spoon,
scrape out and discard the seeds.
Coarsely grate the cucumber.

In a glass jar, with a tight-fitting lid, stir together the first 7 ingredients and store in the refrigerator. Prepare cucumbers and store in a glass bowl. Just before serving, drain cucumbers and stir in the sour cream mixture. Yields about 1 1/2 cups sauce.

Herbed Scallops with Butter & Garlic

   4 shallots, finely chopped
   4 cloves garlic, put through a press
   1 teaspoon paprika
1/4 cup (1/2 stick) butter

   1 pound scallops, cut into 1/2-inch slices
   1 tablespoon lemon juice or more to taste

1/4 cup dry white wine
   1 tablespoon chopped parsley
   2 tablespoons chopped chives
      salt and pepper to taste

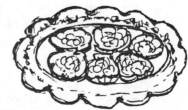

Saute shallots and garlic in paprika and butter for 3 minutes or until shallots are transparent. Add the scallops and lemon juice and continue sauteing for about 6 or 7 minutes or until scallops are cooked through. Add the remaining ingredients and cook until wine is reduced to 1/2. Serve in individual au gratin dishes and sprinkle each top with about 1 tablespoon Garlic Crumbs. Serves 4 or 5.

Garlic Cheese Crumbs

1/4 cup (1/2 stick) butter
   3 cloves garlic, put through a press
1/4 teaspoon thyme
1/2 tablespoon chopped parsley
1/2 teaspoon paprika

   3 tablespoons dry white wine
   1 tablespoon grated Parmesan cheese
      salt and pepper to taste
   3 slices fresh egg bread, made into crumbs in a
         blender or food processor

Combine butter, garlic, thyme, parsley and paprika and cook for 2 minutes. Add wine and cook for 2 minutes or until wine is almost evaporated. Add the remaining ingredients and toss until blended. Store crumbs in a glass jar in refrigerator. Crumbs will stay fresh for 2 weeks. Yields 1 1/2 cups crumbs.

Shrimp & Scallops in Lemon Cheese Sauce

1/2 pound shrimp, shelled and deveined
1/2 pound scallops, cut into 1/4-inch slices
   4 tablespoons butter
   2 cloves garlic, put through a press
1/8 teaspoon thyme flakes
   salt and white pepper to taste

In a large skillet, heat the butter and garlic until the butter is sizzling hot. Add the remaining ingredients and continue cooking and stirring until shrimp and scallops become opaque. Do not overcook. Divide mixture between 6 scallop shells. Divide Creamed Lemon Cheese Sauce between the 6 shells and sprinkle top with Garlic Crumbs.

Just before serving, place in a 350° oven until heated through. Broil tops for a few seconds to lightly brown. Serves 6 as a first course.

Creamed Lemon Cheese Sauce

3/4 cup cream
3/4 cup sour cream
   2 tablespoons lemon juice
1/3 cup chopped green onions
   1 cup grated Swiss cheese
1/2 cup grated Parmesan cheese
   2 tablespoons chopped parsley

Combine all the ingredients and stir until blended.

Garlic Crumbs

3 tablespoons butter
2 cloves garlic, put through a press

1 cup fresh bread crumbs (about 2 slices fresh egg bread)
2 tablespoons grated Parmesan cheese

In a skillet, saute garlic in butter for about 1 minute. Add the crumbs and cheese, and toss and stir until blended.

Shrimp with Emerald Garlic Butter

2 pounds raw shrimp, peeled and deveined

Emerald Garlic Butter:
   2 tablespoons lemon juice
1/4 cup fresh egg bread crumbs

   1 cup butter, softened
   2 shallots, minced
   4 cloves garlic, mashed to a paste
   2 tablespoons parsley, finely chopped
   2 tablespoons chopped chives
1/4 teaspoon thyme flakes
   salt and pepper to taste

Place shrimp in one layer in a porcelain baker. In a bowl, combine lemon juice and bread crumbs. Add the remaining ingredients and stir until blended. Butter can be stored in the refrigerator for 2 weeks.

Spread about 1/2 cup Emerald Garlic Butter on shrimp. Bake in a 350° oven for about 10 or 12 minutes, stirring once or twice, until shrimp are opaque. Do not overcook. Serves 5 or 6.

Note: – This lovely butter is grand on other shellfish and fish. It is especially good with fillets of sole.
*   – Also excellent on broiled tomatoes or sauteed mushrooms.*

Shrimp Provencal with Tomato Mushroom Garlic Sauce

2 pounds raw shrimp, shelled and black veins removed.
Sprinkle generously with garlic powder, paprika,
salt and pepper. Dust lightly with flour.

1/2 cup (1 stick) butter, or more as needed
6 cloves garlic, put through a press
1/4 teaspoon thyme
2 tablespoons minced parsley
1 teaspoon paprika

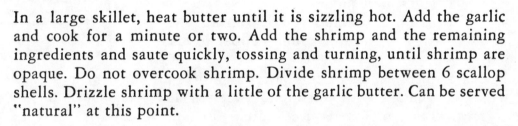

In a large skillet, heat butter until it is sizzling hot. Add the garlic and cook for a minute or two. Add the shrimp and the remaining ingredients and saute quickly, tossing and turning, until shrimp are opaque. Do not overcook shrimp. Divide shrimp between 6 scallop shells. Drizzle shrimp with a little of the garlic butter. Can be served "natural" at this point.

However, the following sauce is irresistible. Drizzle hot Tomato Mushroom Garlic Sauce over the shrimp, sprinkle with grated Parmesan and serve with pride. Serves 6.

Tomato Mushroom Garlic Sauce

1/4 pound mushrooms, cleaned and sliced and tossed with
1 teaspoon lemon juice
4 cloves garlic, put through a press
4 tablespoons olive oil

1 can (1 pound) stewed tomatoes, very finely chopped
1 can (8 ounces) tomato sauce
1 teaspoon sugar
4 green onions, finely chopped
1/4 teaspoon each thyme and basil
2 tablespoons chopped parsley
salt and pepper to taste

Saute mushrooms and garlic in oil until mushrooms are tender. Add the remaining ingredients and simmer sauce for 10 minutes.

Shrimp with Butter & Garlic in Tomato & Clam Sauce

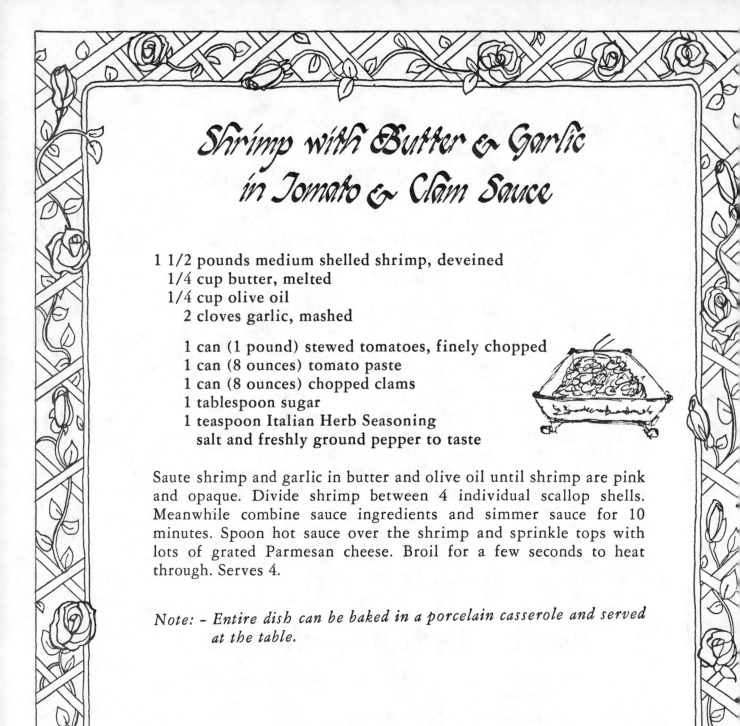

1 1/2 pounds medium shelled shrimp, deveined
1/4 cup butter, melted
1/4 cup olive oil
  2 cloves garlic, mashed

  1 can (1 pound) stewed tomatoes, finely chopped
  1 can (8 ounces) tomato paste
  1 can (8 ounces) chopped clams
  1 tablespoon sugar
  1 teaspoon Italian Herb Seasoning
  salt and freshly ground pepper to taste

Saute shrimp and garlic in butter and olive oil until shrimp are pink and opaque. Divide shrimp between 4 individual scallop shells. Meanwhile combine sauce ingredients and simmer sauce for 10 minutes. Spoon hot sauce over the shrimp and sprinkle tops with lots of grated Parmesan cheese. Broil for a few seconds to heat through. Serves 4.

Note: – Entire dish can be baked in a porcelain casserole and served at the table.

Shrimp with Garlic Herb Wine Sauce

1 1/2 pounds raw shrimp, shelled and deveined
1/2 cup (1 stick) butter, melted
2 cloves garlic, put through a press
2 shallots, finely minced
1/2 cup dry white wine

1 tablespoon chopped parsley
1 tablespoon chopped chives
2 tablespoons lemon juice
1/2 cup cream

salt and white pepper to taste

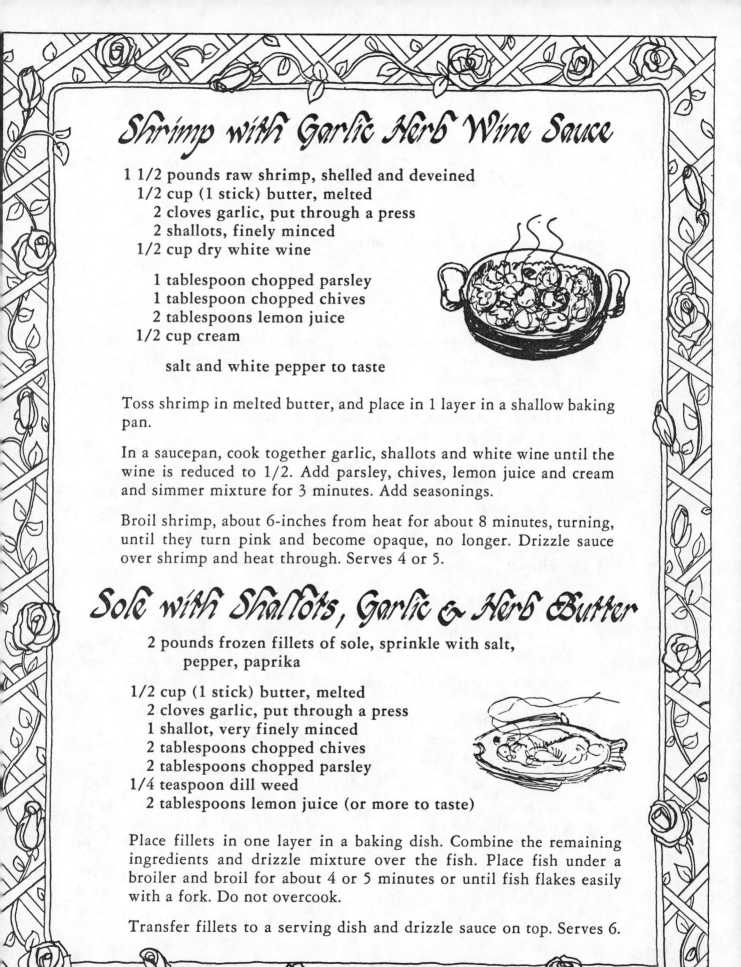

Toss shrimp in melted butter, and place in 1 layer in a shallow baking pan.

In a saucepan, cook together garlic, shallots and white wine until the wine is reduced to 1/2. Add parsley, chives, lemon juice and cream and simmer mixture for 3 minutes. Add seasonings.

Broil shrimp, about 6-inches from heat for about 8 minutes, turning, until they turn pink and become opaque, no longer. Drizzle sauce over shrimp and heat through. Serves 4 or 5.

Sole with Shallots, Garlic & Herb Butter

2 pounds frozen fillets of sole, sprinkle with salt,
pepper, paprika

1/2 cup (1 stick) butter, melted
2 cloves garlic, put through a press
1 shallot, very finely minced
2 tablespoons chopped chives
2 tablespoons chopped parsley
1/4 teaspoon dill weed
2 tablespoons lemon juice (or more to taste)

Place fillets in one layer in a baking dish. Combine the remaining ingredients and drizzle mixture over the fish. Place fish under a broiler and broil for about 4 or 5 minutes or until fish flakes easily with a fork. Do not overcook.

Transfer fillets to a serving dish and drizzle sauce on top. Serves 6.

Fillets of Sole with Mushroom Tomato Garlic Sauce

Mushroom Tomato Garlic Sauce:

1/2 pound mushrooms, sliced
    4 cloves garlic, put through a press
1/4 cup butter (1/2 stick)

    1 can (1 pound) stewed tomatoes, drained, seeded and
        chopped. Reserve juice for another use. Discard seeds.
1/2 cup chopped green onions
    2 tablespoons chopped fresh parsley
    2 tablespoons lemon juice (or more to taste)
    salt and pepper to taste

In a skillet, saute mushrooms and garlic in butter until the mushrooms are tender and liquid is absorbed. Add the remaining ingredients and saute for 5 minutes. Sauce is now ready to serve.

The Fillets:

    2 pounds fillets of sole. Sprinkle them with salt, pepper,
        garlic powder and paprika to taste. Sprinkle each
        fillet with about 1 teaspoon lemon juice.
1/4 cup butter, melted

1/2 cup grated Parmesan cheese

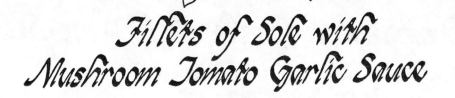

Lay fillets in one layer in a 12 x 16-inch roasting pan. Drizzle fillets with the melted butter. Broil for about 4 minutes, or just a little longer for thicker fillets, but in any case, broil only until the fish flakes easily with a fork. Do not overcook.

Spoon Tomato Garlic Sauce evenly over the fillets and sprinkle the Parmesan cheese evenly over all. Broil for another few seconds to brown cheese. Serve at once. Serves 6.

Note: – Sauce can be made earlier in the day and refrigerated. Heat sauce separately before serving. Fish should be broiled just before serving.

Batter Fried Fillets of Sole

Batter:

  1 cup flour
  2 eggs
  1 cup milk
  1/4 cup grated Parmesan cheese
    salt and pepper to taste
    pinch of nutmeg

Fish:
2 pounds fillets of sole, cut into 3 to 4-inch pieces

Beat together the batter ingredients until the mixture is blended. Heat a skillet with about 1/2-inch oil until a drop of water skitters around. Dip the fillets into the batter and fry until brown. Turn and brown other side. Do not crowd pan and do not overcook fish.

Place cooked fillets in one layer in a 9x13-inch porcelain baking dish. Spoon Sauce Provencal over the top and heat in a 350° oven until heated through. Serves 6.

Sauce Provencal

  3 tablespoons butter
  3 tablespoons olive oil
  2 cups chopped onions
  2 cloves garlic put through a press

  1 can (16 ounces) stewed tomatoes, finely chopped.
    Do not drain.
1/2 can (3 ounces) tomato paste
  1 tablespoon sugar
1/2 teaspoon thyme flakes
1/2 teaspoon oregano
    salt and pepper to taste

Saute onions and garlic in butter and oil until the onions are transparent. Add the remaining ingredients and simmer sauce for 20 minutes, uncovered.

Note: – Sauce can be made earlier in the day or a day or two earlier and refrigerated. Fish can be fried earlier in the day and refrigerated. Sprinkle a little grated cheese over the top as a delicious optional.

Herbed Fillets of Sole with Lemon Souffle

A delicate herb and butter stuffing and a tangy lemon souffle add glamor and excitement to the fillets of sole. If you prepare the Herb Butter earlier in the day then this becomes a very simple dish

6 fillets of sole, pat dry, and sprinkle with lemon juice
    salt and white pepper

Herb Butter:
1/2 cup butter (1 stick) softened
  4 tablespoons chopped parsley
  4 tablespoons chopped chives
1/2 teaspoon dill weed
  1 clove garlic, put through a press
    salt and pepper to taste

  6 tablespoons Ritz cracker crumbs

Lemon Souffle Topping:
1/2 cup mayonnaise
  4 ounces cream cheese with chives
  2 tablespoons lemon juice or more to taste
  1 egg white, beaten stiff

Stir together all the ingredients in Herb Butter, except the cracker crumbs, until the mixture is blended. Divide Herb Butter between each slice of sole, and spread evenly. Sprinkle cracker crumbs on each fillet and roll up.

Place each fillet, seam side down in individual ramekins and bake in a 350° oven for about 20 or 25 minutes or until fish flakes easily with a fork. Do not overcook. Remove juices forming on the bottom.

Beat together the ingredients for the Lemon Souffle Topping until fluffy. Divide souffle mixture between each fillet and spread to cover fish. Broil until topping is puffed and a lovely golden color. Serves 6.

Note: – If you do not have individual ramekins, these can be prepared in a shallow flameproof baker. Spread the sauce over all the fillets, broil and then serve.
*   – Fillets can be spread with butter and cracker crumbs, rolled and set in pan earlier in the day.*
*   – Pat fish dry with paper towellings so that excessive juices do not form.*

Fillets of Sole in Tomato, Onion & Wine Sauce

1 pound fillets of sole, cut into 4-inch pieces. Sprinkle
    with salt, pepper and garlic powder. Drizzle tops
    with 2 tablespoons melted butter.

2 onions, chopped
2 cloves garlic, put through a press
2 tablespoons butter

1/4 cup dry white wine

1 can (1 pound 12 ounces) stewed tomatoes, chopped
    and drained. Reserve juice for another use.
1 tablespoon chopped parsley
    salt and pepper to taste
1 tablespoon lemon juice
1/4 teaspoon thyme flakes

Prepare fillets in one layer in a 9 x 13-inch roasting pan. Bake fillets
in a 350° oven for about 12 to 15 minutes or until fish flakes easily
with a fork. Do not overcook.

Meanwhile, saute onions and garlic in butter until onions are
transparent. (Onions should still have a crunch.) Add wine and
continue cooking until wine is almost evaporated, about 3 minutes.
Now add the remaining ingredients and simmer sauce for about
10 minutes.

Remove fish to a pretty oval platter and spoon a little sauce over
each fillet. Spoon remaining sauce around the edges. Sprinkle top
with additional parsley. Serves 4.

*Note: - The sauce should not be overcooked. It should be like a
fresh tomato sauce, light and crunchy.*

Fillets of Sole with Mushrooms & Shallots in Wine Sauce

1 pound fillets of sole, cut into 4-inch pieces. Sprinkle
    with salt, pepper and garlic powder. Drizzle tops
    with 2 tablespoons melted butter.

1/2 pound mushrooms, cleaned and sliced
  2 cloves garlic, put through a press
  4 shallots, finely chopped
  4 tablespoons butter

1/4 cup dry white wine
  1 tablespoon chopped parsley
  2 tablespoons chopped chives
  1 tablespoon lemon juice
    salt and pepper to taste

Prepare fillets in one layer in a 9 x 13-inch roasting pan. Bake fillets
in a 350° oven for about 12 to 15 minutes or until fish flakes easily
with a fork. Do not overcook.

Meanwhile, saute mushrooms, garlic and shallots in butter until
mushrooms are tender and liquid is absorbed. Add wine and cook
until wine is reduced to 1/2. Add the remaining ingredients and
heat through.

Remove fish to a lovely platter and spoon mushroom sauce over the
top. (This is not a soupy sauce, but basically mushrooms in a little
wine.) Sprinkle top with a little parsley and serve 4 or 5.

Note: – Sauce can be made 1 day earlier and refrigerated. Heat
      before serving.
    – Bake fish just before serving.

Red Garlic Mayonnaise for Soups & Stews

(Sauce Rouille)

This is an excellent sauce to serve with Bouillabaisse or other fish chowders. A dollup (or two) spooned into the soup or stew adds a fantastic depth to the broth.

   1 cup mayonnaise
1/4 cup sour cream
   6 cloves garlic
   1 jar (2 ounces) pimiento strips
   2 tablespoons lemon juice
1/8 teaspoon paprika
     salt and red pepper to taste

Combine all the ingredients in a blender or food processor and puree mixture. Yields about 1 1/2 cups sauce.

Note: – Sauce should be stored in the refrigerator until serving time.
*   – To serve, place in a lovely bowl and allow each guest to serve himself. This sauce is not for the faint of heart.*

Garlic Mayonnaise for Fish & Vegetables

(Aioli)

   1 cup mayonnaise
1/2 cup cream, whipped
   2 teaspoons Dijon mustard
   2 tablespoons lemon juice
   6 cloves garlic, mashed to a paste
     salt and white pepper to taste
1/2 cup fresh bread crumbs

Combine all the ingredients and stir until blended. Place sauce in a glass jar and store in the refrigerator until serving time. This sauce is very good in fish stews or chowders. Serve it, also, with cold poached fish, mushrooms or vegetables.

To serve, place sauce in a bowl and allow each guest to serve himself. Yields about 1 3/4 cup sauce.

Royal Sauce Verte with Shallots & Herbs

3/4 cup mayonnaise
1/2 cup sour cream
1/4 cup cream
   2 tablespoons lemon juice
   1 shallot
   1 green onion
   6 sprigs of parsley, discard the stems
     and use the leaves
1/4 teaspoon thyme
1/8 teaspoon garlic powder
   salt to taste

1/2 cup frozen spinach, defrosted and drained

Combine all the ingredients (except the spinach) in a food processor or blender container and puree until smooth. Stir in the spinach until blended. Refrigerate until ready to use.

Serve with cold poached fish. Good for dipping with raw vegetables. Yields about 1 1/2 cups sauce.

Sauce Remoulade for Cold Fish & Shellfish

   1 cup mayonnaise
1/2 cup sour cream
   1 teaspoon Dijon mustard
   2 tablespoons lemon juice
   2 green onions
   2 tablespoons parsley

   2 to 3 tablespoons sweet pickle relish
1/2 teaspoon anchovy paste (optional)

Puree first 6 ingredients in a food processor or blender. Place mixture into a glass jar with a tight-fitting lid and stir in the pickle relish. Sauce should be stored in the refrigerator until serving time. Yields about 1 3/4 cup sauce.

Meats

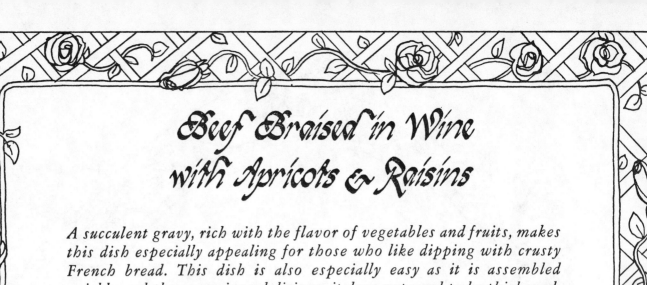

Beef Braised in Wine with Apricots & Raisins

A succulent gravy, rich with the flavor of vegetables and fruits, makes this dish especially appealing for those who like dipping with crusty French bread. This dish is also especially easy as it is assembled quickly and the gravy is so delicious, it does not need to be thickened.

1 brisket of beef, about 4 pounds, lean and trimmed of fat.
   Sprinkle with salt and pepper, paprika and lots of
   garlic powder

1 package (6 ounces) dried apricots
1/2 cup raisins
6 medium carrots, peeled and cut in 2-inch slices
6 small whole onions

3 teaspoons beef stock base
3 tablespoons dried onion flakes
1/3 cup brown sugar
3 tablespoons ketchup
1 cup dry white wine
1/4 teaspoon thyme

In a 9x13-inch roasting pan, place meat. Arrange the apricots, raisins, carrots and onions around meat. Combine the remaining ingredients and stir until blended. Pour this mixture over the meat.

Cover the pan tightly with foil and place in a 350° oven. Bake for about 2 to 3 hours or until meat is fork tender. Remove from the oven and allow to cool. Remove every trace of fat.

Slice meat and return it to the pan. Store in the refrigerator until serving time. Heat in a 350° oven for about 30 minutes or until heated through. Serve with the fruit and vegetables on the side. Serves 6.

Note: – It's especially good prepared 1 day earlier and stored in the refrigerator, allowing flavors to blend.

Paupiettes de Boeuf Bourgignon in Easiest & Best Mushroom & Wine Sauce

This is one of my favorite dishes. A succulent herb stuffing surrounded by the most tender, savory steak is indeed fit for a king. Served with a delicate Mushroom Wine Sauce, adds excitement and a touch of glamor. Entire dish can be assembled and prepared one day earlier.

18 thin slices spencer steak, cut from the small end, about
     a little less than 1/4-inch thick, each. Sprinkle each
     with salt, pepper and garlic powder.

1 package (6 ounces) Stove Top Stuffing Mix, Chicken Flavor
1/4 teaspoon thyme flakes
1/8 teaspoon poultry seasoning
  1 egg, beaten

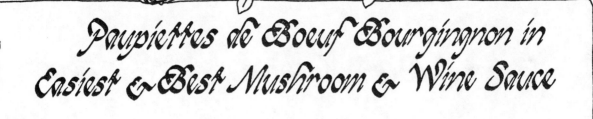

1/4 cup each butter and olive oil
1/4 cup Cognac

Prepare stuffing mix according to directions on the package. Stir in herbs and beaten egg until blended. Place 1 heaping tablespoon stuffing on the small end of the steak, roll up, and fasten with a wooden toothpick.

Roll each paupiette in Seasoned Flour. In a large skillet, heat together butter and olive oil and lightly brown each paupiette on all sides. Do not overcook. Paupiettes should brown in a few minutes. (Don't worry if there are a few pink areas. These will cook when reheating the rolls.) Place paupiettes in one layer in a roasting pan. Heat the Cognac in a brandy warmer, ignite and pour carefully over the paupiettes. Can be held at this point.

When ready to serve, place paupiettes in a 350° oven and heat for about 25 minutes or until heated through. Serve on your loveliest platter with lots of parsley, and serve the Mushroom Wine Sauce on the side. Depending on appetites, figure about 1 paupiette for a woman and 2 for a man.

Easiest & Best Mushroom & Wine Sauce

Saute 1/2 pound sliced mushrooms, 2 cloves mashed garlic, and 1 finely chopped shallot in 3 tablespoons butter, until mushrooms are tender. Add 1/4 cup dry white wine and simmer mixture until wine has evaporated. Add 1/2 cup canned beef broth, 1 teaspoon Bovril, 1 tablespoon Sauce Robert, 1 tablespoon each chopped chives and parsley, and salt and pepper to taste. Simmer mixture for 2 or 3 minutes and serve hot. (Sauce can be made 1 day earlier and refrigerated.)

Seasoned Flour: Combine in a plastic bag, 1 cup flour, 2 teaspoons garlic powder, 2 teaspoons paprika, 1/4 cup grated Parmesan cheese, and 1 teaspoon salt, and shake until blended. Store unused seasoned flour in the refrigerator. Can also be used on fish and chicken.

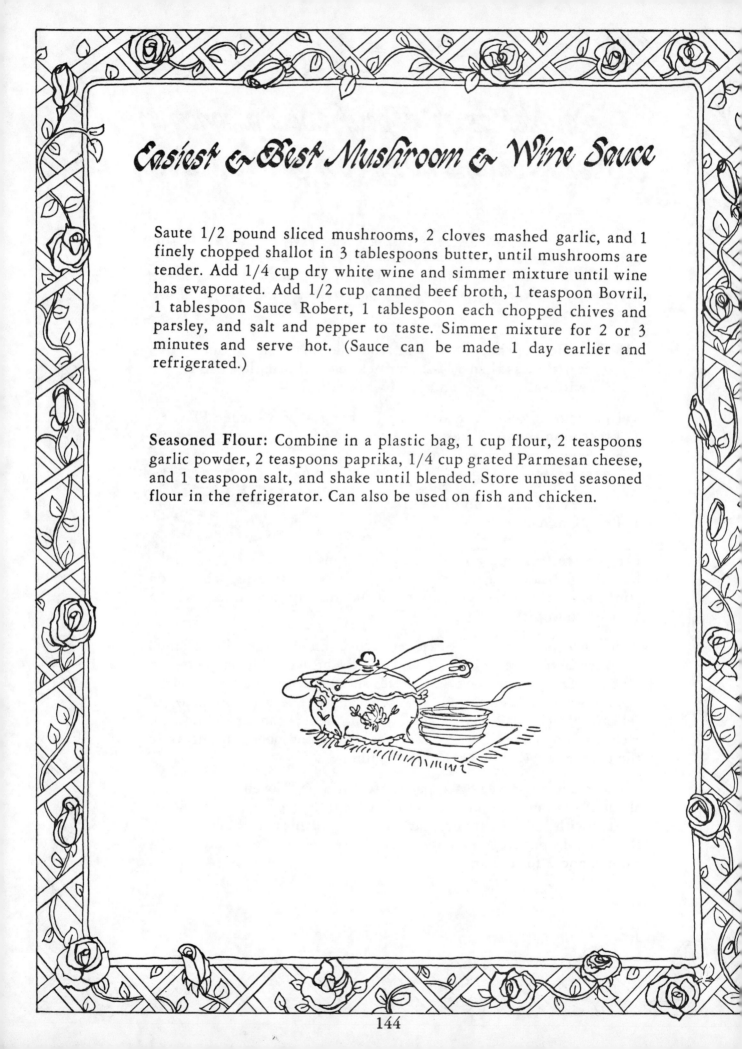

Country Style Stuffed Flank Steak with Carrots & Prunes Sauce

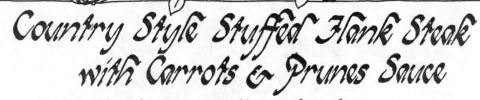

2 flank steaks, about 2 to 2 1/2 pounds each.
Ask your butcher to butterfly these. Sprinkle
with salt, pepper and garlic powder.

1 package (6 ounces) Stove Top Chicken Flavored
    Stuffing Mix
1 1/2 cups chicken broth
4 tablespoons melted butter
1/4 pound lean ground beef
1/4 pound mushrooms, sliced
1 tablespoon butter

Heat together the seasoning packet in the stuffing mix with the chicken broth and butter. Bring to a boil and add the bread cubes. Stir until well mixed. Saute together meat and mushrooms in 1 tablespoon butter until meat loses its pinkness. Add to the stuffing mixture.

Lay out the prepared flank steaks, cut side up. Divide the stuffing mixture on the long side (with the grain of the meat) and roll it up. Skewer it or tie it securely with string, making certain to skewer the ends.

Place roasts in a 12x16-inch pan. Place Carrot and Prune Sauce evenly over the top. Cover pan tightly with foil and bake in a 350° oven for about 2 hours or until meat is tender. Remove skewers or string.

Slice and serve with the carrots and prunes on the side. Spoon some of the delicious gravy on the top. Serves 8.

Carrots & Prunes Sauce

3 carrots, scraped and cut into 2-inch pieces
12 prunes, pitted
1 onion, cut into 1/2-inch slices
1 can (12 ounces) beer
1/4 cup brown sugar
1/2 envelope dehydrated onion soup
    salt to taste

Combine all the ingredients and pour mixture evenly over the flank steaks.

French Potted Beef with Red Wine & Vegetables

Although this dish appears lengthy, it is really so simple, I hope you do not pass it by. It is incredibly rich and delicious and a wonderful dish to consider when it is drenching outside and the spirit is needing a little tender loving care. Serve it with rice or noodles. If you choose potatoes, cook them separately so the gravy does not cloud. Gravy is delicious and does not need to be thickened.

2 onions, chopped
2 carrots, grated
1/4 cup chopped celery
3 cloves garlic, finely minced
3 pounds boneless chuck, cut into 1-inch cubes
    and dusted lightly with flour
3 tablespoons butter
3 tablespoons oil

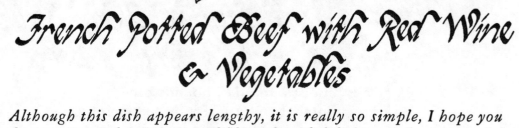

2 tomatoes, canned or fresh, drained and chopped
1/2 cup dry red wine
1 can (10 1/2 ounces) beef broth
1 teaspoon Bovril, meat extract
1 tablespoon tomato paste
1/4 teaspoon thyme
1/2 bay leaf
    salt and pepper to taste
4 slices bacon, cooked crisp, drained and crumbled

In a Dutch oven, combine first 7 ingredients together and cook over moderately high heat, tossing and stirring until meat is beginning to brown.

Add the remaining ingredients and stir until blended. Bring mixture to a boil, lower heat and simmer stew, covered for about 2 hours or until meat is tender. Remove bay leaf. Serves 6.

Note: – This is excellent made 1 day earlier and stored in the refrigerator overnight.

Carbonades of Beef with Fluffy Dumplings

A rich and flavorful combination of beef and onions with a hint of sweetness. The Fluffy Dumplings are tender and the gravy is subtle and pleasant tasting. This is a lovely dish for informal dinners with family and friends.

1/3 cup oil
   3 pounds boneless chuck, cut into 1-inch cubes. Remove
      any fat and toss lightly in flour.
   1 bag (1 pound) frozen, small whole onions
   1 teaspoon minced garlic

   1 can (12 ounces) beer
   1 can (10 1/2 ounces) beef broth
   3 tablespoons brown sugar
   2 tablespoons currant jelly
   1 tablespoon ketchup
1/2 teaspoon thyme flakes
   1 bay leaf
   salt and pepper to taste

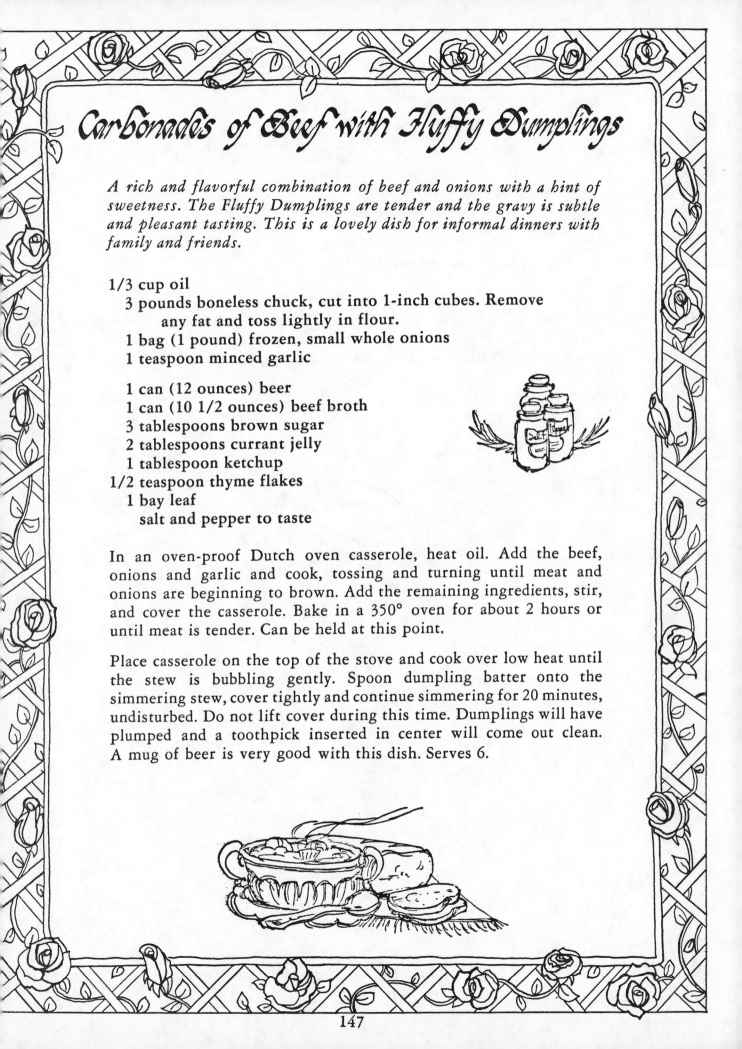

In an oven-proof Dutch oven casserole, heat oil. Add the beef, onions and garlic and cook, tossing and turning until meat and onions are beginning to brown. Add the remaining ingredients, stir, and cover the casserole. Bake in a 350° oven for about 2 hours or until meat is tender. Can be held at this point.

Place casserole on the top of the stove and cook over low heat until the stew is bubbling gently. Spoon dumpling batter onto the simmering stew, cover tightly and continue simmering for 20 minutes, undisturbed. Do not lift cover during this time. Dumplings will have plumped and a toothpick inserted in center will come out clean. A mug of beer is very good with this dish. Serves 6.

Fluffy Parsleyed Dumplings

    2 cups prepared biscuit mix
    1 tablespoon dried onion flakes
    1 teaspoon parsley flakes
3/4 cup milk
    2 tablespoons melted butter

Place all the ingredients in a bowl and stir lightly with a fork until the mixture is blended and smooth. Spoon batter onto simmering stew, cover tightly and continue simmering for 20 minutes, undisturbed. Yields 10 dumplings.

Rib Steak in Red Wine Jody Gillis

4 tablespoons butter
2 rib or club steaks
  salt and pepper to taste

1 tablespoon butter
2 green onions, chopped
1 heaping tablespoon chopped shallots

1 cup dry red wine
  drop of vinegar

1/4 cup whipping cream

Melt butter in a large frying pan. When very hot, add steaks and pan fry on both sides to desired doneness. Season with salt and pepper to taste. Remove and keep warm.

Add 1 tablespoon butter to skillet and saute onion and shallots until tender, about 3 to 5 minutes. Add wine and vinegar and cook rapidly until sauce is reduced by half. Add 1/4 cup cream and correct seasoning. Sprinkle with some chopped parsley, pour over the steaks and serve two lucky people.

Note: - Serve with mashed potatoes and crisp French bread to soak up the delicious gravy.

Easy Steak Diane in Red Wine & Herb Sauce

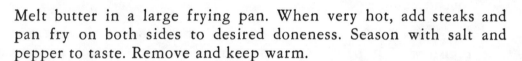

1 sirloin steak, about 1 1/2-inches thick, about 2 pounds
3 tablespoons butter
2 tablespoons chopped chives
2 teaspoons chopped parsley
1 teaspoon Bovril meat extract
1 teaspoon Dijon mustard
1/3 cup red wine
  salt and pepper to taste

Broil steak to desired doneness. Combine the remaining ingredients and cook rapidly until sauce is reduced by one-third. (Optional but excellent: Heat 2 tablespoons Cognac and flame steak.) Pour sauce over the steak and slice it on the diagonal when serving. Serve at once. Serves 3 or 4 depending on the accompaniments.

Rack of Lamb Coated with Mustard & Garlic

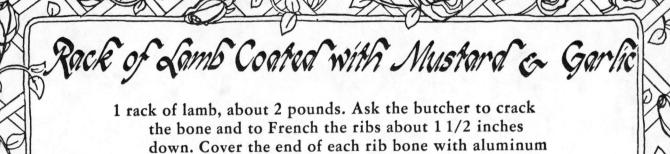

1 rack of lamb, about 2 pounds. Ask the butcher to crack the bone and to French the ribs about 1 1/2 inches down. Cover the end of each rib bone with aluminum foil. Sprinkle lamb with salt and pepper.

2 cloves garlic, mashed
2 teaspoons Dijon mustard
2 tablespoons melted butter

Combine garlic, mustard and butter and rub lamb with this mixture. Place lamb, fat side up, in a shallow roasting pan. Insert meat thermometer in thickest part of the meat, being careful not to touch the bone.

Bake in a 300° oven for about 1 hour or until meat thermometer registers 170° or 175° for medium lamb. Carve lamb at the table and serve with Instant Mushroom and Wine Sauce. Serves 2 or 3.

Instant Mushroom Wine Sauce

1/4 pound mushrooms, sliced
   1 clove garlic
   1 tablespoon butter
   2 tablespoons dry white wine
1/4 cup beef broth
1/2 teaspoon Bovril, meat extract
   1 teaspoon Sauce Robert
   1 teaspoon each chopped chives and parsley

Saute mushrooms and garlic in butter until mushrooms are tender. Add the remaining ingredients and simmer mixture for 1 minute. Yields about 3/4 cup sauce.

Note: - Recipe can be doubled.

Lamb Shanks with Garlic, Tomatoes, Onion & Beer

4 lamb shanks, sprinkle with salt and pepper. Dust
    lightly with flour. Coat with mixture of
    2 tablespoons butter and 2 mashed cloves garlic.

2 onions, finely chopped
1 carrot, grated
2 tomatoes, fresh or canned, peeled, seeded
    and chopped
1 cup beer
1 can (10 1/2 ounces) beef broth
3 tablespoons brown sugar
1/4 teaspoon thyme flakes
    salt and pepper to taste

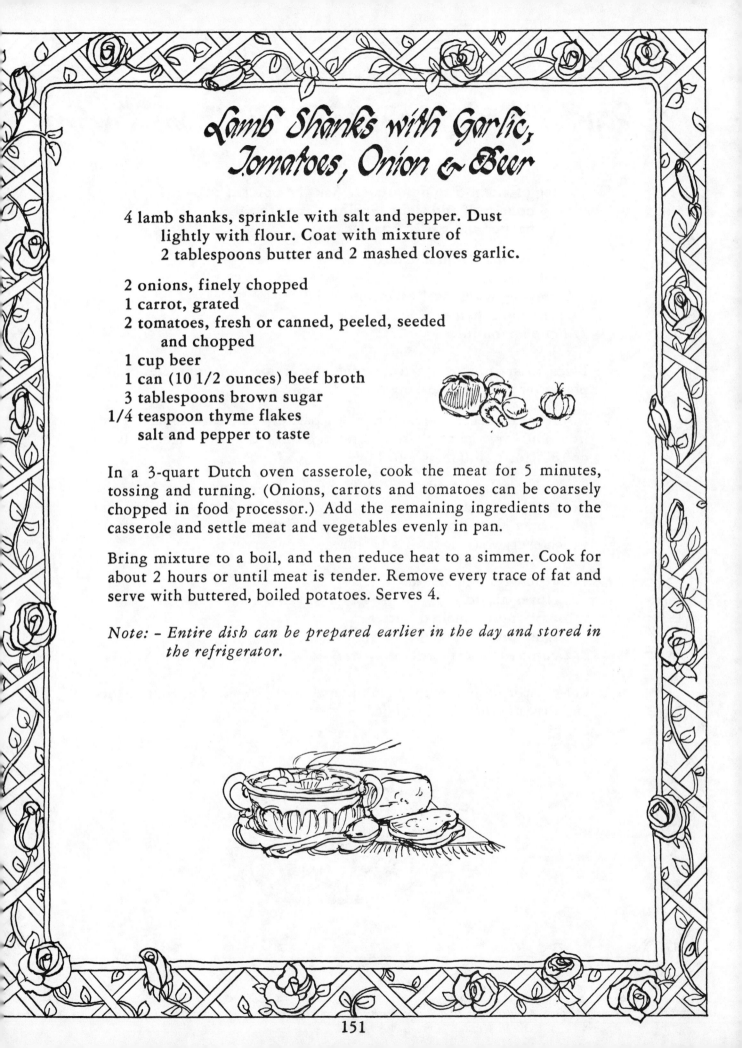

In a 3-quart Dutch oven casserole, cook the meat for 5 minutes, tossing and turning. (Onions, carrots and tomatoes can be coarsely chopped in food processor.) Add the remaining ingredients to the casserole and settle meat and vegetables evenly in pan.

Bring mixture to a boil, and then reduce heat to a simmer. Cook for about 2 hours or until meat is tender. Remove every trace of fat and serve with buttered, boiled potatoes. Serves 4.

Note: – Entire dish can be prepared earlier in the day and stored in the refrigerator.

Roast Leg of Lamb with Garlic Crumb Coating

1 leg of lamb (5 to 6 pounds). Ask the butcher to
  bone, roll and tie it. Sprinkle it with salt,
  pepper and garlic powder.

2 teaspoons Dijon mustard
4 tablespoons oil
2 cloves garlic, finely minced
1/2 teaspoon thyme
1/4 cup lemon juice

Place roast in a pan. Stir together the remaining ingredients and pour over the lamb, coating it on all sides.

Insert meat thermometer in thickest part of the meat and bake lamb in a 350° oven until thermometer registers 170° for medium lamb or 180° for well-done lamb.

Sprinkle Garlic Crumb Coating over the lamb and return it to the oven to bake another 5 or 10 minutes. Remove lamb from pan and place on a heated platter. Slice at the table and pass the gravy, from which every trace of fat has been removed. Serves 6.

Garlic Crumb Coating:
3 cloves garlic
3 tablespoons melted butter
2 tablespoons chopped parsley
1/2 cup fresh bread crumbs

Cook garlic in butter for 1 minute. Add the remaining ingredients and toss and turn until blended.

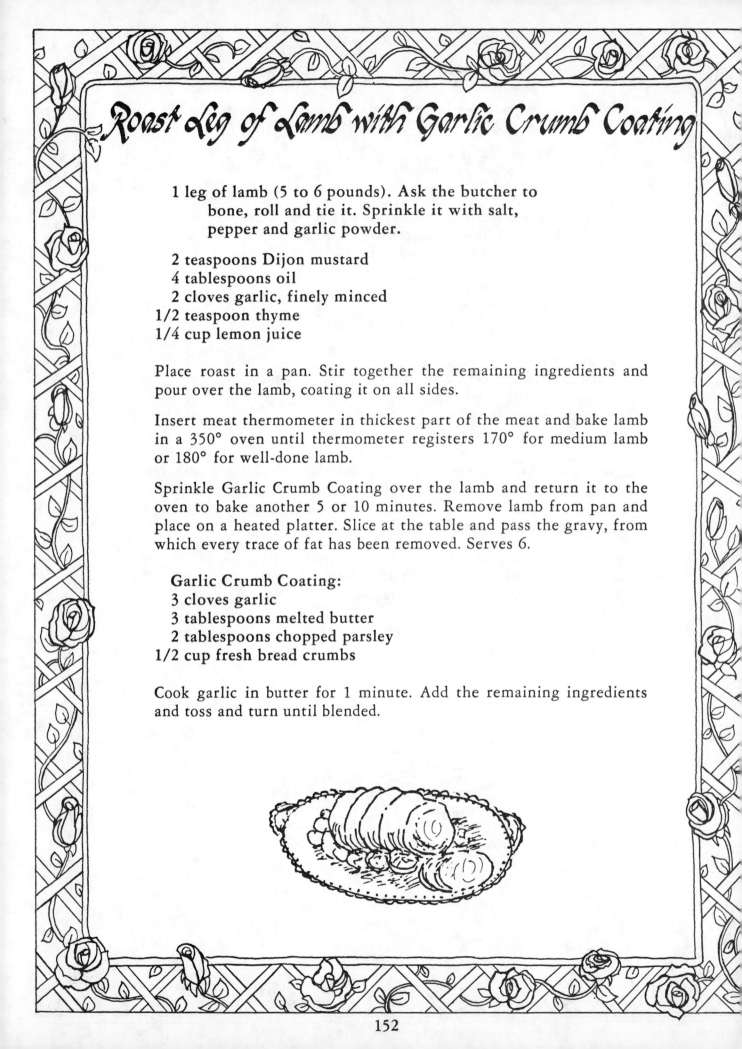

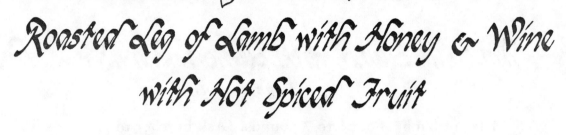

Roasted Leg of Lamb with Honey & Wine with Hot Spiced Fruit

1 leg of lamb (5 to 6 pounds). Ask the butcher to
    bone, roll and tie it. Sprinkle it with salt
    and pepper and garlic powder.

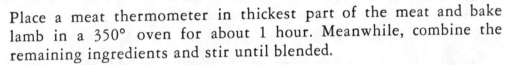

1/2 cup honey
1/2 cup dry white wine
  4 cloves garlic, mashed
  1 tablespoon lemon juice
  3 tablespoons butter

Place a meat thermometer in thickest part of the meat and bake lamb in a 350° oven for about 1 hour. Meanwhile, combine the remaining ingredients and stir until blended.

Baste lamb with honey mixture every 15 minutes until thermometer registers 170° for medium lamb. Remove lamb from pan and place on a heated platter. Slice at the table and serve with Hot Spiced Fruit on the side. Serves 6 to 8.

Note: – *Lamb can be prepared a little earlier in the day. In that case, leave the last 30 minutes of roasting for reheating at serving time.*
     – *If gravy is thin, reduce it rapidly over moderately high heat.*

Hot Spiced Fruit

1 cup dried apricots
1 cup pitted prunes
1/2 cup sugar
1 cup orange juice
1/2 teaspoon cinnamon, or more to taste
2 tablespoons lemon juice

Combine all the ingredients in a saucepan and simmer mixture for about 15 minutes or until fruit is tender.

Imperial Lamb with Lemon, Garlic & Herbs

(Gigot d'Agneau Roti)

1 leg of lamb, about 6 to 7 pounds. (Ask butcher to
   bone, roll and tie it.)

1/4 cup oil
1/3 cup lemon juice
   3 cloves garlic, put through a press
1/4 teaspoon thyme flakes
   salt and pepper to taste

Place lamb in a large bowl. Combine oil, lemon juice, garlic, salt, pepper and thyme and pour mixture over the lamb, making certain that the lamb is well coated. Marinate the lamb in the refrigerator for 24 hours, turning now and again.

Place lamb in a roasting pan with the marinade and roast it in a 425° oven for 20 minutes. Lower temperature to 300° and continue roasting lamb until meat thermometer, placed in the thickest part of the meat, registers approximately 150° for medium-rare, 170° for medium and 180° for well-done. Baste frequently during baking time.

About 30 minutes before lamb is done, carefully sprinkle Garlic Herb Coating over the lamb and continue baking until thermometer registers desired doneness. To make gravy, remove lamb from the pan and strain the juices. Remove any trace of fat. Carve the lamb and spoon some of the pan juices over the top. Serves 8.

Garlic Herb Coating

1/3 cup bread crumbs
   3 cloves garlic, put through a press
1/4 teaspoon thyme flakes
   2 tablespoons melted butter
   1 tablespoon chopped parsley

Combine all the ingredients and stir until blended.

Glazed Ham with Apples & Raisins in Spiced Wine

This is a spectacular dish at serving time. A beautifully glazed ham surrounded by spiced apples and raisins is very exciting. And ham is very good served cold, the next day ... if you can manage to have any leftovers.

1 canned ham (about 5 pounds). Score top of ham in a
    diamond pattern with the tip of a knife. Do not cut
    deep into the meat. Place 1 clove in each diamond.

1 cup apricot jam
1/4 cup apple juice

Bake ham according to the directions on the can. About 30 minutes before ham is finished cooking, combine jam and apple juice and baste ham with this mixture. Return ham to a 350° oven and continue baking until ham is cooked. (Meat thermometer should register about 160°.) Cut into slices and pass Spiced Apples and Raisins on the side. Serves 8.

Apples & Raisins in Spiced Wine

1/2 cup sweet sauternes
1/2 cup apple juice
1/2 cup orange juice
3/4 cup sugar
2 tablespoons butter
6 apples, peeled, cored and sliced into quarters
1/2 cup yellow raisins
1 tablespoon grated orange peel
2 thin slices of lemon
1/2 teaspoon cinnamon
    pinch powdered cloves

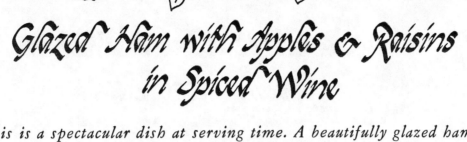

Combine all the ingredients in a saucepan and simmer mixture until apples are soft. Serve warm with pork or lamb. Serves 8.

Note: – Fruit can be made 1 day earlier and stored in the refrigerator.

Honey-Glazed Baked Ham with Raisin Pecan Sauce

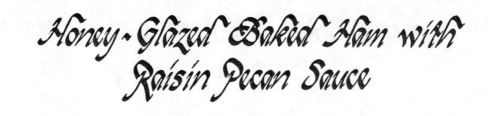

Glazing ham and serving it with spice-drenched fruit can transform a traditional baked ham into a bacchanalian repast. Mounded high with a colorful array of fruits and surrounded by tangy, spicy sauce adds excitement and gaiety to your party.

1 canned ham (about 5 pounds). Remove gelatin and any excess fat. Score top of ham in a diamond pattern with the tip of a knife. Do not cut deep into meat. Place 1 clove in each diamond.

Raisin Pecan Sauce

1 cup raisins
1 cup orange juice
1/2 cup currant jelly
1/2 cup honey
1/3 cup brown sugar
1/4 teaspoon cinnamon
1/4 teaspoon ground cloves
1/4 teaspoon dry mustard
1 cup pecan halves

Bake ham according to directions on the can or at 325° until meat thermometer registers 140°.

Meanwhile, combine the remaining ingredients and simmer mixture about 5 minutes or until raisins are plump. About 30 minutes before the end of baking time, baste generously with Raisin Pecan Sauce. About 15 minutes later, pour remaining sauce over ham and continue baking until sauce is hot and ham is glazed. Serves 8.

Sweet & Sour Braised Pork with Sauerkraut & Raisins

This is a wonderful peasant dish that is very flavorful and delicious. Serve it with some crusty bread to dip into the marvelous gravy. It is exceedingly simple to prepare and a quite economical dish too.

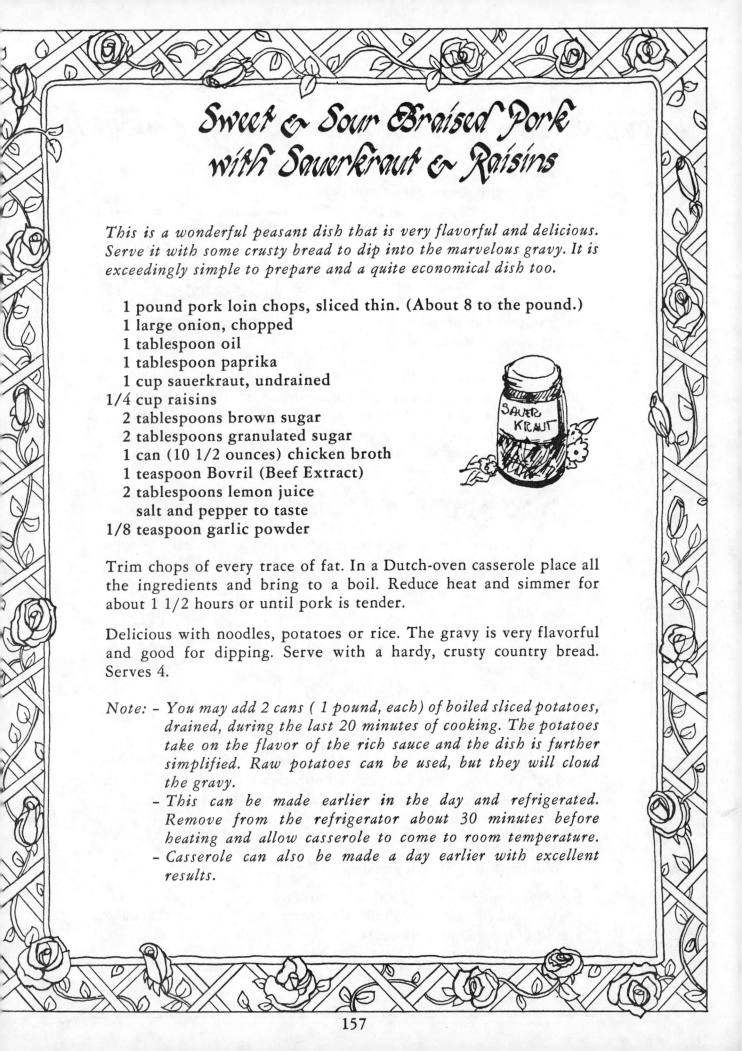

1 pound pork loin chops, sliced thin. (About 8 to the pound.)
1 large onion, chopped
1 tablespoon oil
1 tablespoon paprika
1 cup sauerkraut, undrained
1/4 cup raisins
2 tablespoons brown sugar
2 tablespoons granulated sugar
1 can (10 1/2 ounces) chicken broth
1 teaspoon Bovril (Beef Extract)
2 tablespoons lemon juice
salt and pepper to taste
1/8 teaspoon garlic powder

Trim chops of every trace of fat. In a Dutch-oven casserole place all the ingredients and bring to a boil. Reduce heat and simmer for about 1 1/2 hours or until pork is tender.

Delicious with noodles, potatoes or rice. The gravy is very flavorful and good for dipping. Serve with a hardy, crusty country bread. Serves 4.

Note: – You may add 2 cans (1 pound, each) of boiled sliced potatoes, drained, during the last 20 minutes of cooking. The potatoes take on the flavor of the rich sauce and the dish is further simplified. Raw potatoes can be used, but they will cloud the gravy.
– This can be made earlier in the day and refrigerated. Remove from the refrigerator about 30 minutes before heating and allow casserole to come to room temperature.
– Casserole can also be made a day earlier with excellent results.

Glazed Pork with Cinnamon, Orange & Brandy

1 pork tenderloin (about 1 1/2 pounds). Sprinkle with
  salt, pepper and garlic powder.

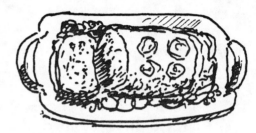

Cinnamon Orange Glaze:

1/2 cup honey
1/2 cup orange marmalade
  1 tablespoon lemon juice
  2 tablespoons brandy
1/2 teaspoon cinnamon

Place the pork in a shallow roasting pan and bake at 350° for about
30 minutes. Heat the remaining ingredients in a saucepan and stir
until blended. Baste with marmalade mixture every 15 minutes,
until meat thermometer registers 175°, about another 30 or 40
minutes. Serve with Cinnamon Brown Rice and Glazed Carrots.

Roast Pork with Apples & Cream

1 pork loin roast (about 4 pounds). Sprinkle with salt,
  pepper and garlic powder.

1/2 cup dry white wine
  2 tablespoons butter
1/2 cup apple jelly
1/2 cup applesauce
1/2 cup cream
  3 apples, cored and cut in half, crosswise
  6 tablespoons brown sugar
1/2 teaspoon cinnamon

Place roast, bone side down in a 9 x 13-inch roasting pan and bake
at 350° for about 45 minutes to 1 hour. Drain off all the fat. (I find
it simpler to remove the roast and place it in a different pan.)

Heat together the wine, butter, apple jelly, applesauce and cream,
until mixture is blended. Place apples around roast and sprinkle
with brown sugar and cinnamon.

Baste pork and apples with wine mixture, every 15 minutes, until
pork is cooked through and meat thermometer registers 175°, about
1 hour longer. Serve pork surrounded with apples. Serves 6.

Roast Pork with Glazed Apples in Honey Wine Sauce

This dish is a triumph of simplicity and good taste. Succulent roast pork surrounded by honey-glazed apple rings and a delicious brown rice is a wonderful choice for an informal dinner.

> 1 tenderloin of pork (about 1 1/2 pounds). Sprinkle with
> salt, pepper, garlic and 1 tablespoon butter, melted.

> 8 apple slices (1-inch, each), core but do not peel

1/4 cup dry white wine
1/2 cup honey

Roast pork in a 9x13-inch pan in a 350° oven for about 20 minutes. Now place apple rings around the pork and baste apples and pork with mixture of wine and honey. Tent roast loosely with foil and continue baking and basting for another 40 minutes or until meat thermometer registers 180°.

Place roast on a platter and surround with apple slices. Decorate with lots of parsley. Serve with Brown Rice with Mushrooms and Onions. Serves 4.

Brown Rice with Mushrooms & Onions

> 1 cup brown rice
> 2 cups chicken broth, homemade or canned
> salt and pepper to taste
> 3 tablespoons butter

1/4 pound mushrooms, sliced
> 1 onion, chopped
> 3 tablespoons butter

In a saucepan, place rice, broth, seasonings and butter. Cover pan and simmer rice until rice is tender and liquid is absorbed. Meanwhile, saute mushrooms and onion in butter until onions are tender. Toss mushroom mixture into cooked rice until mixed. Serves 4 to 5.

Veal Scallops with Boursin & Bacon

8 veal scallops, 1/8-inch thick. Sprinkle with salt,
    pepper and garlic powder. Dust lightly with flour.

8 ounces Boursin cheese (creamed cheese with
    garlic and herbs)
8 slices bacon

Place 1 ounce of Boursin on each veal scallop and roll it up. Spiral
one slice of bacon around each scallop and fasten it with a toothpick.

In a skillet, saute scallops for a few minutes on each side. When
bacon is crisp, scallops are done. Do not overcook. Cheese will have
softened. Serve at once. Mushrooms, sauteed in butter, is a very nice
accompaniment. Serves 4.

Note: – *This dish is assembled and cooked in minutes, so reserve it
     for a night when you are running late.*
    – *Entire dish can be assembled earlier in the day and
     refrigerated. Saute just before serving.*

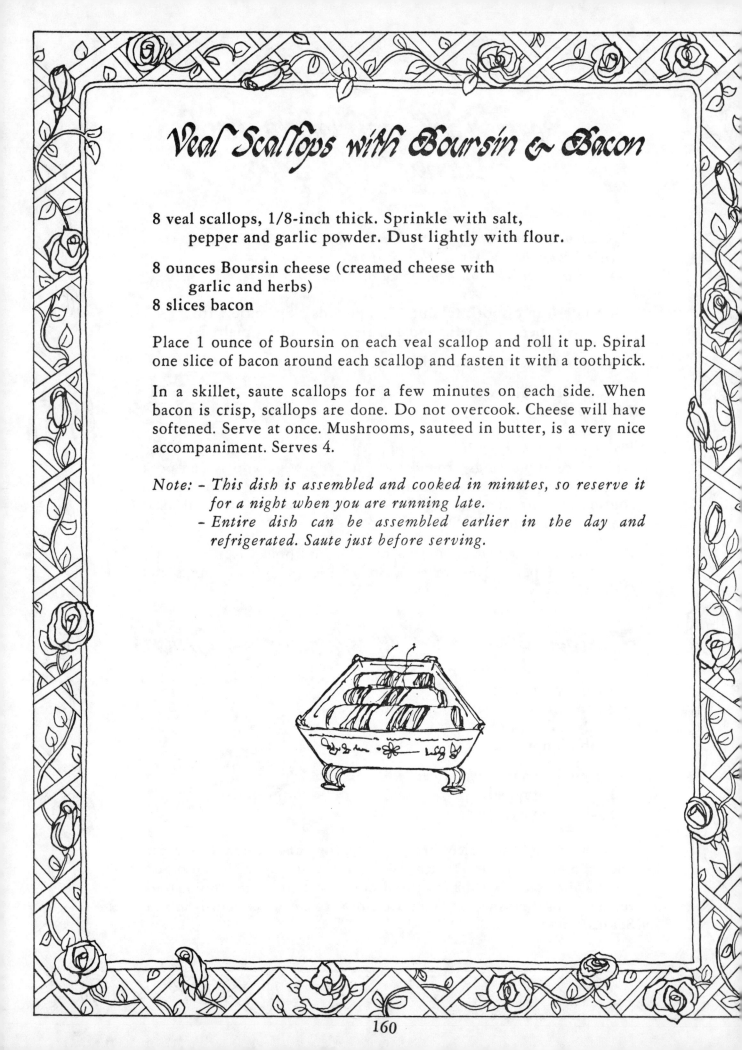

Veal Normandy with Apples, Cinnamon & Cream

Although veal is delicate and succulent, it does need a good, flavorful accompaniment to enrich its rather subtle flavor. This dish is especially delicious, sparkled with apples, cinnamon and cream.

2 pounds veal scallops (about 12 slices), sprinkle with salt, pepper, garlic powder and dust lightly with flour
butter
1/4 cup **Cognac**

4 apples, peeled and sliced
2 tablespoons cinnamon sugar
2 tablespoons chopped shallots
4 tablespoons butter

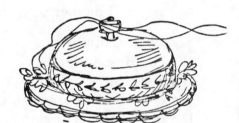

1 1/2 cups apple juice
1 cup cream
1/2 cup sour cream
salt to taste

Saute the scallops in butter, a few at a time and a few minutes on each side, until the meat loses its pinkness. In a brandy warmer, heat the cognac, ignite it, and carefully pour it over the meat. When the flames are out, remove the meat to a porcelain baker.

In the same pan you cooked the veal, saute apples, cinnamon, sugar and shallots in the butter until the apples are firm tender, about 10 minutes. Add apple juice, increase heat to high, and reduce apple juice to half. Stir in creams and salt.

Place apple mixture evenly over the veal. Can be held at this point. Heat in a 325° oven until warmed through. Sprinkle top with parsley and serve with glazed carrots and cinnamon rice. Serves 6.

Note: - Entire dish can be prepared earlier in the day and refrigerated. Allow about 20 to 25 minutes to heat. Do not overcook, simply heat it through.
- Apples should be nice and soft, but not mushy.

Veal Rolls with Herbed Stuffing & Wine & Cream Sauce

Stuffing:

1/4 pound ground pork
1/4 pound ground mushrooms
1 cup garlic croutons, crushed and soaked in
    1/2 cup cream
2 tablespoons grated Parmesan cheese
1 egg
1 tablespoon chopped parsley
    pinch of thyme
1/4 teaspoon poultry seasoning
    salt and papper to taste

Seasoned Crumbs:

1/4 cup bread crumbs
1/4 cup flour
1/4 cup grated Parmesan cheese
1/8 teaspoon garlic powder
1/2 teaspoon paprika

1 1/2 pounds veal scallops (about 12 slices), sprinkle with
    salt, white pepper and garlic powder

1/4 to 1/2 cup butter, for sauteing veal
1/4 cup cognac
1/2 cup cream
1/2 cup white wine

Combine the Stuffing ingredients and set aside. Combine the Seasoned Crumbs ingredients and set aside.

Place 1 tablespoon stuffing on each veal slice. Roll each slice up and secure it with a toothpick. Roll the veal in the Seasoned Crumbs and saute them quickly in butter for about 5 minutes or until the meat loses its pinkness. Do not overcook. Warm the Cognac in a brandy warmer, ignite and carefully pour over the veal. When the flames are out, transfer the veal to a lovely porcelain baker.

Place cream and wine into pan where veal was sauteed and cook it until sauce is reduced to one-half. Ladle a little sauce over each veal roll when serving. Sprinkle with a little parsley and serve with pride. Serves 6.

Note: – Veal rolls and sauce may be made earlier in the day, but take care not to overcook when reheating.

Old-Fashioned Stuffed Breast of Veal with Raisin Sauce

On a cold, frosty night, this is a dish that memories are made of. A garlic-studded stuffing in a succulent gravy (that need not be thickened) is a delight for family and friends. Be certain to serve a crusty French bread to dip into the delicious gravy.

1 breast of veal, about 2 1/2 pounds. Ask your butcher
    to bone it. Sprinkle it with salt and pepper and
    lots of garlic powder.

1 onion, finely chopped
1 carrot, grated
6 cloves garlic, put through a press
4 tablespoons butter

1 package (6 ounces) Stove Top Chicken Flavored
    Stuffing Mix

Saute onion, carrot and garlic in butter until onions are soft. Meanwhile, prepare stuffing mix according to directions on the package. Add the sauteed vegetables to the prepared stuffing and toss and turn until well blended.

Lay out the prepared breast of veal, cut side up. Place the stuffing mixture on the long side of the breast and roll it up. Skewer it or tie it securely with a string, making certain to skewer the ends.

Place roast in a 9x13-inch pan. Pour Raisin Sauce ingredients over the top. Cover the pan tightly with foil and bake in a 350° oven for 1 1/2 to 2 hours or until the meat is tender. Remove skewers or string.

Slice and serve with a spoonful of sauce on top. Serves 4 to 5.

Raisin Sauce

  1 cup beer
  1 envelope dry onion soup mix
1/2 cup currant jelly
  2 tablespoons brown sugar
1/4 cup ketchup
3/4 cup yellow raisins

Combine all the ingredients and stir until blended. Pour over veal roast.

Braised Veal in Tomato, Onion & Wine Sauce

Some evening when you are planning a leisurely and casual dinner with family and friends, you might enjoy serving this very simple and hearty dish. Serve it informally with lots of crusty French bread to soak up the delicious gravy. Rich and full of flavor, it does wonders for the body and the spirit.

3 pounds boneless veal stew meat, cut into 1-inch cubes. Sprinkle these with salt, pepper and lots of garlic powder (coarse grind). Dust lightly with flour.

3 tablespoons oil (can use part olive oil)
1 bag (12 ounces) frozen chopped onions (or 3 large onions, chopped)
1 carrot, grated
1/4 cup green pepper, chopped
4 cloves garlic, put through a press
2 cans (1 pound, each) stewed tomatoes, finely chopped
1 can (8 ounces) tomato paste
1 cup dry white wine
1 tablespoon sugar
1/2 teaspoon each basil and thyme
3 teaspoons chicken seasoned stock base
salt and pepper to taste

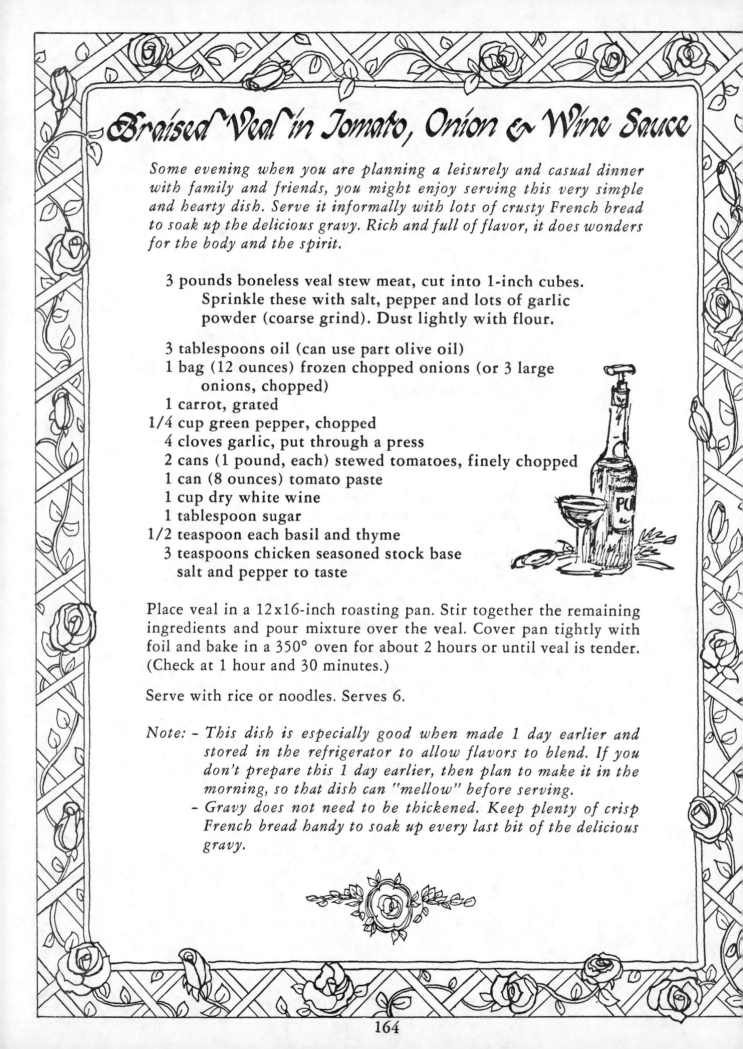

Place veal in a 12x16-inch roasting pan. Stir together the remaining ingredients and pour mixture over the veal. Cover pan tightly with foil and bake in a 350° oven for about 2 hours or until veal is tender. (Check at 1 hour and 30 minutes.)

Serve with rice or noodles. Serves 6.

Note: – This dish is especially good when made 1 day earlier and stored in the refrigerator to allow flavors to blend. If you don't prepare this 1 day earlier, then plan to make it in the morning, so that dish can "mellow" before serving.
– Gravy does not need to be thickened. Keep plenty of crisp French bread handy to soak up every last bit of the delicious gravy.

Paupiettes de Veau with Herbed Stuffing & Sour Cream Wine Sauce

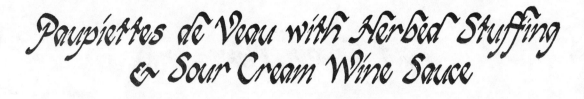

If you are planning a very special dinner, this is a very impressive dish to consider. It can be prepared in advance but must be heated carefully so as not to overcook the tender succulent veal. The Herb Stuffing is deeply flavorful and the Sour Cream Wine Sauce is a perfect accompaniment.

1 1/2 pounds veal scallops (about 12 slices),
    sprinkle with salt, white pepper and
    garlic powder. Sprinkle with flour.

Herb Stuffing:
  1 onion, chopped
  2 tablespoons butter

  1 egg, beaten
  6 cups fresh white bread, cubed (about 12 slices).
    Remove crusts.
1/2 teaspoon paprika
1/2 teaspoon poultry seasoning
    pinch thyme (a good pinch)
  2 teaspoons chicken stock base
    stirred in 1/2 cup water
  2 tablespoons minced parsley
  6 tablespoons melted butter
1/2 teaspoon salt
  pepper to taste

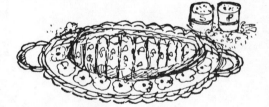

Saute onion in butter until tender. In a large bowl, mash all the ingredients together until thoroughly blended. Stuffing should be moist but on the dry side.

Divide stuffing between the 12 veal scallops. Roll each slice up and secure it with a toothpick. Saute rolls quickly in butter until meat loses its pinkness (about 5 minutes). Do not overcook.

Place veal rolls in a porcelain oval baker. When ready to serve, heat in a 350° oven until just heated through. Do not overcook. Serve with Sour Cream Wine Sauce spooned on the top. Pass the remaining sauce. Garnish with parsley and whole spiced apricots. Serves 6.

Sour Cream Wine Sauce

1/2 cup finely chopped onion
1/2 pound thinly sliced mushrooms
  4 tablespoons butter
  2 tablespoons flour
  1 cup cream
  1 cup sour cream
  3 tablespoons dry white wine

Saute onion and mushrooms in butter until tender. Add flour and cook for 2 minutes. Add remaining ingredients and cook and stir until thickened. Do not boil.

Poultry & Dressings

I often wonder what it is about chicken that lends itself so well to such a variety of preparations. Its versatility never fails to amaze me. And for as many chicken recipes as exist, there are an infinite number waiting to be discovered by creative cooks, everywhere.

During my visits to France, some of the most glorious meals we had were chicken. The French use it extensively and a "chicken-in-every-pot" could have been written by a Frenchman.

Chicken can be a masterpiece, prepared and served in a baronial manner. It is also a grand dish for a picnic on a rolling meadow. Plain or fancy, it can be served hot or cold, with an infinite variety of sauces.

Chicken symbolizes family and friends and informal dinners. Can it be Sunday without chicken and dumplings and biscuits with creamy butter and honey? It is a good choice for family dinners for everyone likes chicken in one form or another ... with honey and wine or glazed or stuffed, with tomatoes or cheese, lemon or garlic.

The recipes that follow reflect this diversity. Chicken with honey, oranges, fruit pudding, wine, cream, peppers, garlic, apples, onions, applesauce, raisins, almonds, brandy, peaches, chestnuts, a noble feast for every Sunday for at least 6 months.

And all of the recipes are basic enough so that even beginners to cooking will create grand dishes with total confidence. And for those that are skilled and accomplished in the culinary arts, I hope you find the recipes exciting and imaginative.

Honey-Glazed Roast Chicken with Old Fashioned Fruit Pudding

This dish is the quintessence of Sunday family dinners. While it is so simple to prepare it adds a great deal of glamor and excitement to a plain roast chicken. The fruit pudding is a family favorite and I hope it will be for yours, too.

2 fryer chickens, cut into serving pieces (about 2 1/2 to 3 pounds, each). Sprinkle generously with salt, pepper and garlic powder.

Honey Glaze:
  4 tablespoons butter (1/2 stick)
1/2 cup honey
1/4 cup undiluted concentrated frozen orange juice

Roast chicken at 325° for 40 minutes, in one layer, in a 12x16-inch pan. Meanwhile, heat together butter, honey and orange juice until mixture is warm and blended. Baste chicken with the Honey Glaze and continue roasting and basting for another 35 minutes or until chicken is tender and a beautiful golden color. Serve with Fruit Pudding, glazed carrots and biscuits with sweet whipped butter. Serves 6.

Old Fashioned Fruit Pudding

  2 cups bread crumbs
1/2 cup sugar
1/4 cup sweet sauternes
  1 cup grated apples
1/2 cup yellow raisins
1/2 cup finely chopped dried apricots
1/2 cup finely chopped dried peaches
  3 eggs
  6 tablespoons melted butter

Combine all the ingredients and mix until thoroughly blended. Spoon mixture into a greased 1 1/2-quart souffle dish and bake in a 350° oven for about 45 minutes or until pudding is set and top is golden brown. Serves 6.

Note: – If apricots and peaches are not soft (these can sometimes be hard and dry) then heat them in some orange juice to soften a little.

Chicken in a Delicate Instant Wine & Cream Sauce

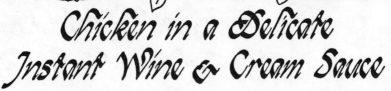

This is a fine chicken dish to serve for family or company dinners. It prepares easily, but you must be careful not to overcook the chicken breasts which will make them tough and chewy. The wine sauce is very simple and delicate and can be prepared in advance.

4 chicken breasts, boned and cut in half. Dust lightly with
    flour and baste with 4 tablespoons melted butter.
    Sprinkle with salt, white pepper and garlic powder.

Instant Wine and Cream Sauce:
  2 shallots, finely chopped
  2 cloves garlic, put through a press
  1 tablespoon butter

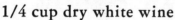

1/4 cup dry white wine
1/4 cup chicken broth (can use canned broth, undiluted)
  2 tablespoons parsley
    pinch of thyme

  1 cup cream
  1 teaspoon lemon juice

Place chicken in a 9x13-inch roasting pan and bake in a 325° oven for about 15 to 20 minutes or until they are just cooked through. Do not overcook.

Meanwhile, saute shallots and garlic in butter until the shallots are soft, but not browned. Add wine and broth and cook over medium-high heat until liquid is reduced to about one-half. Add the remaining ingredients and simmer sauce until slightly thickened, about 3 minutes.

Place the warm chicken on a lovely platter and spoon the sauce over all. Serve with a lovely Green Rice with Herbs and buttered carrots. Serves 4.

Note: – Sauce can be prepared earlier in the day and reheated at time of serving.
    – If you are planning a casual dinner, you can substitute 2 small fryer chickens (about 2 1/2 pounds), cut into pieces, for the chicken breasts.
    – You can substitute 1/4 cup green onions for the shallots.

Chicken with Mushrooms & Onions in Wine Sauce

(Coq au Vin)

This is a simplified version of the wonderful Coq au Vin. It is a delicious dish and very suitable for casual dinners with family and friends. If you have a large porcelain casserole, it is just lovely for the final baking and serving. In absence of one, use a Dutch oven that is ovenproof.

    2 chickens (about 2 1/2 pounds, each) cut into pieces
    2 pounds small white onions, peeled and left whole
      salt and pepper
1/2 cup butter (1 stick), melted

1/4 cup butter (1/2 stick)
    1 pound mushrooms, cleaned and sliced
    4 tablespoons minced shallots
    3 cloves garlic, put through a press

1/4 cup Cognac

    2 cups Burgundy wine

    1 can (10 1/2 ounces) beef broth
    1 tablespoon tomato paste
    1 teaspoon Bovril (beef extract)
1/2 teaspoon thyme flakes
      salt and pepper to taste

In a 12x16-inch baking pan, place chicken and onions in 1 layer. Sprinkle with salt and pepper and drizzle with melted butter. Bake in a 350° oven for 40 minutes, basting now and again.

Meanwhile, in a large skillet, melt the 1/2 stick butter. Saute mushrooms, shallots and garlic in butter until the mushrooms are tender. Warm the Cognac in a brandy warmer, ignite and pour it over the mushrooms. When the flames subside, add the wine and simmer mixture until the wine is reduced to 1 cup. Stir in the remaining ingredients and simmer sauce for 5 minutes.

Place chicken and onions in a Dutch oven or porcelain casserole. Pour sauce over the chicken. Cover and return to oven and continue baking for about 30 minutes or until chicken is tender. Serve with brown rice and buttered peas. Serves 8.

Chicken with Orange Currant Glaze

(Poulet a l'Orange)

1 fryer chicken (about 2 1/2 to 3 pounds) cut up.
    Sprinkle with salt and garlic powder.
1/4 cup butter, melted

1/2 cup currant jelly
1/4 cup frozen orange juice, undiluted
  1 tablespoon Dijon-style mustard
  1 clove garlic, put through a press
1/4 cup butter, melted
  2 tablespoons ketchup
  1 tablespoon grated orange peel

Place chicken in a baking dish and baste with the melted butter. Cook chicken in a 350° oven for about 40 minutes.

Meanwhile, place the remaining ingredients in a saucepan and heat until jelly is melted and mixture is blended. Baste chicken with jelly mixture and continue baking and basting for another 40 minutes. Chicken will be a deep golden color.

Serve with Brown Rice with Raisins and Almonds as a lovely accompaniment. Serves 4.

Sesame Chicken with Honey Glaze

2 fryer chickens (about 2 1/2 to 3 pounds, each) cut up
    and sprinkled with salt, pepper and garlic powder
1 cup honey
1/2 cup ketchup
1/2 cup barbecue sauce
  sesame seeds

Place chicken in a shallow roasting pan and bake in a 350° oven for 30 minutes. Combine honey, ketchup and barbecue sauce and stir until blended. Baste chicken with honey mixture and continue baking and basting for another 30 minutes. Sprinkle sesame seeds on glazed chicken and bake for an additional 10 minutes. Chicken will be a rich golden color and seeds will be lightly browned. Serve with fried rice and glazed carrots. Serves 8.

Chicken with Sweet Red Peppers & Garlic

Tender, succulent chicken breasts, served with sauteed green and red peppers, strongly accented with garlic, all add to a wonderful dish for informal dinners. Serve this over a simple pilaf or buttered noodles (the very fine vermicelli), or pasta tossed with butter and grated Parmesan cheese. Delicious!

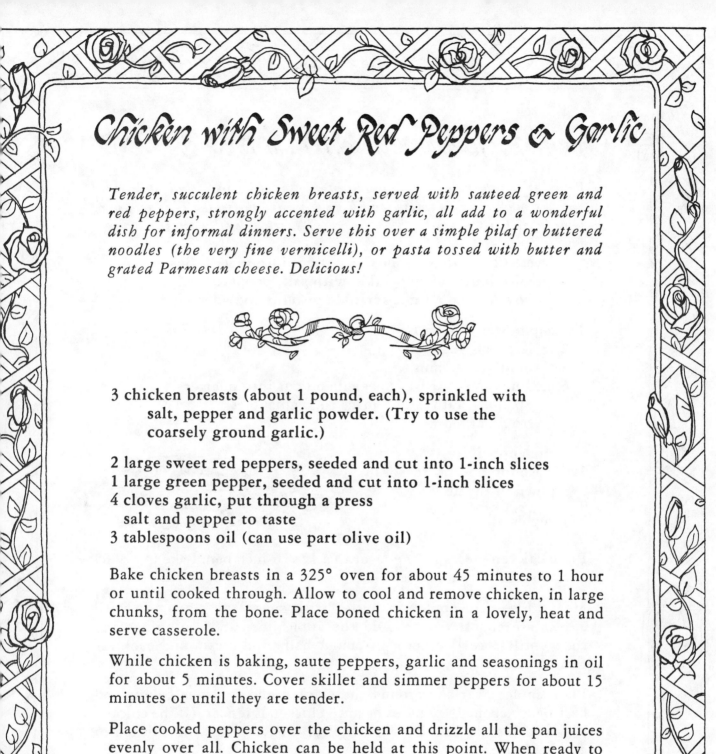

3 chicken breasts (about 1 pound, each), sprinkled with
     salt, pepper and garlic powder. (Try to use the
     coarsely ground garlic.)

2 large sweet red peppers, seeded and cut into 1-inch slices
1 large green pepper, seeded and cut into 1-inch slices
4 cloves garlic, put through a press
   salt and pepper to taste
3 tablespoons oil (can use part olive oil)

Bake chicken breasts in a 325° oven for about 45 minutes to 1 hour or until cooked through. Allow to cool and remove chicken, in large chunks, from the bone. Place boned chicken in a lovely, heat and serve casserole.

While chicken is baking, saute peppers, garlic and seasonings in oil for about 5 minutes. Cover skillet and simmer peppers for about 15 minutes or until they are tender.

Place cooked peppers over the chicken and drizzle all the pan juices evenly over all. Chicken can be held at this point. When ready to serve, heat in a 325° oven until heated through. Serves 4 to 6.

Note: - A lovely addition would be the sprinkling of a little grated Parmesan over the peppers before reheating. Do this only if you are not serving cheese with the noodles or pasta.
       - Keep the accompaniments simple because this is an extremely flavorful dish.

Chicken Normandy with Apples & Cream

Fruit is a marvelous accompaniment to chicken...and it always amazes me as to how many combinations are possible. This is a very simple dish to prepare, but the results are literally fit for a king.

2 fryers (2 1/2 to 3 pounds, each) cut into pieces. Baste
with butter and sprinkle with salt, pepper, garlic
powder and a light sprinkle of onion powder.

1/2 cup butter (1 stick)
2 tablespoons sugar
1/4 teaspoon cinnamon
6 medium apples, cored, peeled and cut into quarters.
Sprinkle with lemon juice to keep apples
from darkening.

1 cup apple juice
1/4 teaspoon poultry seasoning
pinch of thyme

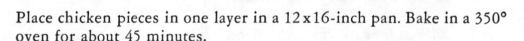

1 cup cream

Place chicken pieces in one layer in a 12 x 16-inch pan. Bake in a 350° oven for about 45 minutes.

Meanwhile saute apples in butter with sugar and cinnamon until apples are almost tender. Add the apple juice and seasonings and cook until sauce is reduced to about half. Add cream and cook for 5 minutes.

Place apples over and around the chicken and continue baking and basting for about 15 minutes or until chicken is tender. (If the chicken has rendered any fat or a lot of juice, then transfer the chicken to another pan.)

Serve this delectable dish with cinnamon rice or cinnamon noodles. Serves 6 to 8.

*Note: – To make a simple cinnamon rice or noodles, toss in melted
butter and sprinkle lightly with cinnamon.*

Chicken Dijonnaise with Onions & Sour Cream

2 fryer chickens (about 2 1/2 pounds, each), cut up and
    brushed with Dijon mustard. Sprinkle with salt,
    pepper and garlic powder.

2 onions, finely chopped
2 cloves garlic
1 tablespoon brown sugar
3 tablespoons butter

1/4 cup white wine

1 tablespoon paprika
1 can (10 1/2 ounces) chicken broth
1 teaspoon chicken stock base
   salt and pepper to taste

1 cup sour cream

Prepare chickens and set aside. In a Dutch oven, saute onions and
garlic with butter and sugar until the onions are soft. Add wine and
cook for a minute or 2 until wine has evaporated. Add seasonings,
chicken broth and chicken stock base and stir until blended. Bring
mixture to a boil.

Arrange chicken pieces over the sauce, cover and simmer for about
1 hour and 15 minutes or until chicken is tender. Just before serving,
add sour cream and heat through. Serve on a bed of noodles or rice.

Note: – Chicken can be cooked earlier in the day and refrigerated.
    However, add the sour cream just before serving.

Sweet & Sour Country Chicken with Carrots & Raisins

Serve this succulent chicken dish with a crusty French bread to soak up the delicious gravy.

2 fryer chickens (about 2 1/2 pounds to 3 pounds, each) cut up. Sprinkle with salt, pepper and garlic powder.

1 tablespoon oil
1 can (16 ounces) tomato sauce
1 carrot, grated
1 onion, finely chopped
1 cup sauerkraut, undrained
1/2 cup brown sugar
1/2 cup yellow raisins
    salt and pepper to taste

Sprinkle chicken with salt, pepper and garlic powder and set aside.

In a Dutch oven, combine the remaining ingredients and bring mixture to a boil. Set chicken pieces evenly in the pan. Cover and simmer mixture for about 1 1/2 hours or until chicken is tender.

This dish is particularly good on the second day, or when made earlier in the day. So plan to make it early. Serve with whole wheat noodles or brown rice. Don't forget the crusty French loaf. Serves 8.

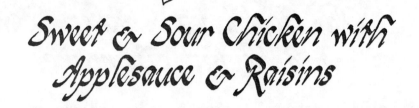

Sweet & Sour Chicken with Applesauce & Raisins

If you ever had to describe a dish as "pure and simple" this would have to be it. It assembles in minutes and produces the finest tasting gravy. Serve with French bread for dipping.

2 fryer chickens (about 2 1/2 pounds, each) cut up.
    Sprinkle with salt, pepper and garlic powder.

1 can (1 pound) stewed tomatoes, finely chopped
2 cans (8 ounces, each) tomato sauce
3 cloves garlic, put through a press
1 onion, finely chopped
1/2 teaspoon thyme flakes
1/4 teaspoon oregano
1/2 cup applesauce
3/4 cup yellow raisins
2 to 3 tablespoons lemon juice
    salt and pepper to taste

Place chicken in one layer in a 12x16-inch roasting pan. Combine the remaining ingredients and pour sauce over the chicken. Tent chicken lightly with foil and bake in a 350° oven for about 1 1/2 hours or until chicken is tender. Remove foil at about 1 hour of cooking time. Serve with rice or noodles. Serves 6 to 8.

Note: – Entire dish can be prepared earlier in the day (or 1 day earlier) and stored in the refrigerator. Heat through in a 350° oven.

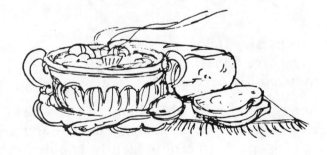

Old-Fashioned Chicken Stew
with Herbed Dumplings

2 fryer chickens (about 2 1/2 to 3 pounds, each) cut into
     8 pieces, drumsticks, thighs, and breasts cut into
     fourths. Do not use backs and necks for the stew.
2 onions, chopped
3 small carrots, sliced
1 rib celery, scraped and thinly sliced
1 clove garlic, put through a press
4 tablespoons butter

2 cans chicken broth, (10 1/2 ounces, each)
1 teaspoon Bovril beef extract*
2 tablespoons tomato paste
1 teaspoon dried thyme flakes
  salt and pepper to taste
1/4 teaspoon paprika

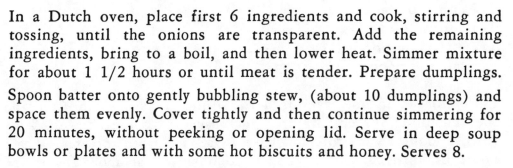

In a Dutch oven, place first 6 ingredients and cook, stirring and tossing, until the onions are transparent. Add the remaining ingredients, bring to a boil, and then lower heat. Simmer mixture for about 1 1/2 hours or until meat is tender. Prepare dumplings.

Spoon batter onto gently bubbling stew, (about 10 dumplings) and space them evenly. Cover tightly and then continue simmering for 20 minutes, without peeking or opening lid. Serve in deep soup bowls or plates and with some hot biscuits and honey. Serves 8.

Note: - *Yes, this is correct. The beef flavor does wonders in this
      stew. The tomato paste and paprika are not traditional
      but add a great deal of depth and character to the gravy.
   - Entire dish can be made earlier in the day and stored in
      the refrigerator.

Herbed Dumplings

1 egg
2/3 cup milk
2 teaspoons parsley flakes
2 teaspoons chive flakes
2 cups prepared biscuit mix

Beat together egg and milk until blended. In a bowl, place parsley, chives and biscuit mix. Pour in egg mixture and stir with a fork until blended. Spoon batter onto gently bubbling stew. Yields 10 dumplings.

Roast Chicken Breasts in Tomato & Wine Sauce

Be sure to serve some crusty French bread with this dish, to soak up the delicious gravy.

4 chicken breasts, boned and cut in half. Dust lightly with
   flour and baste with 4 tablespoons melted butter.
   Sprinkle with salt, white pepper and garlic powder.

1/2 pound mushrooms, thinly sliced
  1 carrot, thinly sliced
  1 onion, finely chopped
  1 shallot or green onion, finely chopped
  4 tablespoons butter

  1 teaspoon chicken stock base
1/4 cup dry white wine
  1 tablespoon chopped parsley
  1 tablespoon lemon juice
  1 can (1 pound) stewed tomatoes, finely chopped, undrained
    pinch of thyme
    salt and pepper to taste

Place chicken in a 9x13-inch roasting pan and bake in a 325° oven for about 15 to 20 minutes or until cooked through. Do not overcook.

Meanwhile saute together the next 5 ingredients until the carrots are tender. Add the remaining ingredients and cook sauce, uncovered, until it is slightly thickened, about 20 minutes.

Place chicken in a lovely porcelain baker and pour vegetables on top. Heat through before serving. Serve with Pink Rice or noodles tossed with butter and bread crumbs. Serves 4 to 6.

Note: - Two small fryer chickens (about 2 1/2 pounds, each), cut
*   into pieces, can be substituted for the chicken breasts.*
*   - Entire dish can be prepared earlier in the day and heated*
*   at time of serving.*

Country Chicken & Fresh Vegetables

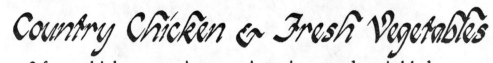

2 fryer chickens, cut into serving pieces and sprinkled
  with salt, pepper, garlic powder and paprika
4 tablespoons melted butter, 1/2 stick

1 clove garlic, put through a press
1/4 pound mushrooms, sliced
1 onion, minced
1/2 green pepper, cut into 1-inch strips
2 carrots, peeled and grated
4 tablespoons butter, 1/2 stick

2 tomatoes, peeled and chopped (use fresh or canned)
1 teaspoon paprika
1 can (10 1/2 ounces) chicken broth
  salt and pepper to taste

Place chicken pieces in a 12x16-inch pan in one layer and drizzle with melted butter. Bake in a 325° oven for 1 hour 15 minutes, basting from time to time with the juices forming in the pan.

Meanwhile, in a large skillet, saute together the garlic, mushrooms, onion, pepper, carrots in 4 tablespoons butter until the vegetables are tender. Add the tomatoes, paprika, chicken broth and seasonings and cover and continue cooking at a simmer for 20 minutes. In a lovely porcelain baker, place the chicken and cover with the sauce. Heat in a 350° oven until piping hot. Serve with Pink Rice and Chives. Serves 6 to 8.

Pink Rice & Chives

2 tablespoons butter
1 cup rice
1 can (10 1/2 ounces) chicken broth
3/4 cup water
2 tablespoons tomato paste
2 tablespoons chives
  salt and pepper to taste

Place all the ingredients in a saucepan and cover pan. Simmer mixture until rice is tender and liquid is absorbed, about 30 minutes. Serves 6.

Crusty Chicken with Garlic, Lemon & Herbs

2 fryer chickens (2 1/2 to 3 pounds, each). Sprinkle with
salt, pepper and garlic powder.

1/2 cup butter
   3 cloves garlic, put through a press
   3 tablespoons lemon juice
   1 tablespoon chopped chives
   1 tablespoon chopped parsley
1/2 teaspoon thyme flakes
   1 teaspoon Dijon mustard

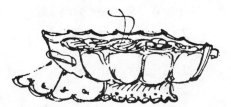

Place chicken pieces in one layer in a 12x16-inch pan. In a saucepan,
heat together the remaining ingredients until butter is melted. Baste
chicken generously with butter mixture. Bake chicken in a 350° oven
for 30 minutes, basting frequently.

Sprinkle Seasoned Crumbs over the chicken and continue baking
for 45 minutes or until chicken is tender. Serves 6 to 8.

Seasoned Crumbs:
1/2 cup Ritz cracker crumbs
1/2 cup grated Parmesan cheese
1/4 teaspoon garlic powder
1/4 teaspoon thyme flakes
1/4 cup melted butter

Combine all the ingredients and toss until blended.

*Note: - This dish is just marvelous served with Casserole with
Noodles, Cheese and Herbs. Add a simple buttered
vegetable as an excellent accompaniment. Keep dessert
light. A lovely Lemon Souffle or Lemon Ice would be nice.*

Chicken with Tomatoes, Peppers & Onions

2 fryer chickens (about 3 pounds, each) cut up.
Sprinkle with salt and pepper. Brush chicken
with 1/4 cup melted butter.

Tomato, Pepper and Onion Sauce:

2 shallots, minced
1/4 cup melted butter
2 onions, finely chopped
1 green pepper, chopped
1 can (1 pound) stewed tomatoes, chopped.
Use the juice, too.
1 teaspoon Italian Herb Seasoning
2 cloves garlic, put through a press
salt and pepper to taste

Lay chicken pieces in one layer in a 12x16-inch roasting pan. Bake in a 350° oven for 40 minutes. Combine sauce ingredients in a saucepan and simmer for 30 minutes. Pour sauce over the chicken and continue baking for 40 minutes. Serve over a bed of Rice with Onions and Peas or simply, buttered noodles. Serves 6 to 8.

Chicken with Mushrooms in Wine & Cream Sauce

This dish is the essence of simplicity, yet is so delicious that you will enjoy serving it on special occasions. The sauce is a delicate blend of wine and cream, onions and mushrooms.

4 chicken breasts, boned and cut into 1-inch pieces.
    Sprinkle with salt, pepper, garlic powder and paprika.
6 tablespoons butter

2 onions, finely chopped
1/2 pound mushrooms, thinly sliced
1/4 cup dry white wine

2 tablespoons flour
2 tablespoons paprika

1 cup (10 1/2 ounces) chicken broth
1 cup cream
  salt and pepper to taste

In a Dutch oven, saute chicken in butter until chicken is opaque and cooked through. This will only take a few minutes, so don't overcook chicken. Remove chicken with a slotted spoon and set aside.

In the Dutch oven, saute onions and mushrooms (add a little butter, if necessary) until onions are soft. Add wine and cook until wine has evaporated. Add flour and paprika and cook and stir for about 3 minutes. Add broth and cream and taste for salt and pepper. Cook until sauce has thickened. Finally, add chicken and heat through.

Serve over a bed of buttered noodles or rice. Serves 6.

Note: – Entire dish can be prepared earlier in the day and heated at time of serving.

Chicken in Tomato Chive Cream Sauce

Try this delicious dish some Sunday when you are having family and friends for dinner. Serve it with hot biscuits to soak up the delicious gravy.

    2 fryer chickens (about 3 pounds, each) cut up.
        Sprinkle with salt, pepper, garlic powder.
    4 tablespoons melted butter

    4 tomatoes, peeled and chopped or 1 can (16 ounces)
        stewed tomatoes, chopped
    3 tablespoons chopped chives
    1 tablespoon chopped parsley
1/4 teaspoon poultry seasoning
    2 tablespoons butter
      salt and pepper to taste

    1 cup sour cream
1/2 cup cream

Prepare chicken with seasonings and brush with melted butter. Bake in a 350° oven for about 1 hour and 15 minutes or until chicken is tender. Remove chicken to a porcelain baker.

While chicken is baking, prepare sauce. Combine tomatoes, chives, parsley, poultry seasoning, butter and salt and pepper and simmer mixture until tomatoes are softened and liquid is absorbed. Add any pan dripping from the cooked chicken. Add the creams to sauce and stir until everything is nicely blended. Pour sauce over the chicken.

Heat in a 325° oven until heated through. Do not overheat. Serve with rice or noodles. Serves 6.

Note· – Entire dish can be prepared earlier in the day and refrigerated. Take care in reheating so that you don't allow the dish to boil. Heat in a 325° oven until heated through and serve with majesty and pride.

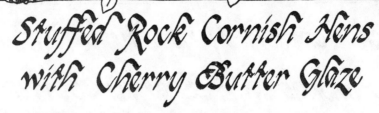

Stuffed Rock Cornish Hens with Cherry Butter Glaze

6 Rock Cornish Hens, sprinkled with salt, pepper, garlic powder and paprika. Brush generously with melted butter.

1 package (8 ounces) herb seasoned stuffing mix
1/4 teaspoon paprika
1/4 teaspoon poultry seasoning
1/4 cup melted butter (1/2 stick)

1 onion, very finely chopped
1/4 cup very finely chopped celery
1/4 cup butter (1/2 stick)

1 can (10 1/2 ounces) chicken broth

Prepare hens. In a large bowl place stuffing mix, paprika, poultry seasoning and melted butter. Toss to combine.

Saute onion and celery in 1/4 cup butter until vegetables are soft. Place vegetables in bowl with stuffing mix. Now add just enough broth to hold stuffing together.

Stuff hen cavities about 3/4 full and skewer them with pins or toothpicks. Bake in a 325° oven for about 45 minutes, basting now and again with butter. Increase oven temperature to 350° and baste hens with Cherry Butter Glaze every 5 minutes for the next 30 minutes or until hens are cooked and glaze is a lovely amber color. Serves 6.

Cherry Butter Glaze

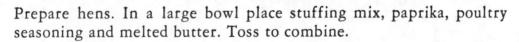

1 can (8 ounces) dark sweet cherries, drained.
    Reserve juice for another use.
1/2 cup black cherry preserves
1/4 cup butter
2 tablespoons dry white wine

Combine all the ingredients and heat until blended.

Note: – Do not stuff hens before baking. Stuffing can be made earlier in the day and refrigerated. Hens can be seasoned and brushed with butter earlier in the day and refrigerated.

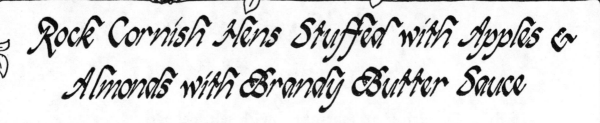

Rock Cornish Hens Stuffed with Apples & Almonds with Brandy Butter Sauce

6 Rock Cornish hens (about 16 to 20 ounces, each)
  Sprinkle hens with salt, pepper, garlic powder
  and paprika. Dust lightly with flour.

Apple Almond Stuffing:
  1 package, 8 ounces, herb seasoned stuffing mix
  1 apple, peeled and grated
1/2 cup butter, melted
  2 teaspoons chicken seasoned stock base
  1 cup apple juice, more or less as needed
3/4 cup sliced almonds, lightly toasted in a 350° oven
      for 8 minutes
1/8 teaspoon poultry seasoning
    salt and pepper to taste

Combine all the ingredients, adding only enough apple juice to hold stuffing together. Stuff hen cavities about 3/4 full and skewer them with toothpicks or skewers.

Baste hens generously with Brandy Butter mixture and bake in a 325° oven for 1 hour 10 minutes. Baste often during baking time, turning once or twice. Hens will turn a lovely golden color. Remove skewers and decorate platter with lots of parsley, crab apples and orange slices. Serves 6.

Brandy Butter Sauce

1/2 cup butter (1 stick)
  2 tablespoons apricot flavored brandy
  2 tablespoons honey

Combine butter, brandy and honey in a saucepan and heat until butter melts and mixture is blended.

Note: – If hens are browning too rapidly, tent the roasting pan loosely with aluminum foil.

Honeyed Duck with Glazed Peaches & Peach Brandy

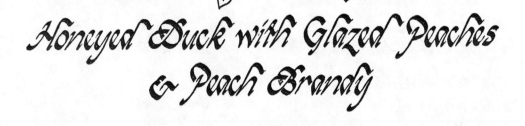

This is a variation of an old favorite, Duck a l'Orange. Somehow, people shy away from serving duck, these days. "It's kinda' fatty," they complain, "and there's hardly any meat on the bones." All true. But it does have a unique and delicious flavor. Roasting it in quarters helps to drain the fat and crisp the skin. Serve it with the Glazed Peaches and a casual dinner will feel like a party.

   1 duck (about 4 to 5 pounds), cut into quarters and
      sprinkled with salt and garlic powder

   1 can (1 pound 12 ounces) peach halves in syrup, drained

1/2 cup peach jam
   2 tablespoons peach brandy or Cognac
1/2 cup honey
1/2 teaspoon cinnamon
   1 tablespoon lemon juice

Place duck in one layer in a 9x13-inch roasting pan. Bake at 350° for 50 minutes. Drain off all of the fat. Place peaches, cut side down, around the duck.

Heat the remaining ingredients in a saucepan and stir until blended. Baste duck and peaches with jam mixture, every 15 minutes, until duck is tender, about 40 minutes more. Duck should be a beautiful golden color. Serve with Glazed Peaches, brown rice and a buttered green vegetable. Serves 3 or 4.

Note: – If peaches are in season, it would be just lovely to use them.
        However, they do have to be peeled.
        – Frozen peaches can also be used.

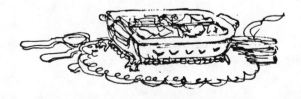

Curried Turkey with Peanuts & Raisins

This is a variation of my favorite curry. Using leftover turkey is especially helpful around holiday time. Cooked chicken is equally good. Serve this with Ginger Rice and Green Onions.

    1 large onion, chopped
    2 cloves garlic, put through a press
    4 tablespoons butter

    1 tablespoon flour
    1 tablespoon curry powder
      salt and pepper to taste

    1 apple, peeled, cored and grated
    1 tablespoon brown sugar
    1 can (10 1/2 ounces) chicken broth

1/2 cup cream
1/2 cup sour cream
1/2 cup yellow raisins
1/2 cup peanuts
    3 cups cooked turkey

Saute onion and garlic in butter until onion is soft, but not brown. Add flour, curry and seasonings and cook for 2 minutes.

Add apple, sugar and broth and cook until sauce thickens. Add the remaining ingredients and heat through. Do not boil.

Serve with Ginger Rice and Green Onions. Serves 4 or 5.

Ginger Rice with Green Onions

    1 cup rice
    2 cups chicken broth
    3 tablespoons butter
      salt and pepper to taste
1/4 teaspoon ginger

1/4 cup chopped green onions

In a saucepan, combine first 5 ingredients. Cover pan and simmer mixture until rice is tender and liquid is absorbed, about 30 minutes. When rice is cooked, stir in the chopped green onions. Serves 4 or 5.

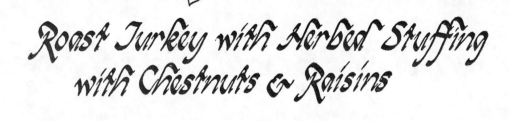

Roast Turkey with Herbed Stuffing with Chestnuts & Raisins

1 turkey, about 15 pounds, thoroughly cleaned and
    patted dry

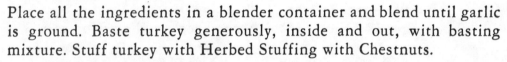

Basting Mixture:
1 cup melted butter
1 teaspoon salt
1/4 teaspoon pepper
1 tablespoon paprika
6 cloves garlic
1/4 teaspoon onion powder

Place all the ingredients in a blender container and blend until garlic is ground. Baste turkey generously, inside and out, with basting mixture. Stuff turkey with Herbed Stuffing with Chestnuts.

Place turkey on a rack in roasting pan, breast side down. (If directions for roasting appear on the wrapper, follow them. If not, figure roughly at 300° for under 15 pounds 25 minutes per pound; for over 15 pounds approximately 20 minutes per pound.) Tent the turkey loosely with foil and baste often with the juices. About 1 hour before turkey is cooked, turn it breast side up, and continue baking, uncovered, until turkey is finished (approximately 185° to 190° on a meat thermometer, inserted in the thickest part of the thigh — not touching the bone.) You can also test for doneness by moving the drumstick up and down. If it gives easily, turkey is done. Remove any fat from the gravy. Gravy is very flavorful and does not need to be thickened.

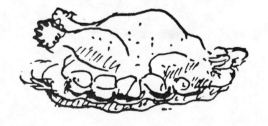

Herbed Stuffing with Chestnuts & Raisins

1 cup butter (2 sticks)
2 cups onions, finely chopped
1 cup celery, finely chopped
2 cloves garlic, put through a press
1 cup yellow raisins
2 cups chestnuts (canned), coarsely chopped
1/4 cup finely chopped parsley
2 teaspoons poultry seasoning
2 teaspoons chicken-seasoned stock base
2 eggs
2 cans (10 1/2 ounces, each) chicken broth
salt and pepper to taste
2 packages (8 ounces, each) herbed seasoned stuffing mix

Saute onions, celery, garlic and raisins in butter until onions are soft. Add remaining ingredients, using only enough broth to hold stuffing together. Will stuff a 15 to 18 pound turkey. Can be baked separately in a casserole, which I prefer and recommend.

Noodles & Rice

Lemon Cheese Noodle Souffle

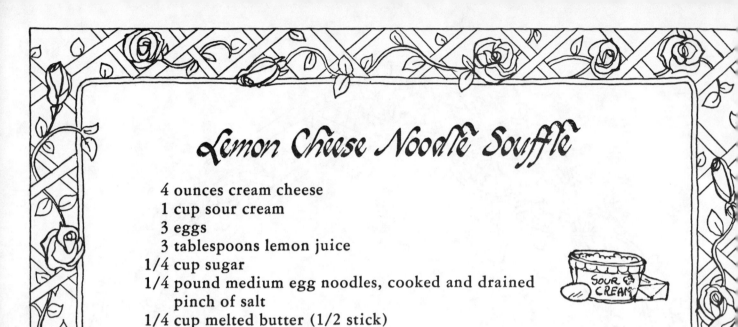

    4 ounces cream cheese
    1 cup sour cream
    3 eggs
    3 tablespoons lemon juice
1/4 cup sugar
1/4 pound medium egg noodles, cooked and drained
    pinch of salt
1/4 cup melted butter (1/2 stick)

In a food processor or in a blender in batches, beat together cream cheese and sour cream until blended. Add the remaining ingredients and blend until noodles are very finely chopped.

Pour mixture into a buttered and sugared 1 1/2-quart souffle dish. Bake in a 350° oven for 45 to 50 minutes, or until top is golden brown and eggs are set. Do not overcook.

Serve with chicken glazed with honey and spiced apricots. Delicious! Serves 5 to 6.

Note: – Entire casserole can be assembled earlier in the day and refrigerated. Bake before serving. Allow 5 to 10 minutes extra baking time if going into the oven straight from the refrigerator.

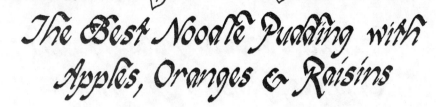

The Best Noodle Pudding with Apples, Oranges & Raisins

This is my favorite noodle pudding. No matter how many times I prepare it, I always receive such animated raves and excited requests for the recipe. I hope you enjoy it, too.

1 package (8 ounces) medium noodles, cooked and drained

1/2 cup (1 stick) butter

2 medium apples, very thinly sliced
4 tablespoons orange juice
1 cup yellow raisins, plumped in orange juice

4 eggs
2 cups sour cream
1/2 cup milk
1 cup sugar
1 teaspoon vanilla
1/2 teaspoon salt

2 tablespoons cinnamon sugar

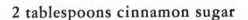

In a 9x13-inch pan, melt the butter. Add the cooked and drained noodles and toss them in the butter until they are completely coated.

Combine the apples, orange juice and raisins and toss with the cooked noodles until evenly mixed.

Beat together the eggs, sour cream, milk, sugar, vanilla and salt until the mixture is nicely blended. Pour the egg mixture evenly over the noodles and spread noodles evenly in the pan. Sprinkle top with cinnamon sugar.

Bake in a 350° oven for 1 hour or until top is golden brown. Cut into squares and serve warm. Serves 10.

Note: - Entire casserole can be assembled and baked 1 day earlier and stored in the refrigerator. Warm in a 325° oven for about 20 to 25 minutes or until heated through.

Creamy Noodle Pudding with Oranges, Raisins & Cinnamon

 1 package (6 ounces) medium noodles, cooked and drained

1/2 cup melted butter

 4 eggs, beaten
 1 cup sour cream
 1 cup cottage cheese
 1 cup sugar
1/2 orange, grated (remove any large pieces of membranes)
 1 can (8 ounces) crushed pineapple, drained
1/2 cup yellow raisins
1/2 teaspoon salt

 cinnamon sugar

In a 9 x 13-inch pan, melt the butter. Toss the cooked noodles in the melted butter until they are nicely coated.

Beat together the next eight ingredients until blended and pour mixture over the noodles. Toss to mix and spread evenly. Sprinkle top with cinnamon sugar.

Bake in a 350° oven for about 1 hour or until top is golden and egg mixture is set. Serves 8 to 10.

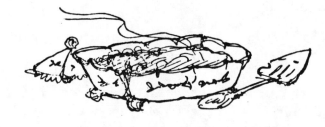

Crown Mold of Noodles
with Cinnamon, Dates & Pecans

1 package (8 ounces) medium noodles, cooked tender
    and very lightly salted
6 tablespoons butter, melted
4 tablespoons cinnamon sugar
1/2 cup finely chopped dates

3 tablespoons butter, melted
3 tablespoons cinnamon sugar
1 cup pecan halves

2 eggs
1/2 cup sour cream
1/2 cup sugar
1/2 teaspoon vanilla

In a bowl, toss together noodles, butter, cinnamon, sugar and dates.

Spray a 2-quart mold with a non-stick coating and butter it heavily. Evenly spread butter, cinnamon sugar and pecans in bottom of ring. Place noodle mixture on top of pecans.

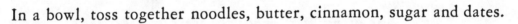

Beat together the remaining ingredients and pour it over the noodles. Place mold on a cookie sheet and bake it in a 350° oven for about 1 hour or until custard is set and top is golden brown. Unmold on a platter and serve with Cinnamon Orange Glazed Pork. Serves 8 to 10.

Note: - Mold can be made earlier in the day and stored in the refrigerator. Reheat before serving.
*   - Fill the center with spiced peaches or apricots.*

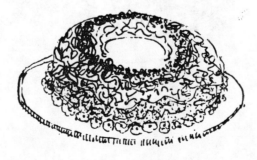

Spinach Noodles with Butter, Lemon & Garlic Sauce

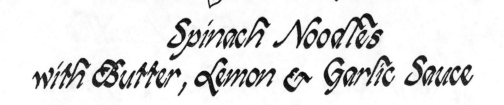

1 package (8 ounces) green noodles, cooked according
    to the directions on the package and drained

6 tablespoons butter
4 cloves garlic, put through a press
4 tablespoons lemon juice
4 tablespoons minced parsley
  salt and pepper to taste

Saute garlic in butter until golden. Add lemon juice and parsley to sauce. Toss cooked noodles with lemon garlic mixture until noodles are thoroughly coated. Add seasonings to taste. Serves 6.

Note: - A delicious optional would be the addition of 1/2 cup toasted
       pine nuts. To toast pine nuts, place in a 350° oven for
       8 minutes.
    - If you are planning to make this casserole earlier in the day,
      refrigerate it but bring it to room temperature before
      reheating. Cover casserole and reheat in a 325° oven until
      heated through, about 20 minutes.

Noodles with Yogurt & Chives

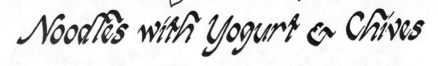

8 ounces medium egg noodles, cooked tender but firm
    and drained
1/4 cup butter, melted

1 cup unflavored yogurt
1/3 cup finely chopped chives
1/4 cup cream
    salt and pepper to taste
1/4 cup grated Parmesan cheese or more to taste

Toss hot, cooked noodles in melted butter. Stir together the yogurt, chives and cream until blended and mix it with the noodles. Season with salt and pepper. Just before serving, sprinkle noodles with grated cheese and toss. Serves 6.

Green Noodles & Mushrooms, Shallots & Cheese

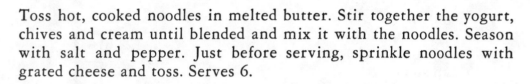

1 package (8 ounces) medium green noodles, cooked
    tender but firm and drained. Sprinkle with salt
    and pepper to taste.
1/4 cup melted butter

1/2 pound mushrooms
2 shallots, minced
1 onion, finely chopped
1/4 cup butter

1/2 cup cream
1 cup grated Swiss cheese

1/4 cup chopped parsley

Toss hot, cooked noodles in melted butter. Set aside. In a large skillet, saute mushrooms, shallots and onion in butter until onions are soft and liquid is evaporated. Add cream and cheese to mushroom mixture and stir, off heat, until blended. Toss mushroom cheese mixture with cooked noodles and transfer to a lovely heat and serve casserole. Sprinkle top generously with parsley. Heat in a 350° oven for about 20 minutes or until heated through. Serve at once. Serves 6.

Noodle Pudding with Cottage Cheese, Cinnamon & Raisins

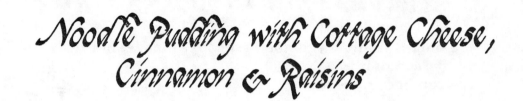

1 package (8 ounces) medium noodles, cooked tender
   and drained
1/2 cup melted butter

5 eggs
2 cups sour cream
1 cup cottage cheese
1 cup sugar
1 teaspoon vanilla
1/2 cup yellow raisins

4 tablespoons cinnamon sugar

Toss cooked and drained noodles with melted butter. Place noodles in a 9 x 13-inch baker.

Beat together eggs, sour cream, cottage cheese, sugar and vanilla until blended. Stir in raisins. Pour egg mixture over cooked noodles. Sprinkle cinnamon sugar evenly over all.

Bake in a 350° oven for about 1 hour or until eggs are set and top is golden brown. Serves 8 to 10.

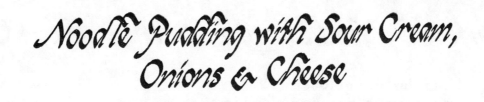

Noodle Pudding with Sour Cream, Onions & Cheese

1 package (8 ounces) medium egg noodles, cooked tender
    and drained
1/4 cup melted butter

5 eggs
2 cups sour cream
1 cup cottage cheese
1/2 cup chopped green onions
2 tablespoons chopped parsley
1/2 cup grated Parmesan cheese
2 tablespoons lemon juice
    salt and pepper to taste

Toss cooked drained noodles with melted butter. Place noodles in a
9 x 13-inch porcelain baker.

Beat together the remaining ingredients until blended, and toss this
mixture with the cooked noodles.

Bake in a 350° oven for about 50 minutes to 1 hour or until eggs are
set and top is golden brown. Serves 8.

Buttered Noodles with Onions & Sour Cream

1 cup chopped onions
1 clove garlic, put through a press
1/4 cup (1/2 stick) butter
1 1/2 teaspoons paprika
1/2 cup bread crumbs

1 teaspoon chicken seasoned stock base
1/4 cup (1/2 stick) melted butter

1 package (8 ounces) medium egg noodles, cooked
     until tender
1/2 cup sour cream

salt and freshly ground pepper to taste

Saute onions and garlic in butter until onions are soft and just beginning to color. Remove from heat and stir in the paprika and bread crumbs until blended. Stir together the melted butter and stock base and add to the onion mixture. Cook for 2 minutes, stirring. In a bowl, stir the cooked noodles with the butter mixture. Stir in the sour cream and toss the noodles until everything is nicely blended.

Place mixture into a lovely heat and serve casserole and heat in a 350° oven until heated through. Serves 6.

Note: - Entire dish can be prepared earlier in the day and refrigerated. Remove from the refrigerator about 30 minutes before you are planning to heat it and allow casserole to come to room temperature. Heat in a 350° oven for about 25 minutes.

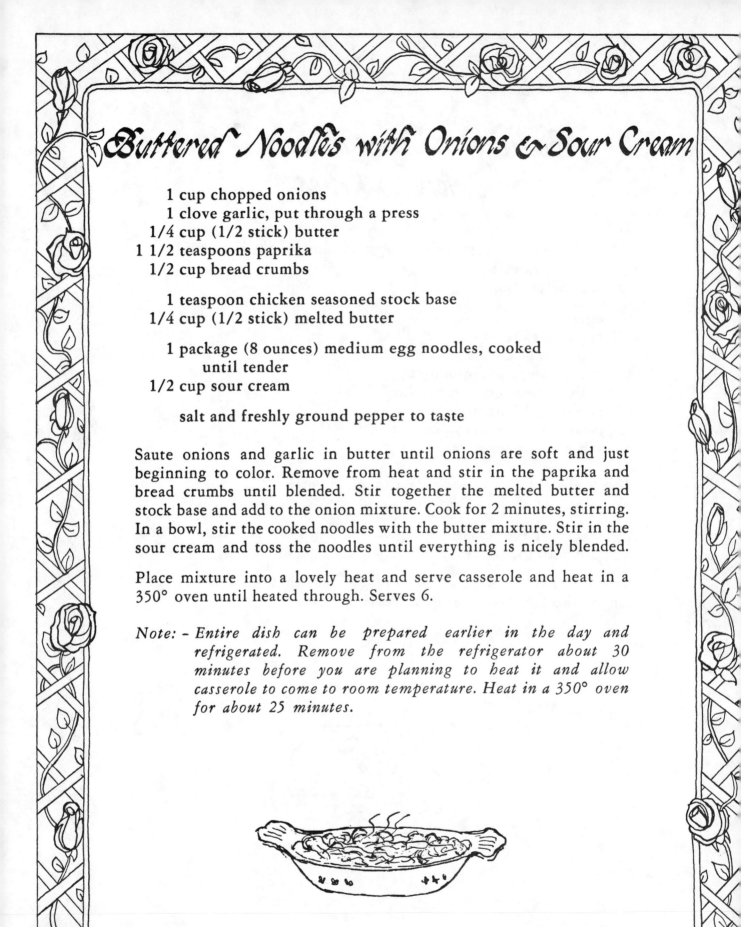

Fideos with Butter, Garlic & Onions

1 package (8 ounces) fideos or vermicelli coils
4 tablespoons butter
1 onion, very finely chopped
2 cloves garlic, put through a press
2 cans (10 1/2 ounces, each) chicken broth
   salt and pepper to taste
2 tablespoons minced parsley

Toast fideos in a 350° oven for about 8 minutes or until golden brown. Set aside. In a saucepan, saute onion and garlic in butter until onions are soft. Add the chicken broth and fideos to the saucepan, stir and simmer mixture covered until the fideos are tender and liquid is absorbed, about 10 minutes. Serves 6.

Rice with Onions & Buttered Peas

2 tablespoons butter
1 onion, chopped

1 cup long-grain rice

1 can (10 1/2 ounces) chicken broth
3/4 cup water
   salt and pepper to taste

2 tablespoons butter
1 package (10 ounces) green peas

Saute onion in butter until onion is transparent. Add rice and saute for two minutes, stirring until rice is completely coated. Carefully add the chicken broth, water and salt and pepper. Stir, cover and simmer mixture until rice is tender and liquid is absorbed.

Meanwhile, saute peas in 2 tablespoons butter until peas are tender but firm, about 5 minutes. Toss cooked peas with the cooked rice. This is a delightful accompaniment to Chicken with Tomato, Pepper and Onions. Serves 6.

Pink Rice in a Light Tomato Sauce

   1 can (10 1/2 ounces) chicken broth
3/4 cup water
   3 tablespoons butter, melted
     salt and pepper to taste

   1 tomato, peeled, seeded and chopped
      (or 1 canned tomato, chopped)
   2 tablespoons tomato sauce
   1 tablespoon chopped parsley
   1 tablespoon chopped chives

   1 cup rice

Combine all the ingredients in a saucepan and stir until mixture is blended. Cover pan and simmer rice until it is tender and liquid is absorbed, about 35 minutes. Serve with chicken or veal, with tomato sauce. Serves 4 or 5.

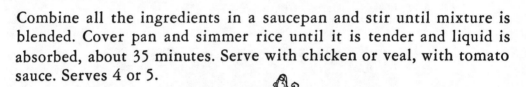

Buttered Lemon Rice with Parsley & Cheese

   1 cup long-grain rice
   2 tablespoons butter
   1 can (10 1/2 ounces) chicken broth
3/4 cup water
     salt and pepper to taste

Combine all the ingredients in a saucepan, cover and simmer mixture until liquid is absorbed and rice is tender, about 25 minutes. When rice is cooked, toss with:

   2 tablespoons butter, melted
   2 tablespoons lemon juice
1/4 cup grated Parmesan cheese
1/4 cup chopped parsley

Serve at once. Or place in a lovely porcelain casserole and cover with foil. Reheat in a 350° oven for about 20 minutes or until heated through. Serves 6.

Brown Rice with Raisins & Almonds

1 1/2 cups brown rice
3 cans (10 1/2 ounces, each) chicken broth
4 tablespoons butter
salt and pepper to taste

1/2 cup toasted slivered almonds
1/2 cup golden raisins, plumped in hot water and drained

Combine rice, broth, butter and seasonings in a medium-sized saucepan. Bring to boil, stir and cover. Reduce heat and simmer rice for about 40 minutes or until rice is tender and liquid is absorbed. Stir in almonds and raisins. Serves 8.

Tomato Rice with Garlic & Herbs

1 cup rice
2 tomatoes, coarsely chopped
2 tablespoons olive oil
1 teaspoon dried sweet basil
2 tablespoons chopped parsley (or 2 teaspoons dried)
1/8 teaspoon garlic powder (or 1 clove minced)
1 can (10 1/2 ounces) chicken broth
1/2 cup water
salt and freshly ground pepper to taste

Combine all the ingredients in a saucepan and stir until blended. Cover pan and simmer mixture until liquid is absorbed and rice is tender. When rice is cooked stir in the following sauce:

1/2 cup tomato sauce
1/2 teaspoon onion flakes
1/2 teaspoon sugar
pinch of Italian Herb Seasoning

Combine tomato sauce, onion, sugar and Italian Seasoning and simmer mixture for 5 minutes. Stir into hot cooked rice.

Brown Rice with Cinnamon & Onions

1 onion, chopped
1 tablespoon brown sugar
3 tablespoons butter

1 1/4 cups brown rice

1 can (10 1/2 ounces) chicken broth
1 can (10 1/2 ounces) beef broth
salt and pepper to taste

Saute onion with brown sugar in butter until onions are soft. Add the rice and cook and stir for 3 minutes. Add the remaining ingredients, cover the pan and simmer rice until liquid is absorbed and rice is tender. This is a delicious accompaniment to pork or lamb. Serves 6.

Green Rice with Chives & Herbs

1 cup rice
3 tablespoons butter
1 can (10 1/2 ounces) chicken broth
1 cup water
3 tablespoons chopped parsley
2 tablespoons chopped chives
1/8 teaspoon poultry seasoning
pinch of thyme
salt and pepper to taste

Combine all the ingredients in a saucepan and cover. Bring mixture to a boil, lower heat and simmer for about 30 minutes or until rice is tender and liquid is absorbed. Serves 4 or 5.

Vegetables

Asparagus Almondine in Lemon Cream Sauce

2 packages (10 ounces, each) frozen asparagus spears,
  cooked firm, but tender. Sprinkle with salt and pepper.

2 tablespoons finely chopped shallots
2 tablespoons butter

1/4 cup dry white wine

3/4 cup cream
3/4 cup sour cream
  1 tablespoon lemon juice (or more to taste)

1/2 cup sliced toasted almonds
1/4 cup Ritz crackers, crushed into fine crumbs
  2 tablespoons melted butter

Place cooked asparagus in a shallow porcelain baker. In a skillet, saute shallots in butter until they are soft. Add wine and continue cooking until wine has almost evaporated.

Stir together cream, sour cream and lemon juice until blended. Add cream mixture to shallots and heat through.

Spoon sauce over the asparagus. Toss together the almonds, crumbs and melted butter until even, and sprinkle crumb mixture over the cream sauce. Bake in a 350° oven until heated through. Do not overcook. Serves 6.

Asparagus with Parmesan & Swiss Cheese

2 packages (10 ounces, each) frozen cut asparagus, cooked
until tender. Salt and white pepper to taste.

1 carton (1 cup) cottage cheese
1 package (8 ounces) cream cheese, at room temperature
1 cup grated Swiss cheese
1/2 cup grated Parmesan cheese
3 eggs
1/2 cup Ritz Cracker crumbs
1 tablespoon minced onion flakes
2 tablespoons lemon juice

Combine all the ingredients and stir until blended. Place mixture
into a heavily buttered 12-inch oval au gratin baker and bake in
a 350° oven for about 55 minutes or until top is golden and mixture
is set. Serve for lunch or a lovely vegetarian dinner. Serves 6 for
lunch, 4 for dinner.

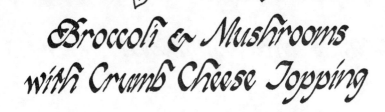

Broccoli & Mushrooms with Crumb Cheese Topping

2 packages chopped broccoli (10 ounces each),
    defrosted and drained

1/2 cup chopped onions
    2 tablespoons butter
1/2 pound mushrooms, cleaned and sliced

    5 eggs, beaten
    1 cup sour cream
1/2 cup bread crumbs
    salt and pepper to taste
    pinch of nutmeg

1/4 cup Ritz cracker crumbs
1/4 cup grated Parmesan cheese

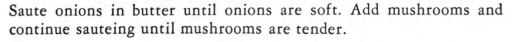

Saute onions in butter until onions are soft. Add mushrooms and continue sauteing until mushrooms are tender.

Beat eggs with the sour cream until blended. In a large bowl, combine the broccoli, mushroom mixture, egg mixture, crumbs and seasonings and stir to mix well.

Place mixture in a buttered 9x13-inch porcelain bake and serve casserole and sprinkle with the cracker crumbs and grated cheese. Bake in a preheated 325° oven for about 35 or 40 minutes or until eggs are set and top is lightly browned. Serves 6.

Note: – Entire casserole can be assembled earlier in the day and refrigerated.

Casserole of Broccoli with Shallots, Cream & Cheese

This is a lovely casserole that serves well as an accompaniment to roast pork or veal. It is also excellent as a main dish for lunch or a meatless light supper.

1/4 cup finely minced shallots
4 tablespoons butter (1/2 stick)

2 packages (10 ounces, each) frozen chopped
    broccoli, defrosted
4 eggs, beaten
1 1/2 cups half and half
3/4 cup grated Swiss cheese
1/2 cup grated Parmesan cheese
1/8 teaspoon nutmeg
salt and pepper to taste
2/3 cup Ritz cracker crumbs

1/4 cup Ritz cracker crumbs
1/4 cup grated Parmesan cheese

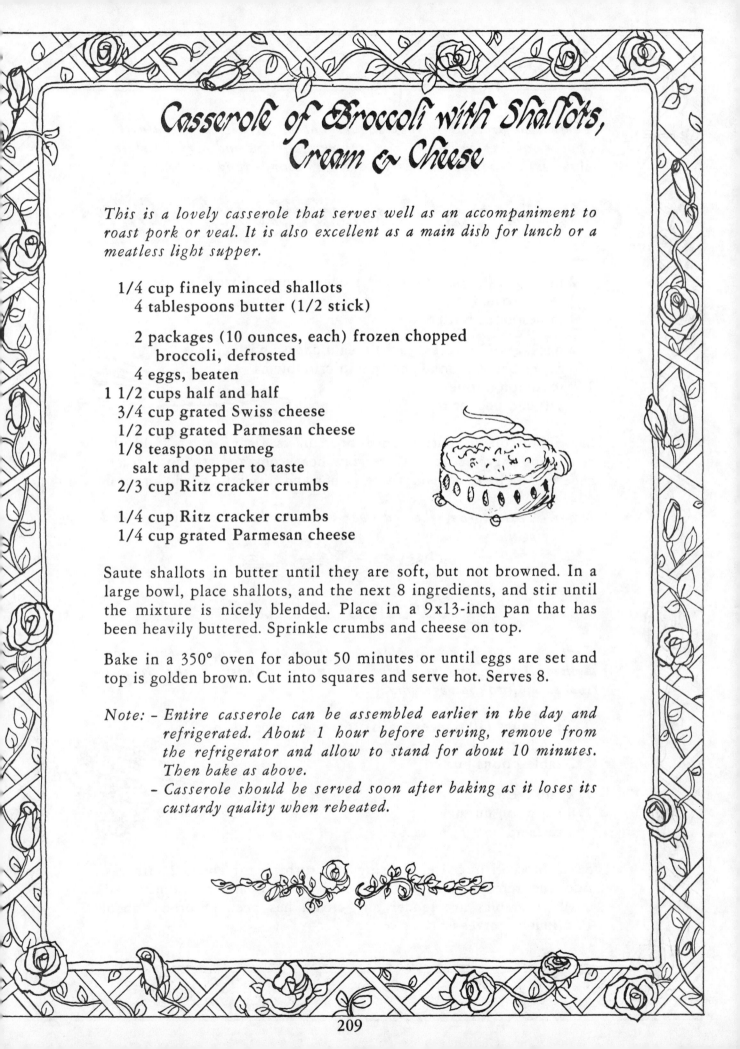

Saute shallots in butter until they are soft, but not browned. In a large bowl, place shallots, and the next 8 ingredients, and stir until the mixture is nicely blended. Place in a 9x13-inch pan that has been heavily buttered. Sprinkle crumbs and cheese on top.

Bake in a 350° oven for about 50 minutes or until eggs are set and top is golden brown. Cut into squares and serve hot. Serves 8.

Note: – Entire casserole can be assembled earlier in the day and refrigerated. About 1 hour before serving, remove from the refrigerator and allow to stand for about 10 minutes. Then bake as above.
– Casserole should be served soon after baking as it loses its custardy quality when reheated.

These two broccoli recipes should not be dismissed because they appear so simple. They are extremely delicious and very satisfying. Make extras, because everyone asks for seconds (and thirds).

Easiest & Best Creamed Broccoli & Chives

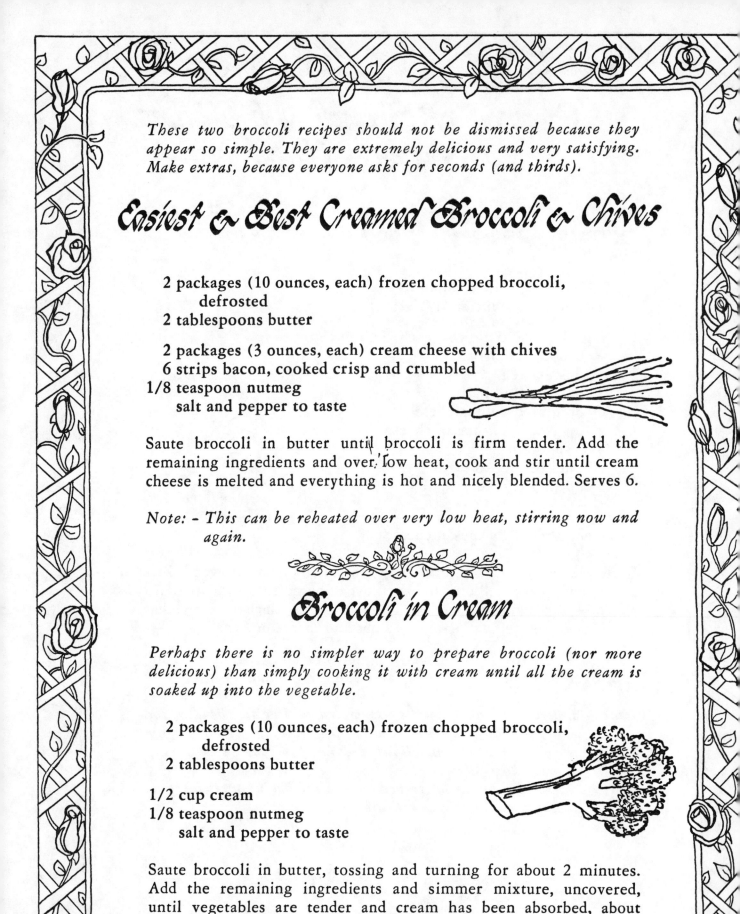

    2 packages (10 ounces, each) frozen chopped broccoli,
        defrosted
    2 tablespoons butter

    2 packages (3 ounces, each) cream cheese with chives
    6 strips bacon, cooked crisp and crumbled
    1/8 teaspoon nutmeg
        salt and pepper to taste

Saute broccoli in butter until broccoli is firm tender. Add the remaining ingredients and over low heat, cook and stir until cream cheese is melted and everything is hot and nicely blended. Serves 6.

Note: – This can be reheated over very low heat, stirring now and again.

Broccoli in Cream

Perhaps there is no simpler way to prepare broccoli (nor more delicious) than simply cooking it with cream until all the cream is soaked up into the vegetable.

    2 packages (10 ounces, each) frozen chopped broccoli,
        defrosted
    2 tablespoons butter

    1/2 cup cream
    1/8 teaspoon nutmeg
        salt and pepper to taste

Saute broccoli in butter, tossing and turning for about 2 minutes. Add the remaining ingredients and simmer mixture, uncovered, until vegetables are tender and cream has been absorbed, about 10 minutes. Serves 6.

Broccoli Mini-Souffle with Onions & Cheese

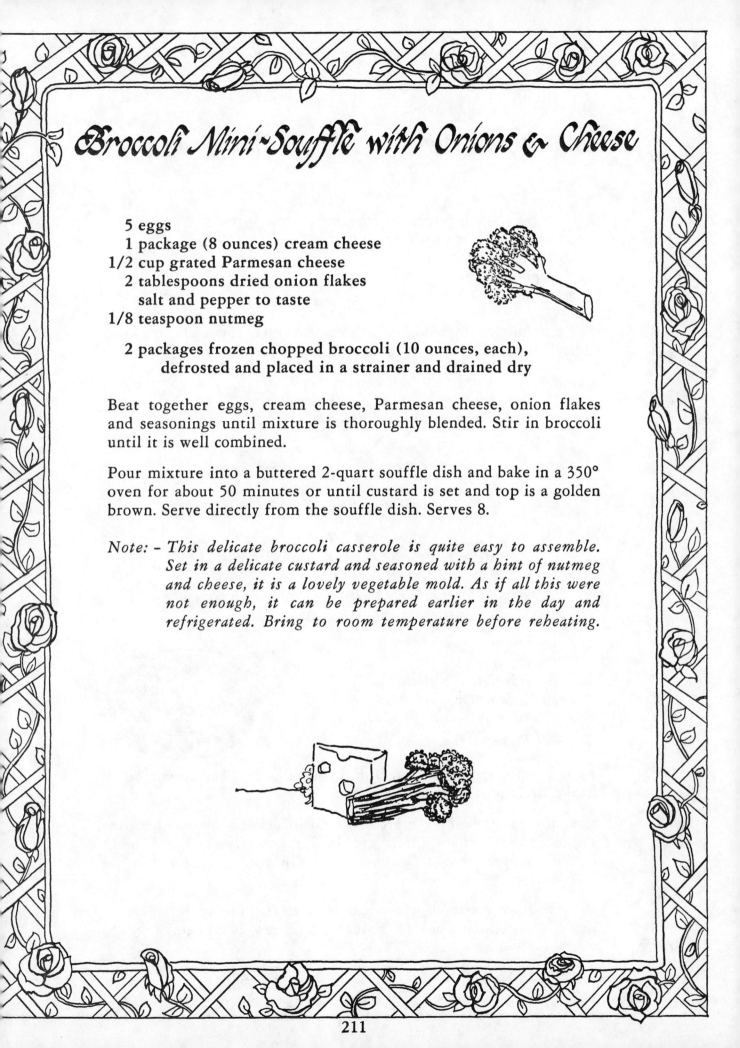

5 eggs
1 package (8 ounces) cream cheese
1/2 cup grated Parmesan cheese
2 tablespoons dried onion flakes
    salt and pepper to taste
1/8 teaspoon nutmeg

2 packages frozen chopped broccoli (10 ounces, each),
    defrosted and placed in a strainer and drained dry

Beat together eggs, cream cheese, Parmesan cheese, onion flakes and seasonings until mixture is thoroughly blended. Stir in broccoli until it is well combined.

Pour mixture into a buttered 2-quart souffle dish and bake in a 350° oven for about 50 minutes or until custard is set and top is a golden brown. Serve directly from the souffle dish. Serves 8.

Note: – This delicate broccoli casserole is quite easy to assemble. Set in a delicate custard and seasoned with a hint of nutmeg and cheese, it is a lovely vegetable mold. As if all this were not enough, it can be prepared earlier in the day and refrigerated. Bring to room temperature before reheating.

Glazed Brussels Sprouts & Onions in Butter

2 packages (10 ounces, each) frozen Brussels sprouts
1 can (1 pound) small whole onions
3 tablespoons butter
1 tablespoon sugar
   salt to taste

Combine all the ingredients in a large skillet, cover and cook for about 5 minutes or until sprouts are firm tender.

Remove cover and continue cooking and turning until butter and sugar become syrupy and most of the liquid is absorbed. Onions will become lightly browned. Serves 8.

Creamed Brussels Sprouts in an Instant Cheese Sauce

2 packages (10 ounces, each) frozen Brussels sprouts
2 tablespoons butter

1/2 cup cream
1/2 cup sour cream
2/3 cup grated Swiss cheese
   2 tablespoons chopped chives
   2 tablespoons lemon juice
   salt to taste

Saute sprouts in butter until firm tender. Place cooked sprouts in an oval porcelain baker or shallow pan.

Combine the remaining ingredients until blended. Spoon this over the cooked sprouts and spread evenly. Sprinkle a few chopped chives or parsley over the top. Can be held at this point and stored in the refrigerator.

Remove from the refrigerator and bring to room temperature. Heat in a 350° oven until heated through and cheese is melted. Serves 8.

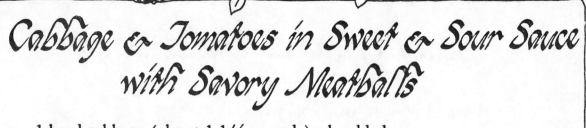

Cabbage & Tomatoes in Sweet & Sour Sauce with Savory Meatballs

1 head cabbage (about 1 1/4 pounds), shredded
1 onion, finely chopped
1 can (1 pound) stewed tomatoes
1 can (8 ounces) tomato sauce
1 can (10 1/2 ounces) beef broth
3 tablespoons lemon juice
1 tablespoon brown sugar
2 tablespoons sugar
salt and freshly ground pepper to taste

Combine all the ingredients in a Dutch-oven casserole and bring to a boil. Lower heat and simmer mixture for about 1 hour or until cabbage is soft. Do not cover casserole tightly, but leave cover slightly ajar. This is a lovely accompaniment to pork or beef. Serves 6, as a side dish.

Note: – This dish can easily be transformed into a main dish by the addition of meatballs after the vegetables have simmered for about 15 minutes. Then, continue simmering for an additional 45 minutes to 1 hour.

– This can be made a day earlier and refrigerated.

 ## Savory Meatballs

1 pound lean ground beef
3 slices white bread, remove crusts and soak in water. Squeeze dry.
1/2 medium onion, grated. This must be grated and not chopped. This can be done with a conventional 4-sided grater or in a processor.
3 tablespoons tomato sauce
1 egg, beaten
salt, pepper, garlic powder to taste

Combine all the ingredients and shape into 1-inch balls. Drop into the simmering vegetables and continue cooking as described above. Yields about 8 meatballs. Serves 4 as a main dish.

Honey Glazed Brandied Carrots

1 bag (1 pound) frozen baby carrots

3 tablespoons butter
3 tablespoons honey
2 tablespoons brandy
1 1/2 tablespoons chopped parsley
    salt and pepper to taste

Cook carrots in salted water until they are tender, and drain.

In a skillet, place carrots and remaining ingredients and cook and stir until carrots are glazed and glossy. Serves 6.

Timbale of Pureed Carrots & Cream

1 bag (1 pound) frozen carrots
1 can (10 1/2 ounces) chicken broth
4 tablespoons butter

2 eggs
1/2 cup cream
    pinch of nutmeg
    salt and pepper to taste

Cook carrots in broth and butter until tender. Remove carrots to a blender or food processor and cook remaining juices over high heat until reduced to 1/4 cup. Coarsely puree carrots.

Beat together eggs, cream and seasonings until blended. Beat in carrots and reduced broth. Place mixture in a heavily buttered 1 1/2-quart souffle dish and bake in a 350° oven for about 40 minutes or until eggs are set. Spoon from the souffle dish to serve. Serves 6.

Molded Carrot Pudding with Oranges & Raisins

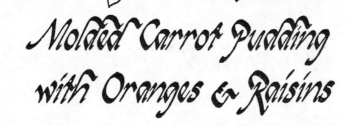

    2 eggs
1/2 cup brown sugar
1/4 cup sugar
1/2 cup butter (1 stick), softened

    1 cup flour
    1 teaspoon baking powder
1/2 teaspoon baking soda
1/4 teaspoon salt

1 1/2 cups grated carrots
    1/2 orange, grated, remove any large pieces
        of membrane
    1/2 cup yellow raisins
        1 tablespoon lemon juice
        1 teaspoon vanilla

Beat together eggs, sugars and butter for 2 minutes at high speed. Beat in dry ingredients and beat for another minute until blended. Beat in the remaining ingredients.

Place mixture into a 2-quart ring mold that has been sprayed with a non-stick coating and heavily buttered and floured. Bake at 350° for about 50 minutes or until a cake tester inserted in center comes out clean. Remove from the oven, loosen edges and carefully invert onto a serving platter. Fill center with spiced fruit or cranberry sauce. Serve with turkey or chicken. Serves 8.

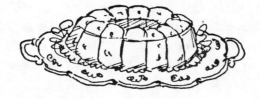

Cauliflower with Butter & Onions

     2 onions, chopped
1/4 cup butter (1/2 stick)
     1 tablespoon sugar

     2 packages frozen cauliflower (10 ounces, each)
1/2 cup canned chicken broth
     1 teaspoon chicken seasoned stock base
     3 tablespoons fresh, chopped parsley (or 1 tablespoon dried)
        salt and pepper to taste

Saute onions in butter until onions are tender. Add sugar and saute for another minute or two. Add the remaining ingredients, stir and cover saucepan. Simmer mixture until cauliflower is tender. Time will depend on the size of the flowerets, but figure about 25 minutes.

Place cauliflower in a lovely heat and serve casserole and sprinkle with Buttered Crumbs. Serve at once, or reheat in a 350° oven until piping hot. Serves 6 to 8.

Buttered Crumbs with Paprika

1/2 cup bread crumbs
     4 tablespoons butter
1/8 teaspoon paprika

In a skillet, combine all the ingredients and cook and stir until crumbs are lightly browned. Sprinkle crumbs over vegetables.

Note: – Entire dish can be assembled earlier in the day and refrigerated. Bring to room temperature and sprinkle with crumbs before reheating.

– You will find that even children will enjoy eating cauliflower served this way.

Cauliflower Casserole with Tomatoes & Cheese

When you are looking to add a little excitement to a simple dinner, you would do well to consider this dish. It is very pretty to look at, so it presents beautifully. It is also very delicious.

4 tablespoons butter (1/2 stick)
2 packages (10 ounces, each) frozen cauliflower

2 tomatoes, peeled and coarsely chopped
2 tablespoons lemon juice
    salt to taste

1 1/2 cups grated Swiss cheese
2 tablespoons chopped chives
2 tablespoons chopped parsley

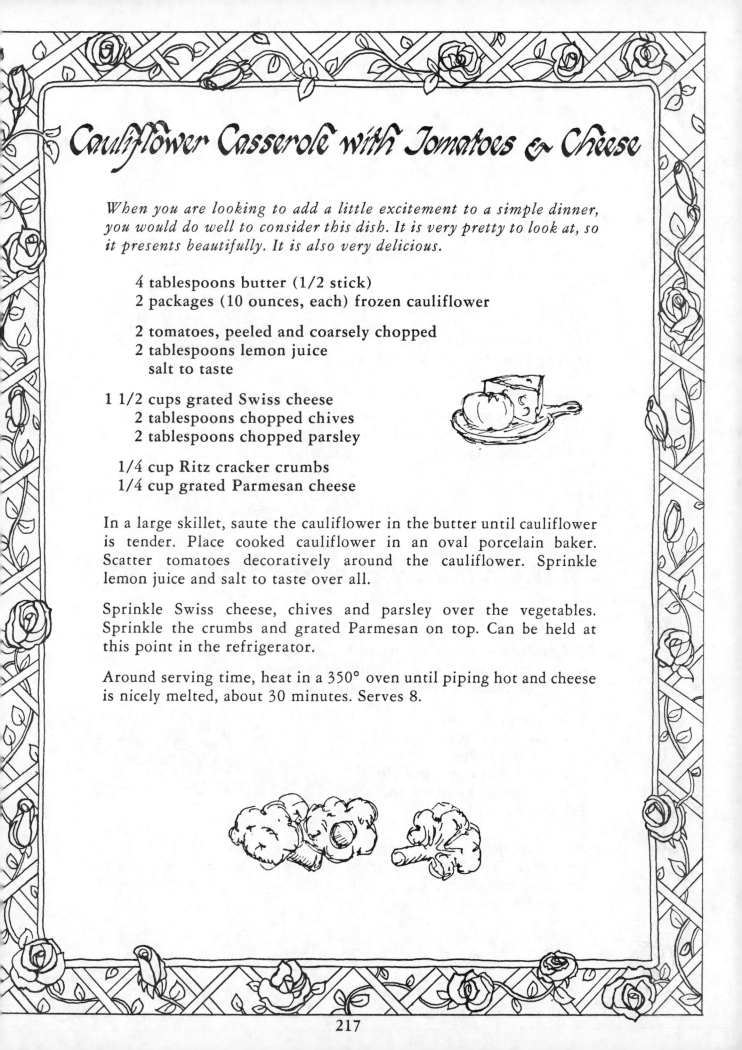

1/4 cup Ritz cracker crumbs
1/4 cup grated Parmesan cheese

In a large skillet, saute the cauliflower in the butter until cauliflower is tender. Place cooked cauliflower in an oval porcelain baker. Scatter tomatoes decoratively around the cauliflower. Sprinkle lemon juice and salt to taste over all.

Sprinkle Swiss cheese, chives and parsley over the vegetables. Sprinkle the crumbs and grated Parmesan on top. Can be held at this point in the refrigerator.

Around serving time, heat in a 350° oven until piping hot and cheese is nicely melted, about 30 minutes. Serves 8.

Casserole of Cauliflower with Onions & Cheese

2 tablespoons butter
1 package (10 ounces) frozen cauliflower
1/2 cup finely chopped onions
    salt and pepper to taste
1/2 cup sour cream
1/2 cup grated Swiss cheese

1/4 cup cracker crumbs
1/4 cup grated Parmesan cheese

Saute cauliflower and onions in butter until vegetables are tender. Stir in seasonings, sour cream and Swiss cheese. Turn mixture into a buttered 1 1/2-quart souffle dish. Sprinkle top with crumbs and grated cheese. Heat in a 350° oven until hot. Serves 4.

Sauteed Cucumbers with Butter & Dill

2 medium cucumbers, peeled and cut in half, lengthwise.
    Scoop out the seeds with a spoon and slice the
    cucumbers, crosswise into thin slices.

2 tablespoons butter
1 teaspoon chicken seasoned stock base
    salt and pepper to taste
2 tablespoons chopped chives
1 tablespoon chopped parsley
1/8 teaspoon dill weed

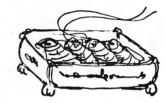

In a saucepan, melt butter with chicken stock base. Add the remaining ingredients and saute mixture for about 10 minutes or until cucumbers are tender and all the liquid has been absorbed. Serve with fish or shellfish. Serves 4.

Sautéed Eggplant & Zucchini with Garlic & Tomatoes

This is an excellent vegetable dish that serves well as an appetizer or a side dish. It is quite delicious served either hot or cold. Put it in a baked pie shell, sprinkle it with Swiss cheese and it transforms into a wonderful vegetable pie.

1 eggplant (about 1 pound), peeled and thinly sliced
1 tablespoon oil

4 zucchini, unpeeled and sliced
2 large onions, peeled and chopped
4 cloves garlic, put through a press
2 tablespoons oil

1 can (1 pound 12 ounces) stewed tomatoes, drained and
    finely chopped. Reserve juice for thinning sauce.
3 ounces tomato paste
1 teaspoon Italian Herb Seasoning
1/2 teaspoon thyme flakes
1 tablespoon chopped parsley
1 teaspoon sugar
   salt and pepper to taste

In a 12x16-inch pan, place eggplant slices and drizzle with 1 tablespoon oil. Cover pan tightly with foil and bake in a 400° oven until eggplant is soft, about 20 minutes.

Meanwhile, in a large skillet, saute zucchini, onions and garlic in oil, until vegetables are soft. Add the remaining ingredients and the eggplant and simmer mixture for about 20 minutes. Add a little of the reserved tomato juice, if necessary, to thin out the sauce. Serve either hot or cold. Serves 6.

Note: – Entire dish can be prepared and stored in the refrigerator two days before serving.

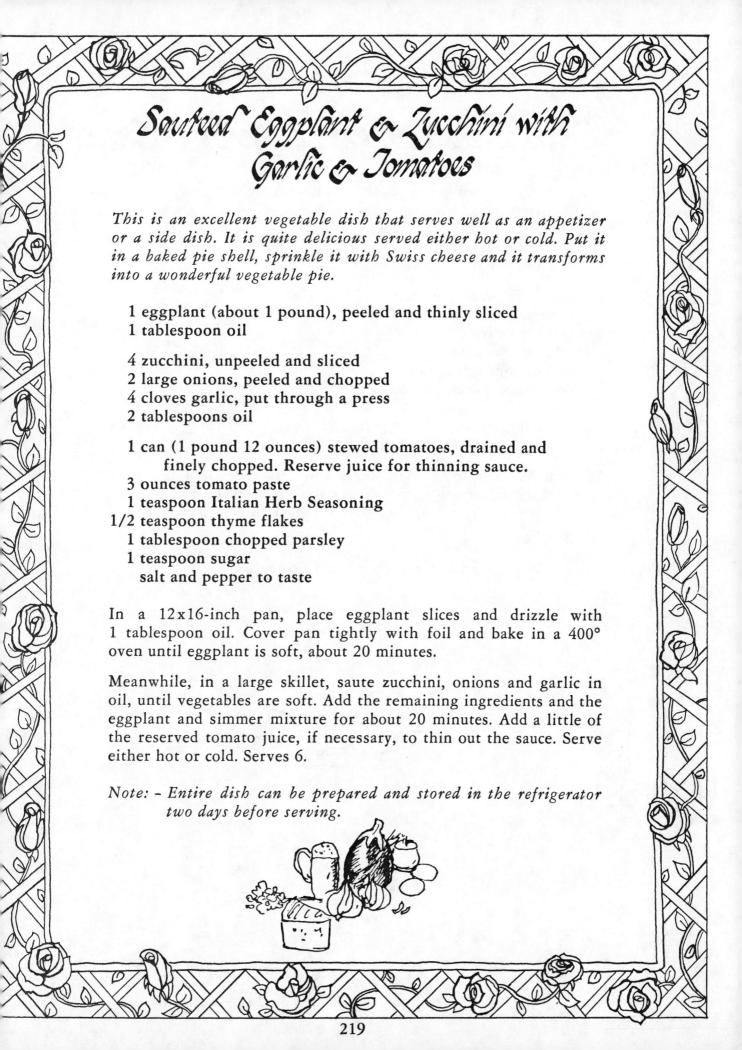

Green Beans with Garlic, Herbs & Cheese

2 packages frozen green beans (10 ounces, each)
   defrosted
2 cloves garlic, finely minced
2 tablespoons butter
   salt and pepper to taste

1/2 cup fresh bread crumbs
   1 tablespoon chopped parsley
1/4 teaspoon thyme
   2 tablespoons butter
   2 tablespoons lemon juice
1/3 cup grated Parmesan cheese

In a large skillet, saute first 4 ingredients together until green beans are tender. Transfer mixture to a pretty porcelain baker.

Combine the remaining ingredients and toss and stir until nicely mixed. Sprinkle crumb mixture over the green beans and bake in a 350° oven until piping hot and top is lightly browned, about 20 minutes. Serves 6 to 8.

Note: – Must use fresh bread crumbs for this recipe.

Green Beans with Onions, Butter & Cream

There is probably no simpler method of preparing green beans ... and it could hardly be more delicious. Green beans, sauteed with onions in butter and enriched with a little cream, is the essence of simplicity. Even children who don't like vegetables will be asking for seconds.

1 onion, finely chopped
3 tablespoons butter

2 packages frozen green beans, (10 ounces, each), defrosted

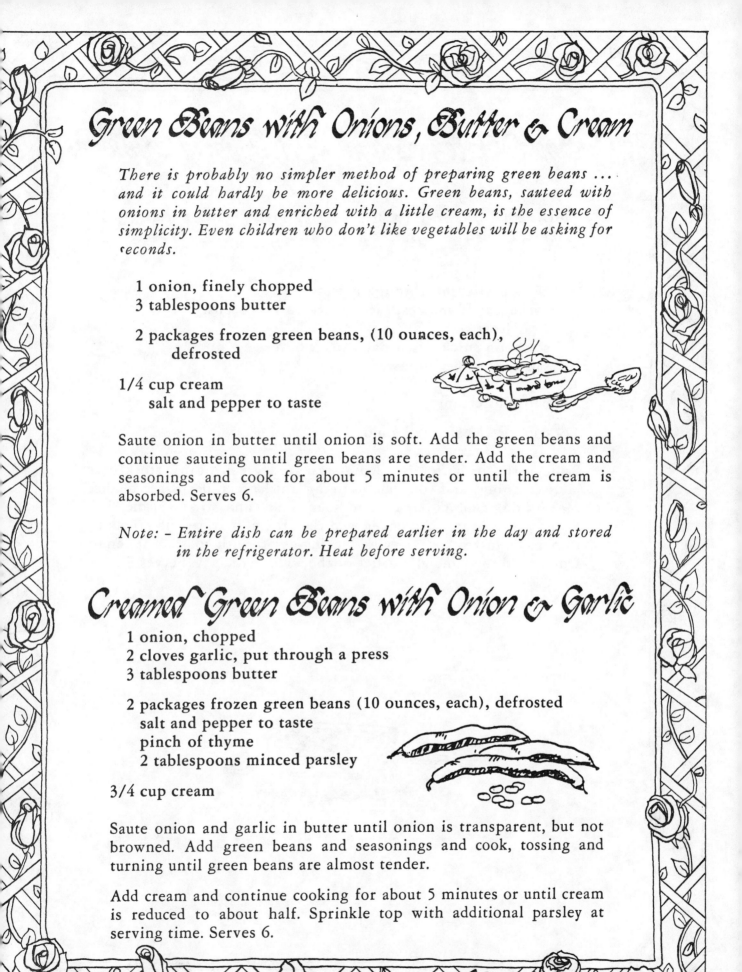

1/4 cup cream
salt and pepper to taste

Saute onion in butter until onion is soft. Add the green beans and continue sauteing until green beans are tender. Add the cream and seasonings and cook for about 5 minutes or until the cream is absorbed. Serves 6.

Note: – Entire dish can be prepared earlier in the day and stored in the refrigerator. Heat before serving.

Creamed Green Beans with Onion & Garlic

1 onion, chopped
2 cloves garlic, put through a press
3 tablespoons butter

2 packages frozen green beans (10 ounces, each), defrosted
salt and pepper to taste
pinch of thyme
2 tablespoons minced parsley

3/4 cup cream

Saute onion and garlic in butter until onion is transparent, but not browned. Add green beans and seasonings and cook, tossing and turning until green beans are almost tender.

Add cream and continue cooking for about 5 minutes or until cream is reduced to about half. Sprinkle top with additional parsley at serving time. Serves 6.

Creamed Green Beans with Toasted Almonds

This is a favorite method of preparing green beans and a very old standby. Using creme fraiche adds a fillip.

4 tablespoons butter
1 clove garlic, put through a press
2 packages (10 ounces, each) frozen green beans,
    defrosted
1 teaspoon chicken seasoned stock base
   salt and pepper to taste
1/4 cup cream
1/4 cup sour cream

1/2 cup toasted slivered almonds

Saute garlic in butter for 2 minutes. Add green beans, stock base and seasonings and continue sauteing until green beans are tender. Meanwhile, combine cream and sour cream and stir until blended. When green beans are tender, add the cream mixture and stir until combined. Just before serving, sprinkle top with toasted almonds. Do not add the almonds earlier or they will get soggy. Serves 6.

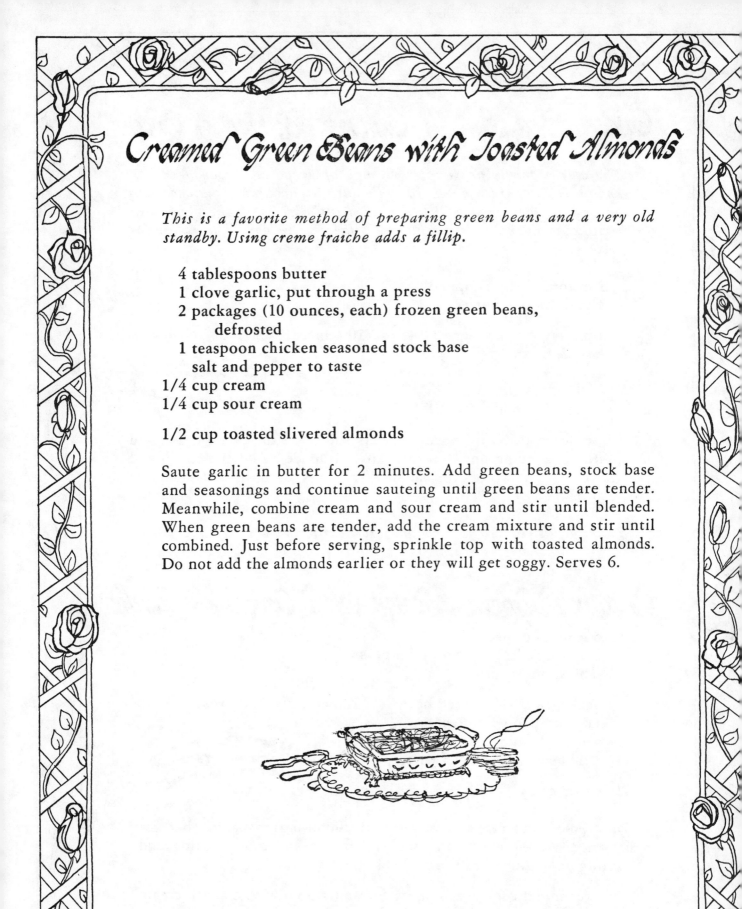

Green Beans with Onions, Lemon Juice & Parsley

2 packages frozen green beans (10 ounces, each) defrosted.
   Either cut beans or French-style beans can be used.

1 onion, chopped
3 tablespoons butter

1 teaspoon chicken stock base
1 teaspoon lemon juice
2 tablespoons chopped parsley
   pinch of thyme
   salt and pepper to taste

Defrost green beans. In a saucepan, saute onion in butter until onion is just beginning to color. Add green beans and stock base and continue to saute until beans are tender. Add the remaining ingredients and toss and stir until blended. Serves 6.

Garlicky Green Beans with Tomatoes & Herbs

1 onion, chopped
2 cloves garlic, put through a press
4 tablespoons butter

2 tomatoes, fresh or canned
1/4 cup tomato sauce
1/4 teaspoon thyme
1/4 teaspoon basil
2 tablespoons chopped parsley

2 packages frozen green beans (10 ounces each) defrosted
   salt and pepper to taste

In a saucepan, saute onion and garlic in butter until onion is just beginning to color. Add tomatoes and tomato sauce and simmer mixture for 10 minutes, uncovered. Add the remaining ingredients and simmer mixture, uncovered, until green beans are tender. Serves 6.

Parsleyed Mushrooms with Tomatoes, Onions & Garlic

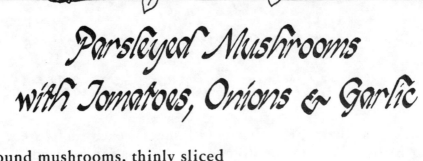

1/2 pound mushrooms, thinly sliced
  4 tablespoons butter
  2 cloves garlic, finely minced

  2 canned tomatoes, drained and finely chopped
  2 green onions, finely chopped
  2 tablespoons chopped parsley
  1 tablespoon lemon juice
    salt and pepper to taste

In a saucepan, saute mushrooms and garlic in butter until mushrooms are tender. Add the remaining ingredients and simmer mixture until juices have evaporated and sauce has thickened. If you are serving these with buttered noodles, a sprinkling of grated Parmesan would be just lovely. Serves 4.

Creamed Mushrooms with Butter, Garlic & Herbs

This is a delightful dish to serve with roast chicken or veal. The mushrooms are lavished with herbs and cream and sparkled with garlic.

1 pound mushrooms, cleaned and sliced
2 tablespoons lemon juice
1 onion, finely minced
4 shallots, finely minced
3 cloves garlic, finely minced
6 tablespoons butter

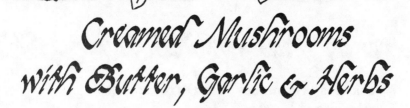

1/4 cup chopped parsley
1/4 cup chopped chives
1/2 teaspoon thyme
1/2 teaspoon poultry seasoning
    salt and pepper to taste

3/4 cup cream

In a large skillet, saute together first 6 ingredients until mushrooms are tender and onion is soft. All the liquid should be absorbed.

Add the remaining ingredients and turn heat to moderately high. Mixture will bubble briskly and cream will evaporate into a shiny sauce. Serves 6.

French Peas with Butter & Shallots

- 2 packages (10 ounces, each) frozen peas
- 3 tablespoons butter
- 1 tablespoon very finely minced shallots
- 1 teaspoon chicken seasoned stock base
- 2 teaspoons sugar
- 2 leaves iceberg lettuce, chopped
- salt and pepper to taste
- 1/4 cup chicken broth

Combine all the ingredients in a 2-quart saucepan and toss to combine. Cover top and simmer peas until they are tender, about 30 minutes. Serves 8.

Peas with Mushrooms, Bacon & Cream

- 1/2 pound mushrooms, cleaned and sliced
- 1 tablespoon finely minced shallots
- 4 tablespoons butter

- 2 packages (10 ounces, each) frozen peas
- 1/2 cup cream

- 8 slices bacon, cooked crisp, drained and crumbled

- salt and pepper to taste

Saute mushrooms and shallots in butter until mushrooms are tender. Add peas and cream and continue cooking until peas are tender. Add bacon and seasonings and toss. Heat through and serve. Serves 8.

Cottage Oven Roasted Potatoes with Onions & Paprika

*(Dedicated to our friend, Peter Greenfield,
who thought these were "the best.")*

Perhaps no other dish summons up memories of childhood better than this old family recipe. Somehow, no matter how large a quantity you make, there never seems to be enough. Sometimes I have gone so far as to prepare a large enough batch for two dinners, but they never make it to the next day. I'm certain they freeze well, but I have never been able to test it.

6 large potatoes, scrubbed, rubbed and tubbed. Do not peel.
3 onions, chopped
1 stick butter, melted
   salt and pepper to taste
1 teaspoon paprika

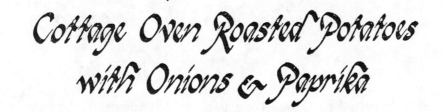

Cut potatoes in half lengthwise. Now cut them crosswise into 1/2-inch slices. In a 9x13-inch roasting pan, toss potatoes and onions in butter until evenly coated. Bake in a 350° oven for about 1 1/2 hours, turning every 15 minutes. After about 1 hour baking time, add seasonings and continue baking until onions are very soft and potatoes are nicely browned. They will not be terribly crisp but should be crusty.

I hesitate to predict how many this will serve, but figure about 4 or 5 servings.

Cottage Potatoes with Onions & Bacon

This is an excellent variation of the above recipe. Follow the instructions exactly with the addition of 8 slices of bacon, cooked crisp, drained and crumbled. Add the bacon about 20 minutes before the potatoes are finished cooking. Enjoy!

Mashed Potato Casserole with Cheese & Chives

4 cups mashed potatoes (can use instant mashed potatoes)
2 cups cottage cheese
1/2 cup sour cream
4 tablespoons butter, softened
4 eggs
1/2 cup chopped chives (can use finely chopped green onions)
    salt and pepper to taste
6 tablespoons grated Parmesan cheese

Combine mashed potatoes, cottage cheese, sour cream, butter, eggs, onions and seasonings in a large bowl and stir until blended. Spread mixture evenly into a buttered 8 x 12-inch porcelain baker. Sprinkle top with grated cheese.

Bake in a 350° oven for about 50 minutes or until top is a golden brown. Serves 8.

Creamed Potatoes with Onions & Cheese

4 large potatoes, thinly sliced, sprinkle with salt,
    pepper and garlic powder
1 can (3 ounces) French Fried Onions
1 cup grated Swiss cheese
6 tablespoons melted butter

3 eggs
1 cup cream
1/4 cup grated Parmesan cheese

Combine potatoes, onions, cheese and butter and toss until mixed. Place mixture into a buttered 9 x 12-inch porcelain baker.

Beat together eggs, cream and grated Parmesan until blended. Pour mixture over the potatoes and spread evenly. Cover casserole with foil and bake in a 350° oven for about 1 hour or until potatoes are practically finished cooking. Remove cover and continue baking until top is nicely browned. Serves 6.

Potato Fans with Chives & Cheese

6 large potatoes, peeled. Cut potatoes into 1/4-inch
thick slices, crosswise, but do not cut through.
Cut to within 1/4-inch from the bottom.
Sprinkle with salt to taste.
1/2 cup butter (1 stick)

1/3 cup chopped chives
1/4 cup grated Parmesan cheese

Melt butter in a roasting pan to comfortably hold the potatoes
without crowding. Place potatoes in pan, fan side up, and baste
thoroughly with butter. Bake in a 350° oven for about 40 minutes,
basting now and again.

Baste the potatoes and sprinkle them with the chives and cheese
and continue baking until potatoes are tender, about 20 minutes.
Keep warm in a low oven. Potatoes can be held for about 20 minutes.
Serves 6.

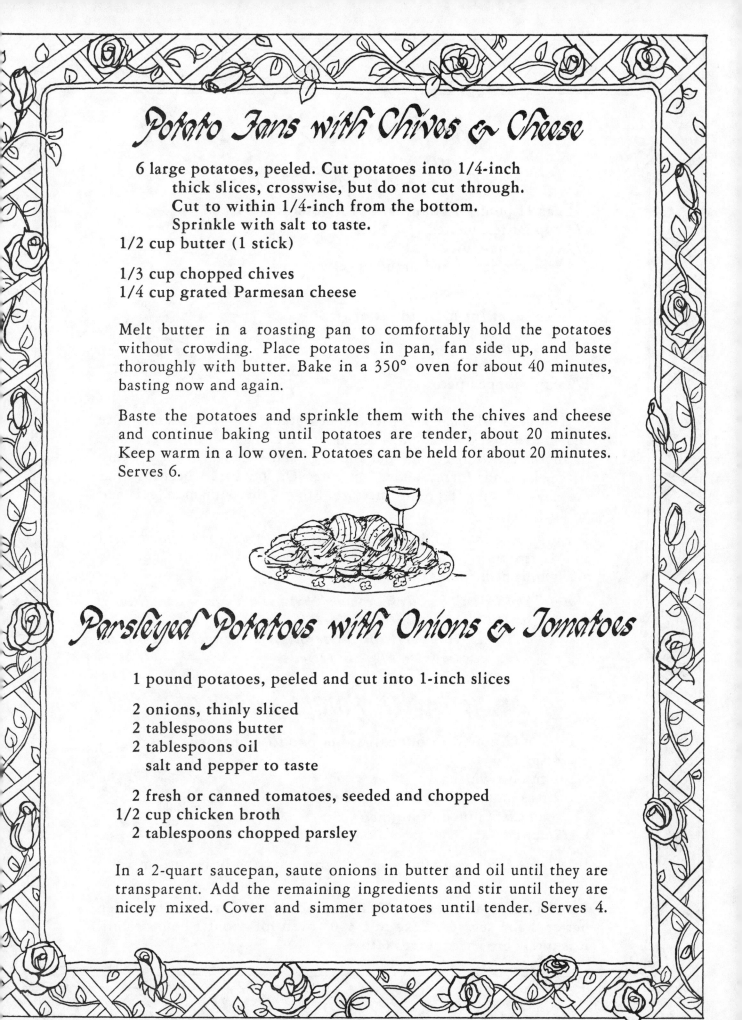

Parsleyed Potatoes with Onions & Tomatoes

1 pound potatoes, peeled and cut into 1-inch slices

2 onions, thinly sliced
2 tablespoons butter
2 tablespoons oil
salt and pepper to taste

2 fresh or canned tomatoes, seeded and chopped
1/2 cup chicken broth
2 tablespoons chopped parsley

In a 2-quart saucepan, saute onions in butter and oil until they are
transparent. Add the remaining ingredients and stir until they are
nicely mixed. Cover and simmer potatoes until tender. Serves 4.

Sweet Potato Mini-Souffle with Oranges & Pecans

1 can (1 pound 13 ounces) sweet potatoes, mashed
1/3 cup butter, melted
1/2 cup orange juice
2 tablespoons grated orange peel

4 eggs
1/2 cup sugar (or more to taste)

1/2 teaspoon cinnamon
1/4 teaspoon salt
1/2 cup chopped pecans

In a large bowl, beat together sweet potatoes, butter, orange juice and grated orange peel until the mixture is as smooth as possible. In another bowl, beat together the eggs and sugar until the mixture is very light and foamy, about 5 minutes. On low speed, beat together the eggs and sweet potato mixture. Stir in the cinnamon, salt and pecans.

Turn mixture into a 1 1/2-quart souffle dish that has been buttered and dusted with sugar. Bake at 325° for about 1 hour, or until it's nicely browned. Serves 6.

Note: – Souffle will be nicely crowned, but not as high as a traditional souffle. Don't think that anything went wrong . . . Taste is delicious. However, this casserole is not sweet. Add a little more cinnamon or sugar to taste.

Spicy Sweet Potato Casserole

1 can (1 pound 13 ounces) sweet potatoes, mashed
4 eggs
1 cup brown sugar
2 teaspoons pumpkin pie spice
an extra pinch of nutmeg
1 1/2 cups cream

In a large bowl, combine all the ingredients and beat until mixture is smooth.

Pour mixture into an 8x12-inch porcelain baker that has been buttered and sugared. Bake in a 350° oven for about 1 hour or until it is nicely browned. Serves 6 to 8.

Spiced Pumpkin Pudding with Cinnamon & Raisins

1 can (1 pound) pureed pumpkin
2 teaspoons pumpkin pie spice
1/2 cup cinnamon sugar
3 eggs
3 tablespoons frozen orange juice concentrate
1 tablespoon grated orange peel
1/2 cup gingersnap cookie crumbs

1/2 cup chopped walnuts
4 tablespoons cinnamon sugar

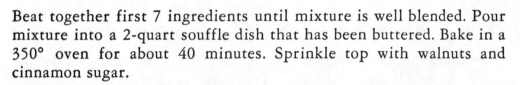

Beat together first 7 ingredients until mixture is well blended. Pour mixture into a 2-quart souffle dish that has been buttered. Bake in a 350° oven for about 40 minutes. Sprinkle top with walnuts and cinnamon sugar.

Return to oven and continue baking for about 10 or 15 minutes or until casserole is set and nuts are lightly browned. Serves 6.

Spiced Pumpkin Casserole with Onions & Cream

1 onion, finely chopped
3 tablespoons butter

1 can (1 pound) pureed pumpkin
3 eggs, beaten
1/3 cup bread crumbs
1/2 cup cream
2 teaspoons pumpkin pie spice
2 tablespoons brown sugar
salt to taste

Saute onion in butter until onion is tender. Combine all the ingredients and beat until blended. Pour mixture into a 2-quart souffle dish that has been buttered. Bake in a 350° oven for about 40 to 45 minutes or until eggs are set. Serves 6.

Creamed Spinach with Instant Crème Fraîche

    2 packages frozen spinach (10 ounces, each), defrosted
        and drained very dry
    2 tablespoons melted butter
    1 teaspoon chicken seasoned stock base
      salt and pepper to taste
      pinch nutmeg

    1 teaspoon lemon juice
1/2 cup cream
1/2 cup sour cream

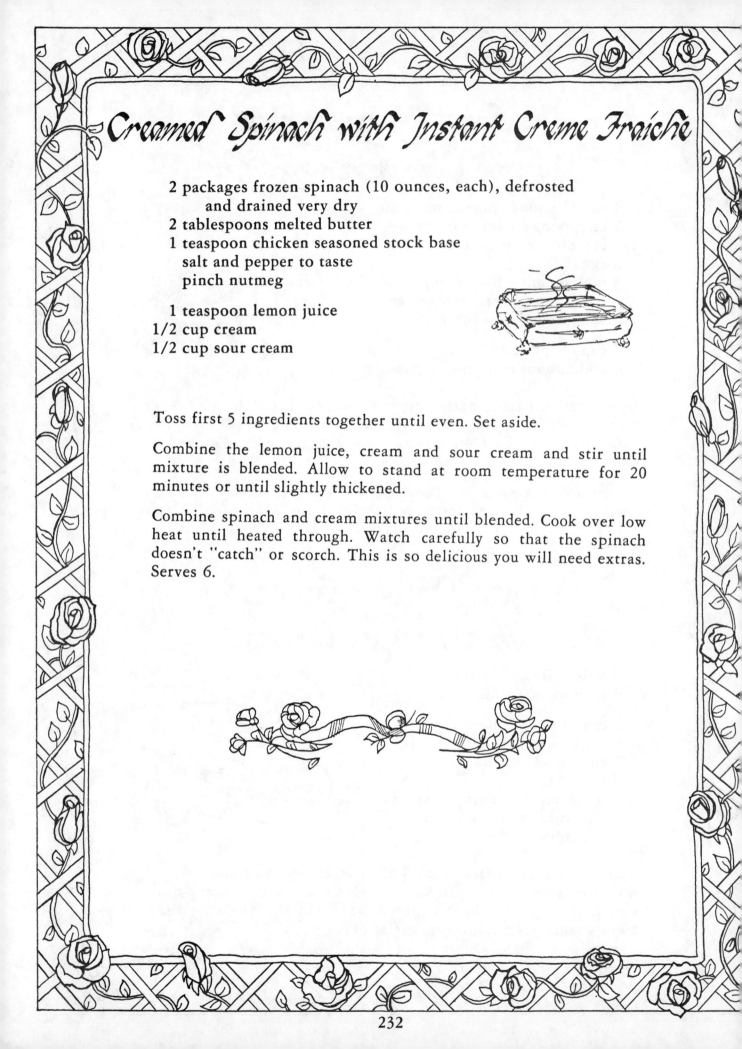

Toss first 5 ingredients together until even. Set aside.

Combine the lemon juice, cream and sour cream and stir until mixture is blended. Allow to stand at room temperature for 20 minutes or until slightly thickened.

Combine spinach and cream mixtures until blended. Cook over low heat until heated through. Watch carefully so that the spinach doesn't "catch" or scorch. This is so delicious you will need extras. Serves 6.

Creamed Spinach with Cheese Crumbs

2 packages (10 ounces, each) frozen chopped spinach,
   defrosted and pressed in a strainer to drain

2 packages (3 ounces, each) cream cheese with chives
1/2 cup sour cream
1 tablespoon flour
1 tablespoon lemon juice
1 cup grated Swiss cheese
   salt and pepper to taste
1/8 teaspoon nutmeg

1/4 cup grated Parmesan cheese
1/4 cup bread crumbs
2 tablespoons melted butter

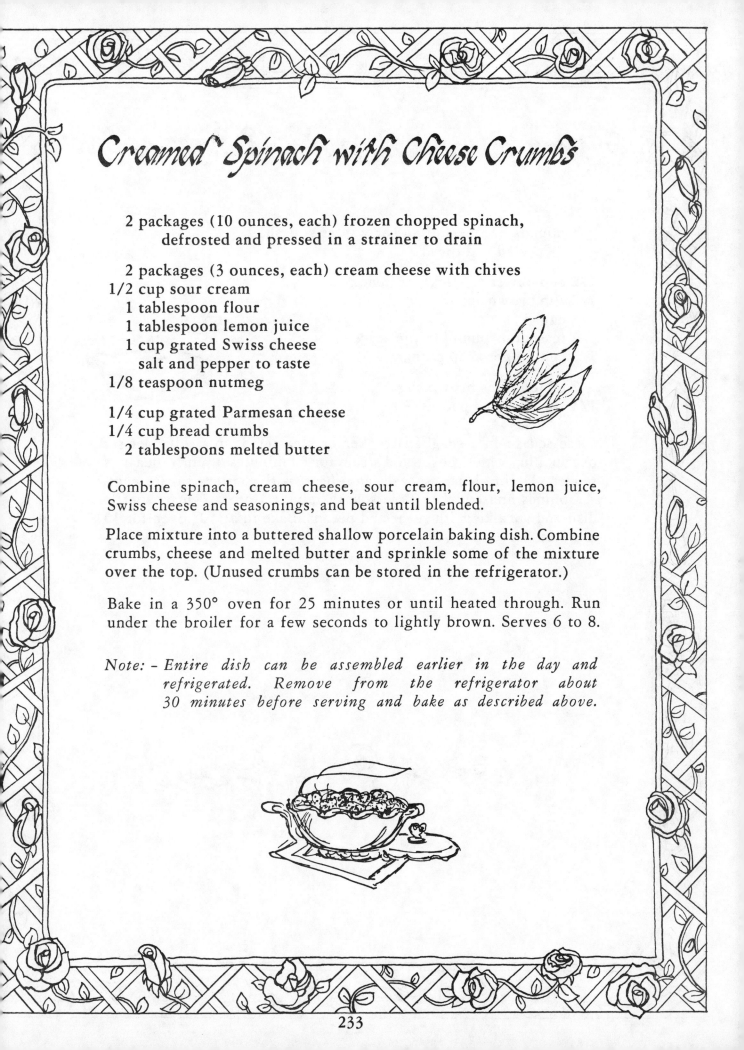

Combine spinach, cream cheese, sour cream, flour, lemon juice, Swiss cheese and seasonings, and beat until blended.

Place mixture into a buttered shallow porcelain baking dish. Combine crumbs, cheese and melted butter and sprinkle some of the mixture over the top. (Unused crumbs can be stored in the refrigerator.)

Bake in a 350° oven for 25 minutes or until heated through. Run under the broiler for a few seconds to lightly brown. Serves 6 to 8.

Note: – Entire dish can be assembled earlier in the day and refrigerated. Remove from the refrigerator about 30 minutes before serving and bake as described above.

Gingery Banana Squash with Sugar & Spice

3 pounds banana squash (or winter squash),
    peeled and diced

1/2 cup butter (1 stick), softened
1/2 cup brown sugar
   2 eggs
   2 teaspoons pumpkin pie spice
1/2 cup ginger snap crumbs

   2 tablespoons brown sugar
1/4 cup chopped pecans

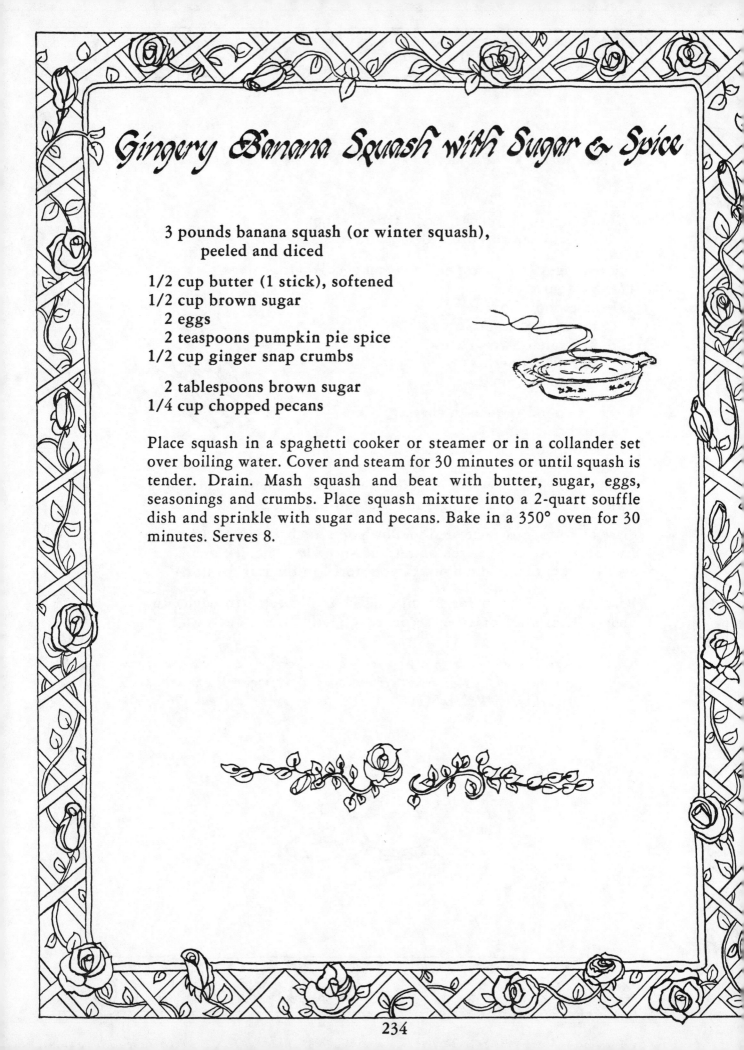

Place squash in a spaghetti cooker or steamer or in a collander set over boiling water. Cover and steam for 30 minutes or until squash is tender. Drain. Mash squash and beat with butter, sugar, eggs, seasonings and crumbs. Place squash mixture into a 2-quart souffle dish and sprinkle with sugar and pecans. Bake in a 350° oven for 30 minutes. Serves 8.

Tomatoes Topped with Garlic & Herbed Crumbs

Thick, juicy slices of tomatoes topped with garlic and herbed crumbs is wonderfully easy and very delicious. In fact, these highly seasoned crumbs will transform any quite average vegetable into an exciting dish. They have a deep and delicious flavor and texture that will add sparkle to most vegetables.

1/2 cup (1 stick) butter
   6 cloves garlic, put through a press
1/4 teaspoon thyme flakes
1/8 teaspoon poultry seasoning
   2 tablespoons chopped parsley
   2 tablespoons dried onion flakes
   1 teaspoon paprika

1/4 cup grated Parmesan cheese
   3 cups Ritz cracker crumbs (or another savory cracker)
   salt and pepper to taste

   tomato slices (figure 2 for each serving)

In a skillet, cook together first 7 ingredients for about 2 minutes. Add the remaining ingredients (except the tomatoes) and turn and toss mixture until the crumbs are nicely coated.

Place crumb mixture into a glass jar with a tight-fitting lid, and store in the refrigerator. Crumbs will stay fresh for 2 weeks. Yields 3 cups seasoned crumbs.

Now, slice tomatoes about 3/4-inch thick and place on a buttered cookie sheet. Cover each top generously with Herbed Crumbs. Bake in a 350° oven for about 20 minutes or until tomatoes are hot and slightly softened.

Note: – If you desire a softer texture, substitute fresh bread crumbs for the cracker crumbs.

Zucchini with Mushrooms, Garlic & Cream

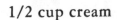

        1 onion, chopped
1 1/2 pounds zucchini, cut into 1/4-inch slices
    1/2 pound mushrooms, thinly sliced
        4 cloves garlic, finely minced
        4 tablespoons butter
        1 teaspoon chicken seasoned stock base
            salt and pepper to taste

    1/2 cup cream

Combine all the ingredients, except the cream, in a Dutch oven casserole and saute until onions are soft and zucchini are tender. Add cream and turn heat to moderately high. Mixture will bubble briskly and cream will evaporate into a shiny sauce. Serves 6.

Zucchini Casserole with Mushrooms, Cream & Cheese

        1 onion, chopped
        1 pound zucchini, cut into 1/4-inch slices
1/4 pound mushrooms, thinly sliced
        3 cloves garlic, finely minced
        4 tablespoons butter

1/2 cup cream
1/2 cup sour cream
    2 eggs
    1 cup grated Swiss cheese
1/3 cup grated Parmesan cheese
    1 tablespoon chopped parsley
        salt and pepper to taste

Saute together first 5 ingredients until zucchini is tender and onion is soft. Place zucchini mixture in a lovely porcelain baker. Combine the remaining ingredients and beat until blended. Pour over cooked zucchini. Sprinkle top with additional grated Swiss cheese. Bake in a 350° oven for about 30 minutes or until eggs are set and top is lightly browned. Serves 6.

Note: – Entire dish can be assembled earlier in the day and stored in the refrigerator. Bake before serving as described above.

Zucchini with Tomatoes & Garlic

1 pound zucchini, do not peal. Cut into 1/4-inch slices.
1 onion, finely chopped
2 cloves garlic, finely minced
3 tablespoons butter

2 canned or fresh tomatoes, seeded and chopped
1 teaspoon chicken seasoned stock base
1 tablespoon chopped parsley
   salt and pepper to taste

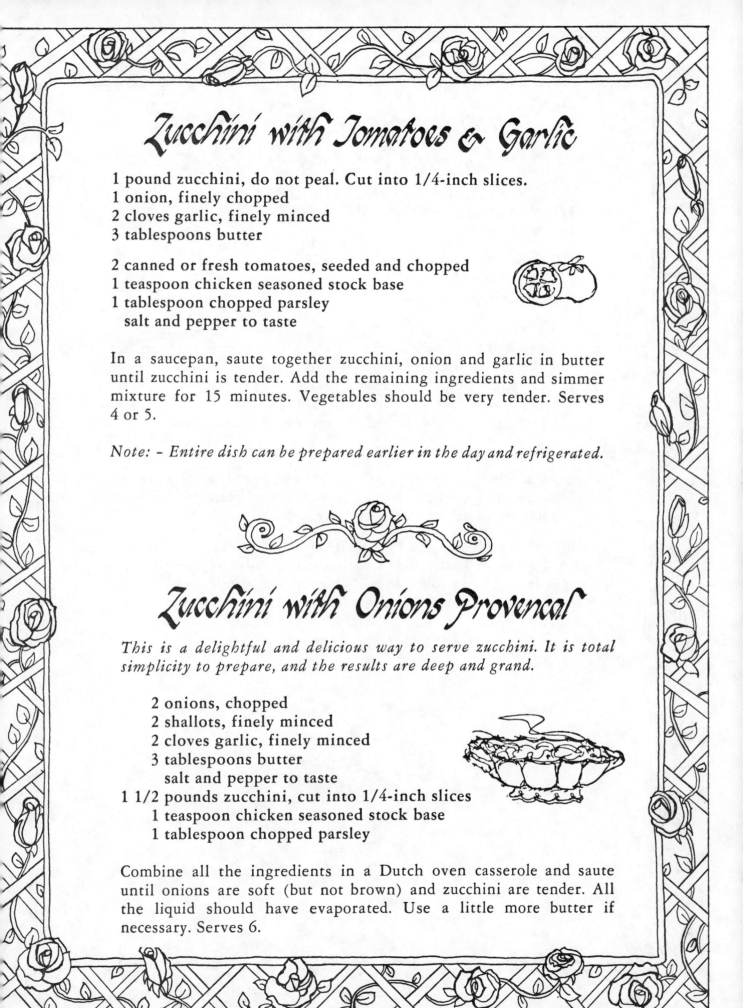

In a saucepan, saute together zucchini, onion and garlic in butter until zucchini is tender. Add the remaining ingredients and simmer mixture for 15 minutes. Vegetables should be very tender. Serves 4 or 5.

Note: – Entire dish can be prepared earlier in the day and refrigerated.

Zucchini with Onions Provencal

This is a delightful and delicious way to serve zucchini. It is total simplicity to prepare, and the results are deep and grand.

2 onions, chopped
2 shallots, finely minced
2 cloves garlic, finely minced
3 tablespoons butter
   salt and pepper to taste
1 1/2 pounds zucchini, cut into 1/4-inch slices
   1 teaspoon chicken seasoned stock base
   1 tablespoon chopped parsley

Combine all the ingredients in a Dutch oven casserole and saute until onions are soft (but not brown) and zucchini are tender. All the liquid should have evaporated. Use a little more butter if necessary. Serves 6.

Zucchini & Noodle Casserole with Tomatoes & Cheese

        1 pound zucchini, unpeeled and sliced
    1/2 pound mushrooms, sliced
    1/4 cup butter

        2 tomatoes, peeled and chopped (fresh or canned)
    1/4 cup chopped chives
    1/4 cup chopped parsley

        4 eggs
        1 cup half and half
        1 cup grated Swiss cheese
    1/2 cup grated Parmesan cheese
        salt and pepper to taste
        1 package (8 ounces) medium noodles, cooked tender
           drained

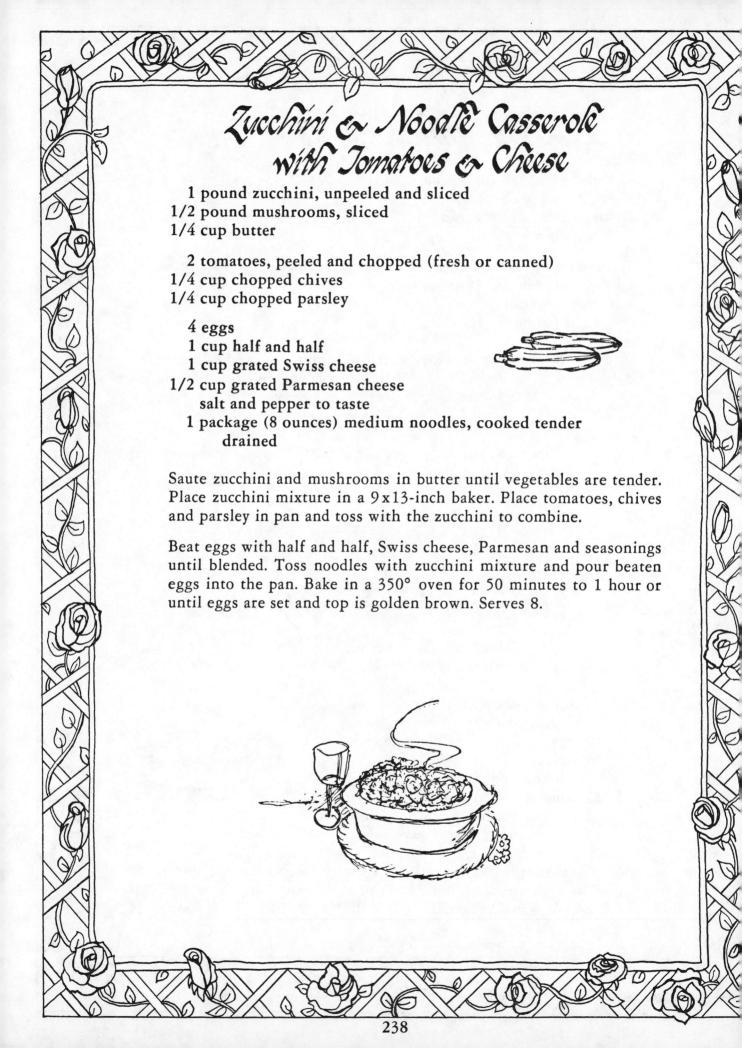

Saute zucchini and mushrooms in butter until vegetables are tender. Place zucchini mixture in a 9 x 13-inch baker. Place tomatoes, chives and parsley in pan and toss with the zucchini to combine.

Beat eggs with half and half, Swiss cheese, Parmesan and seasonings until blended. Toss noodles with zucchini mixture and pour beaten eggs into the pan. Bake in a 350° oven for 50 minutes to 1 hour or until eggs are set and top is golden brown. Serves 8.

Desserts

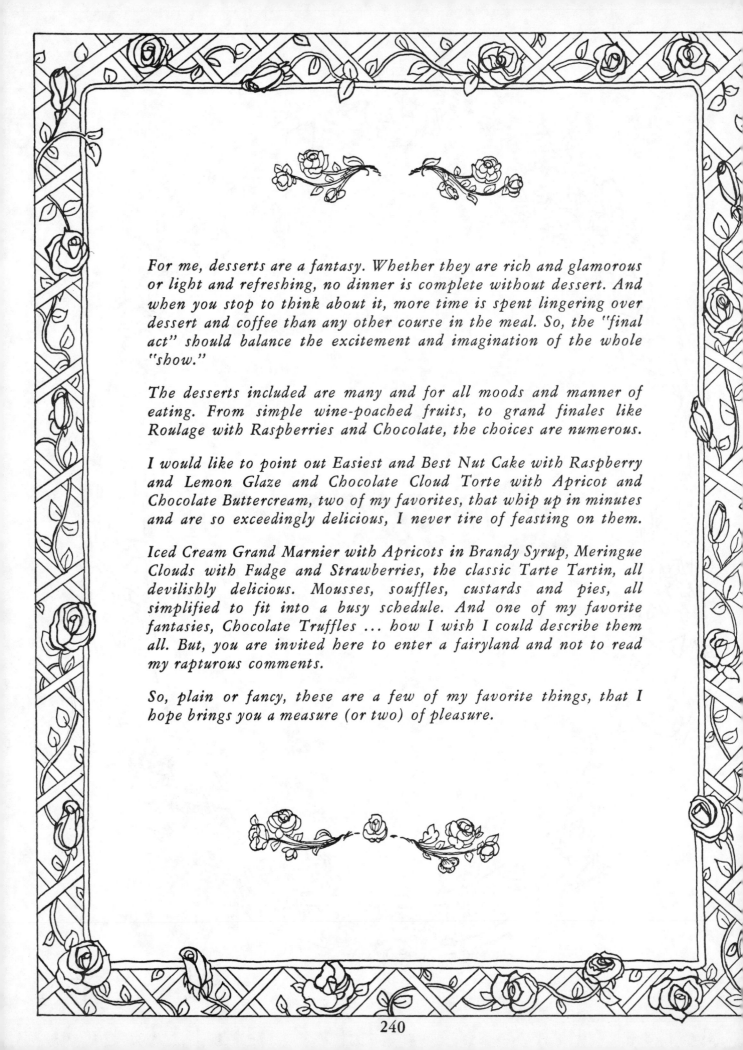

For me, desserts are a fantasy. Whether they are rich and glamorous or light and refreshing, no dinner is complete without dessert. And when you stop to think about it, more time is spent lingering over dessert and coffee than any other course in the meal. So, the "final act" should balance the excitement and imagination of the whole "show."

The desserts included are many and for all moods and manner of eating. From simple wine-poached fruits, to grand finales like Roulage with Raspberries and Chocolate, the choices are numerous.

I would like to point out Easiest and Best Nut Cake with Raspberry and Lemon Glaze and Chocolate Cloud Torte with Apricot and Chocolate Buttercream, two of my favorites, that whip up in minutes and are so exceedingly delicious, I never tire of feasting on them.

Iced Cream Grand Marnier with Apricots in Brandy Syrup, Meringue Clouds with Fudge and Strawberries, the classic Tarte Tartin, all devilishly delicious. Mousses, souffles, custards and pies, all simplified to fit into a busy schedule. And one of my favorite fantasies, Chocolate Truffles ... how I wish I could describe them all. But, you are invited here to enter a fairyland and not to read my rapturous comments.

So, plain or fancy, these are a few of my favorite things, that I hope brings you a measure (or two) of pleasure.

Easiest & Best Nut Cake with Raspberry & Lemon Glaze

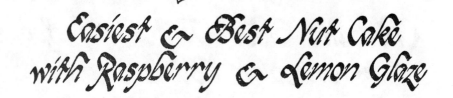

This has got to be my favorite nut cake. It is moist and incredibly delicious, flavored with the raspberry and tart lemon. Not the least of its virtues, it can be assembled in minutes, can be frozen (unglazed) and is elegant enough for the most discriminating dinner.

4 eggs
1 cup sugar

6 tablespoons flour
1 teaspoon baking powder
1 teaspoon vanilla
1 1/3 cups walnuts, processed to resemble coarse meal

1/2 cup seedless red raspberry jam, heated

Beat eggs with sugar for 4 minutes or until eggs are light and foamy. With mixer on lowest speed, beat in the flour, baking powder, vanilla and walnuts until blended.

Pour batter into a greased 10-inch springform pan and bake in a 350° oven for 25 to 28 minutes or until a cake tester, inserted in center, comes out clean. (Do not overbake, or cake will not be moist.) Allow to cool a little and then spread raspberry jam evenly over the top. Allow to cool thoroughly.

Drizzle Lemon Glaze over the raspberries in a decorative fashion and allow some of the raspberry to show through. Run a little glaze down the sides. Allow glaze to set, about 1 hour. Cut into wedges and serve at room temperature. Serves 8.

Lemon Glaze:

Stir together 2 tablespoons lemon juice with about 1 1/4 cups sifted powdered sugar until glaze is of drizzling consistency.

Chocolate Cloud Torte with Apricot & Chocolate Buttercream

This cake is light as air and so delicate you will enjoy serving it with pride. As it contains only 2 tablespoons of flour, the light quality is obtained in the beating of the eggs. Not having to separate eggs either, makes it especially easy for a family dinner. While this cake is simple, it is by no means plain and will do very nicely for a dinner party.

  4 eggs
  1 cup sugar

  1 teaspoon vanilla
  2 tablespoons flour
  1 cup ground walnuts
  2 tablespoons cocoa
  1 teaspoon baking powder

1/3 cup chopped walnuts
1/2 cup apricot jam, heated

Beat eggs with sugar for 4 minutes or until eggs are light and foamy. Beat in vanilla.

With mixer on lowest speed, beat in the flour, walnuts, cocoa and baking powder until just blended. Do not overbeat. Fold in chopped walnuts.

Pour batter into a greased 10-inch springform pan and bake in a 350° oven for 20 to 25 minutes or until a cake tester inserted in center comes out clean. Do not overbake. (Cake will rise and settle a bit. This is normal.) Allow to cool.

Drizzle warm apricot jam evenly over cake. Spread top and sides with Chocolate Buttercream Frosting. Serves 8.

Chocolate Buttercream Frosting

  1 cup butter (2 sticks) at room temperature
3/4 cup sifted powdered sugar
  3 tablespoons sifted cocoa
  1 teaspoon vanilla

Beat butter until light and creamy. Beat in the remaining ingredients until thoroughly blended.

Buché de Noel
(Christmas Chocolate Roll)

Traditionally served at Christmas, but excellent any time of the year is this heavenly, light as air, chocolate roll. Not only is it beautiful to serve, but it is also incredibly delicious. Cake can be baked several days earlier and should be frosted the day before serving.

6 egg whites (at room temperature)
1/2 cup sugar

6 egg yolks
1/2 cup sugar

1 1/2 cups finely grated walnuts
4 tablespoons sifted cocoa
1 teaspoon baking powder

Preheat oven to 350°. Butter a 10x15-inch jelly roll pan. Line it with waxed paper extending 4-inches beyond the ends of the pan. Butter the waxed paper and set it aside. Wet a towel, and squeeze it until it is damp-dry.

In a large mixing bowl, beat egg whites until foamy. Continue beating and adding 1/2 cup sugar slowly, until whites are stiff and glossy.

Beat yolks with 1/2 cup sugar until mixture is very thick. Beat in the walnuts, cocoa and baking powder until blended. Fold in beaten egg whites.

Pour batter into prepared pan and spread evenly. Bake at 350° for about 25 minutes or until top is golden and a cake tester, inserted in center, comes out clean. Immediately cover cake with slightly dampened towel. Allow cake to cool and then refrigerate. Leave towel on cake. This can be done 2 days ahead.

The day before serving, turn cake out on 2 overlapping strips of waxed paper. Remove baking paper and trim edges of cake. Spread Chocolate Whipped Cream over cake. Using the waxed paper to help you, roll cake up from long end, ending seam side down. Sprinkle top with sifted powdered sugar to resemble snow. Serves 10 to 12.

Chocolate Whipped Cream: Beat together 1 1/2 cups cream with 1/3 cup sugar, 3 tablespoons sifted cocoa and 1 teaspoon vanilla until stiff.

Golden Bourbon Fruit & Nut Cake with Bourbon & Honey Glaze

1 1/2 cups butter (3 sticks)
   2 cups sugar

   6 eggs

   3 cups flour
   2 teaspoons baking powder

1/4 cup bourbon
   2 teaspoons vanilla

1/2 pound glaceed cherries
1/2 pound glaceed mixed fruits
   3 cups chopped walnuts or pecans
   1 cup yellow raisins

Cream butter with sugar until light and fluffy. Add eggs, one at a time, beating well after each addition. Beat for 3 minutes more at medium speed. Beat in flour and baking powder until blended. Beat in bourbon and vanilla until blended. Stir in fruits and nuts.

Pour batter into 6 aluminum foil baby loaf pans, 6 x 3 x 2-inches, that have been heavily greased and lightly floured. Bake in a 350° oven for 45 to 50 minutes or until a cake tester, inserted in center, comes out clean. Cool cakes on a rack. While cooling, paint top with Bourbon and Honey Glaze. Decorate top with halved cherries.

When cool, wrap in wax paper and foil. Refrigerate or freeze. Yields 6 baby loaves.

Bourbon and Honey Glaze: Combine together until blended 1/2 cup orange honey and 2 tablespoons bourbon.

Note: – This cake lends itself beautifully to glazing. In this case, do not use the Bourbon and Honey Glaze. Instead, glaze tops with a mixture of 2 tablespoons cream, 1 teaspoon vanilla and 1 1/2 cups sifted powdered sugar. Either spread the glaze on the cake or drizzle it over in a decorative fashion.

Fresh Apple Cake
with Orange, Cinnamon & Walnuts

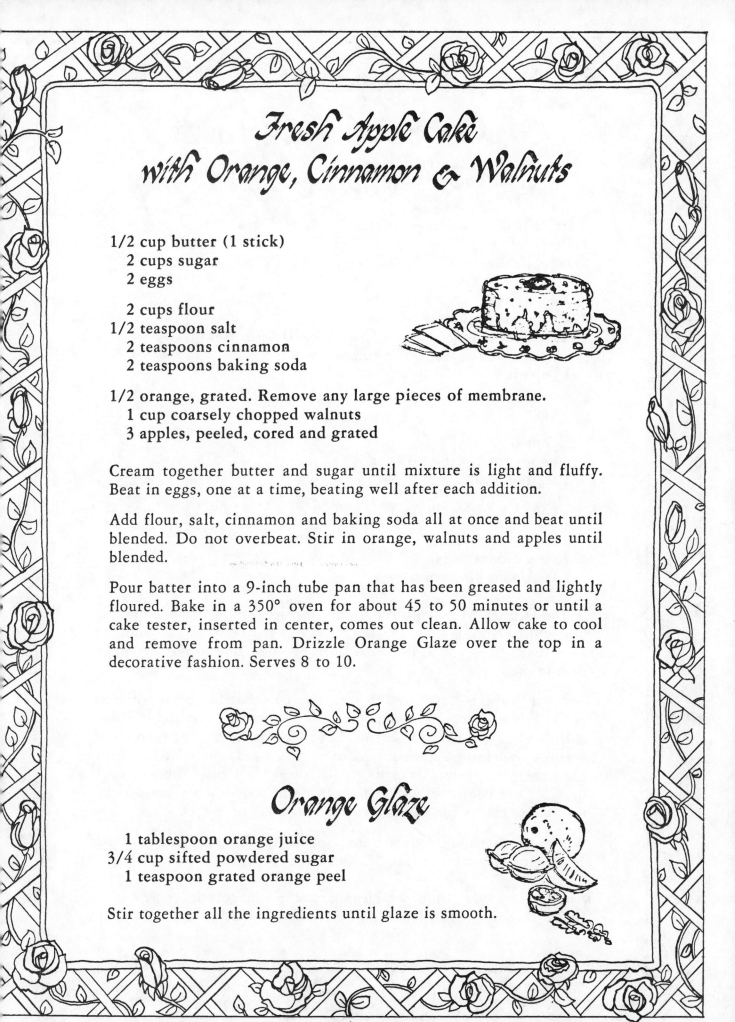

1/2 cup butter (1 stick)
   2 cups sugar
   2 eggs

   2 cups flour
1/2 teaspoon salt
   2 teaspoons cinnamon
   2 teaspoons baking soda

1/2 orange, grated. Remove any large pieces of membrane.
   1 cup coarsely chopped walnuts
   3 apples, peeled, cored and grated

Cream together butter and sugar until mixture is light and fluffy. Beat in eggs, one at a time, beating well after each addition.

Add flour, salt, cinnamon and baking soda all at once and beat until blended. Do not overbeat. Stir in orange, walnuts and apples until blended.

Pour batter into a 9-inch tube pan that has been greased and lightly floured. Bake in a 350° oven for about 45 to 50 minutes or until a cake tester, inserted in center, comes out clean. Allow cake to cool and remove from pan. Drizzle Orange Glaze over the top in a decorative fashion. Serves 8 to 10.

Orange Glaze

   1 tablespoon orange juice
3/4 cup sifted powdered sugar
   1 teaspoon grated orange peel

Stir together all the ingredients until glaze is smooth.

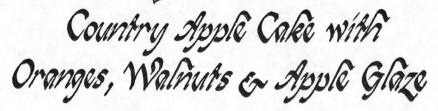

Country Apple Cake with Oranges, Walnuts & Apple Glaze

This is a beautiful cake that I do believe could easily become a favorite at your house. It is deeply delicious with the flavors of orange, cinnamon and apples.

      2 cups sugar
  1/4 cup orange juice
  1/2 medium orange, grated. Use peel and fruit. Remove
          any large pieces of membranes
      1 cup oil
      2 teaspoons vanilla
      4 eggs

      3 cups flour
      3 teaspoons baking powder
  1/2 teaspoon salt

      1 cup chopped walnuts

      2 cups grated apples
      2 tablespoons sugar
      2 teaspoons cinnamon

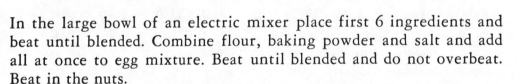

In the large bowl of an electric mixer place first 6 ingredients and beat until blended. Combine flour, baking powder and salt and add all at once to egg mixture. Beat until blended and do not overbeat. Beat in the nuts.

Spoon 1/3 the batter into a 9-inch tube pan that has been buttered and lightly floured. Combine apples, sugar and cinnamon and sprinkle half this mixture over the batter. Cover this with 1/3 the batter and sprinkle remaining apple mixture over the second layer. Top this with the remaining batter. Bake in a 350° oven for 1 hour. Reduce heat to 325° and continue baking for 30 minutes or until a cake tester inserted in center comes out clean. Cool in pan on a rack.

When cool, remove from pan and spoon Apple Glaze over the top and let it run down the sides. Delicious! Serves 12.

Apple Glaze: Combine 3 tablespoons apple juice with 1 1/2 cups sifted powdered sugar. Drizzle mixture over cooled cake.

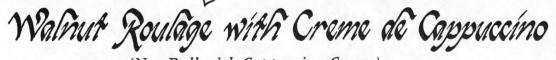

Walnut Roulage with Creme de Cappuccino

(Nut Roll with Cappuccino Cream)

If you are ever looking for a dessert that will earn you a great reputation plus an embrace (or two), you would do well to prepare this heavenly creation. A delicate nut roll, light as air, filled and frosted with an exciting whipped cream flavored with espresso, cocoa and cognac is simply divine.

   6 egg whites
1/2 cup sugar

   6 egg yolks
1/2 cup sugar
   2 teaspoons baking powder
   1 teaspoon vanilla
   1 cup ground walnuts (loosely packed)

Preheat oven to 350°. Grease a 10x15-inch jelly roll pan. Line it with waxed paper extending 4-inches beyond the ends of the pan. Grease the waxed paper. Set aside.

Beat whites until foamy. Gradually add 1/2 cup sugar and continue beating until whites are stiff and glossy. Beat yolks (not necessary to clean the beaters) with 1/2 cup sugar until very thick and pale. Beat in the baking powder, vanilla and ground walnuts until blended. Fold in beaten egg whites until blended. Do not overmix.

Pour batter into prepared pan and bake at 350° for about 20 minutes or until top is dry and a cake tester inserted in center comes out clean. Remove cake from oven and immediately cover with a damp towel. When cool, refrigerate cake until ready to frost. Cake may be baked 2 days before serving.

One day before serving, sprinkle cake with sifted powdered sugar and invert on overlapping sheets of wax paper. Carefully peel off wax paper that roll was baked in. Spread 2/3 of the Creme de Cappuccino on the cake. Using the wax paper to help you, roll cake lengthwise, ending with seam side down. Frost with remaining Cappuccino Creme.   Serves 10.

Creme de Cappuccino

Beat 1 1/2 cups whipping cream with 1 tablespoon Instant Espresso, 1/2 tablespoon cocoa, 2 1/2 tablespoons sugar and 1 tablespoon Cognac until stiff.

Roulage with Raspberries & Chocolate Chip Whipped Cream

This heady and magnificent dessert is really quite easy to prepare. What it actually is is a jelly roll sponge cake filled with raspberries, chocolate and whipped cream. Follow the directions exactly and you will be assured of perfect results every time.

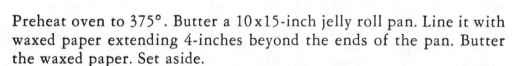

4 eggs
3/4 cup sugar

3/4 cup sifted flour
1 teaspoon baking powder
   pinch of salt

1 teaspoon vanilla

Preheat oven to 375°. Butter a 10x15-inch jelly roll pan. Line it with waxed paper extending 4-inches beyond the ends of the pan. Butter the waxed paper. Set aside.

Spread a thin dish towel out on a counter top. Sprinkle it with sifted powdered sugar.

In large mixing bowl, beat eggs with sugar for about 10 minutes or until mixture is very thick. Combine flour, baking powder and salt and sprinkle on top of egg mixture. With mixer running at lowest speed, beat until batter is just blended. Do not overbeat. Beat in vanilla. Pour batter into prepared pan.

Bake in a 375° oven for 20 minutes or until top is golden brown and a cake tester, inserted in center, comes out clean. Invert cake on prepared towel, remove waxed paper and trim off any crisp edges. Starting on the long end, roll up the cake with the towel and allow to cool.

When cool, unroll the cake, spread with 1/2 of the Raspberry Chocolate Cream. Remove towel and reroll cake. Set on a pretty platter and frost top with the remaining cream. Sprinkle top with grated chocolate. Serves 12.

Raspberry Chocolate Cream: Beat 1 1/2 cups cream with 1 tablespoon sugar until thick. Fold in 3/4 cup frozen raspberries and 1/2 cup crushed chocolate chips until blended. Will fill and frost one 15-inch jelly roll.

Chocolate Roulage with Rum & Chocolate

Making this soft, velvety chocolate roll is worth every bit of the extra effort. Follow the instructions carefully and you will have perfect results every time. The chocolate buttercream frosting is probably one of the very easiest and very best. This magnificent dessert will delight everyone, young and old. Decorate it with shaved chocolate for a lovely effect.

   6 egg whites
   3 tablespoons sugar

   6 egg yolks
3/4 cup powdered sugar
   5 tablespoons cocoa
   1 teaspoon vanilla

Preheat oven to 375°. Grease a 10x15-inch jelly roll pan. Line it with waxed paper extending 4-inches beyond the ends of the pan. Grease the waxed paper. Set aside. Lay out a towel and sprinkle it generously with sifted powdered sugar.

Beat whites until foamy. Gradually add 3 tablespoons sugar and continue beating until whites are stiff and glossy. Beat yolks with sifted powdered sugar until very thick. Beat in cocoa and vanilla. Fold in beaten egg whites. Pour batter into prepared pan and bake at 375° for about 15 minutes or until top is dry and a cake tester inserted in center comes out clean.

Invert cake onto prepared towel and roll it up. Allow to cool. Unroll cake and spread with Chocolate Buttercream Frosting. Reroll and place on a lovely platter. Frost with remaining buttercream. Swirl frosting in decorative fashion. Decorate top with shaved chocolate. Serves 12.

Chocolate Rum Buttercream Frosting

   1 cup butter (2 sticks) at room temperature
3/4 cup sifted powdered sugar
   1 tablespoon rum
   3 tablespoons cocoa
1/2 teaspoon vanilla

(It is important that the butter be at room temperature for creaming and spreading.) Beat butter until light and creamy. Beat in the remaining ingredients until thoroughly blended.

Old-Fashioned Orange Sponge Cake with Strawberries & Whipped Cream

This recipe is a simplified version of the classic sponge cake. Normally, the eggs were separated, beaten, and then folded together. By using the following technique, you can eliminate all these steps and the results are marvelous. The trick is that you beat the eggs and the sugar until they are the texture of lightly whipped cream, frothy and light. Do not underbeat or the cake will lose volume.

The tangy lemon and orange flavor is simply delicious and with the plump strawberries and a little whipped cream, it becomes a memorable dessert.

6 eggs
1 cup sugar

1 cup flour, sifted
1/2 cup grated orange (about 1/2 medium orange)
2 tablespoons grated lemon peel
2 teaspoons vanilla

In the large bowl of electric mixer, beat eggs and sugar at high speed for at least 10 minutes or until eggs have tripled in volume and are light and frothy as lightly whipped cream.

On low speed, beat in flour only until blended. Beat in remaining ingredients, on low speed, until blended. Pour batter into a 9-inch tube pan, ungreased, and place in a 350° oven. Bake for about 40-45 minutes or until a cake tester inserted in center comes out clean. Do not over-bake. Remove from the oven, *invert*, and allow to cool.

Serve with strawberries and whipped cream or simply dusted with a little sifted powdered sugar. Serves 10.

Note: – As I said before, don't underbeat.
– This cake freezes beautifully.

Chocolate Torte Darling
with Chocolate Buttercream Frosting

Makes 1 layer

    4 eggs
7/8 cup sugar
    1 cup pecans
    1 teaspoon vanilla
    2 tablespoons bread crumbs
    2 teaspoons baking powder
    2 tablespoons cocoa

Place eggs in blender container and blend for a few seconds. With the blades running, carefully add the remaining ingredients in the order listed, and blend for 1 minute more.

Pour batter into a 10-inch layer pan with a removable bottom that has been greased and lightly dusted with flour. Repeat for second layer.

Bake layers together in a 350° oven for about 20 to 25 minutes or until a cake tester inserted in center comes out clean. Remove rings when they are cool enough to handle. When layers are cooled, remove them with a sharp knife, scraped along the bottom. Fill and frost with Chocolate Buttercream. Serves 12.

Chocolate Buttercream Frosting

1 1/2 cups butter, at room temperature, but not too soft
    1 cup sifted powdered sugar
    2 tablespoons rum
    3 tablespoons cocoa
    2 tablespoons cream
    1 teaspoon vanilla
    pinch of salt

Combine all the ingredients in a large bowl of mixer and beat at high speed until butter is very light and fluffy, about 4 minutes. Will fill and frost 1 10-inch layer cake. Sprinkle with grated chocolate.

Easiest & Best Chocolate Cake with Chocolate Rum Cream

This is an unbelievably light and finely textured cake. Frosting is a delicate buttercream icing. If you like, sprinkle the top with a little shaved chocolate.

> 5 eggs
> 1 cup sugar
> 1 teaspoon vanilla
> 1 tablespoon rum

1/2 cup flour
1/2 cup cornstarch
1/2 cup ground almonds (or almond meal, purchased at
    health food stores)
> 5 tablespoons cocoa

1/2 cup (1 stick) butter, melted and cooled

Beat eggs with sugar, vanilla and rum for about 10 minutes or until the eggs are very light and fluffy, and tripled in volume. Meanwhile sift together the flour, cornstarch, almonds and cocoa.

With the beaters going at the lowest speed, gently fold flour mixture into the beaten eggs until blended. Gently beat in the melted butter.

Generously grease a 10-inch spring form pan and pour batter into it. Bake in a 350° oven for about 30 minutes or until a cake tester inserted in center comes out clean. Allow cake to cool and then frost with Chocolate Rum Cream. Remove spring form ring, but leave cake on metal bottom. Sprinkle a little shaved chocolate over the top and refrigerate. Remove from the refrigerator about 10 minutes before serving. Serves 10.

Chocolate Rum Cream

2/3 cup semi-sweet chocolate chips
> 1 tablespoon rum
> 6 tablespoons butter (3/4 stick), at room temperature

Melt chocolate with rum over hot, not boiling water. Beat in the butter, 1 tablespoon at a time, until mixture is smooth and velvety. (Frosting will be loose, but will firm up in the refrigerator.) Pour frosting over cooled cake and refrigerate.

Chocolate Chip Chocolate Rum Torte

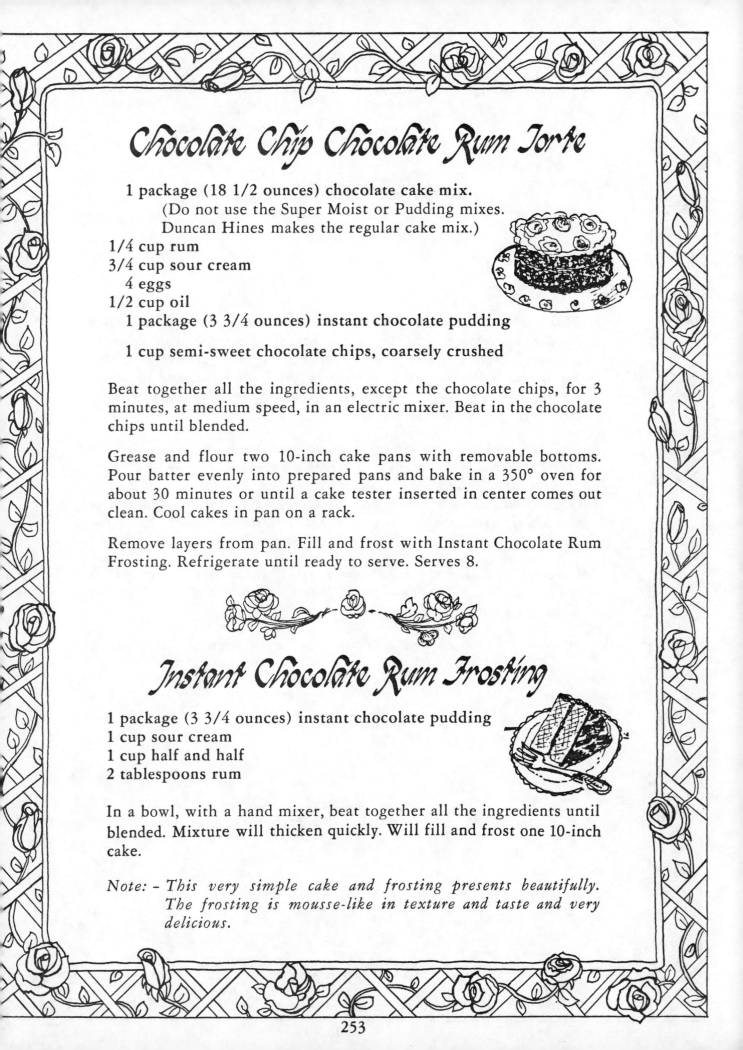

1 package (18 1/2 ounces) chocolate cake mix.
>   (Do not use the Super Moist or Pudding mixes.
>   Duncan Hines makes the regular cake mix.)

1/4 cup rum
3/4 cup sour cream
  4 eggs
1/2 cup oil
  1 package (3 3/4 ounces) instant chocolate pudding

  1 cup semi-sweet chocolate chips, coarsely crushed

Beat together all the ingredients, except the chocolate chips, for 3 minutes, at medium speed, in an electric mixer. Beat in the chocolate chips until blended.

Grease and flour two 10-inch cake pans with removable bottoms. Pour batter evenly into prepared pans and bake in a 350° oven for about 30 minutes or until a cake tester inserted in center comes out clean. Cool cakes in pan on a rack.

Remove layers from pan. Fill and frost with Instant Chocolate Rum Frosting. Refrigerate until ready to serve. Serves 8.

Instant Chocolate Rum Frosting

1 package (3 3/4 ounces) instant chocolate pudding
1 cup sour cream
1 cup half and half
2 tablespoons rum

In a bowl, with a hand mixer, beat together all the ingredients until blended. Mixture will thicken quickly. Will fill and frost one 10-inch cake.

Note: – This very simple cake and frosting presents beautifully. The frosting is mousse-like in texture and taste and very delicious.

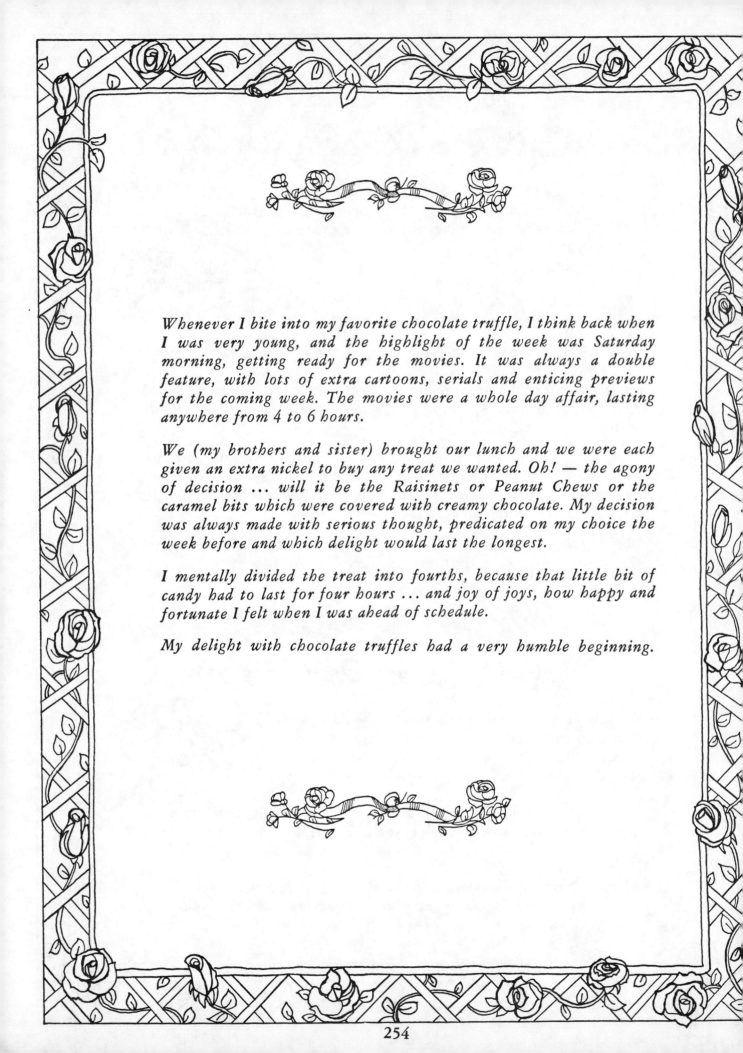

Whenever I bite into my favorite chocolate truffle, I think back when I was very young, and the highlight of the week was Saturday morning, getting ready for the movies. It was always a double feature, with lots of extra cartoons, serials and enticing previews for the coming week. The movies were a whole day affair, lasting anywhere from 4 to 6 hours.

We (my brothers and sister) brought our lunch and we were each given an extra nickel to buy any treat we wanted. Oh! — the agony of decision ... will it be the Raisinets or Peanut Chews or the caramel bits which were covered with creamy chocolate. My decision was always made with serious thought, predicated on my choice the week before and which delight would last the longest.

I mentally divided the treat into fourths, because that little bit of candy had to last for four hours ... and joy of joys, how happy and fortunate I felt when I was ahead of schedule.

My delight with chocolate truffles had a very humble beginning.

Soft Chocolate Truffles Fantasy

Perhaps there is no other chocolate fantasy that is such a delight as Soft Chocolate Truffles. I recently had the good fortune to savor some of these incredible morsels. The most astonishing thing was how the taste lingered for hours, so that even a very small piece was totally satisfying. I simply could not rest until I duplicated them for you. These are very close to the ones I tasted ... very rich, very delicious, and as smooth as satin.

1/2 cup cream
1/4 cup butter (1/2 stick)
1/2 pound semi-sweet chocolate chips
   pinch of salt
  1 teaspoon vanilla

  2 egg yolks
  1 cup sifted powdered sugar
  1 tablespoon Grand Marnier liqueur

  sifted cocoa

In the top of a double boiler, heat cream with butter until butter is melted. Add chocolate chips, salt and vanilla and stir until chocolate is melted. Remove from heat and beat in the yolks until blended. Add sugar and Grand Marnier and beat until mixture is smooth, about 1 minute.

Line an 8x12-inch pan with plastic wrap extended about 4-inches over the sides. Spread chocolate evenly in prepared pan and refrigerate until it is firm. Cut into 1-inch squares and sprinkle top with sifted cocoa. Remove each square and dust it with cocoa on each side. Place in bon bon wrappers and refrigerate until ready to serve. Yields 96, 1-inch squares.

Note: – If you enjoy a slightly more bittersweet taste, add 1 tablespoon sifted cocoa to the melted chocolate.
*   – Freezes beautifully.*

Orange Date Nut Cookies with Lemon Glaze

This little gem produces a lovely, thin, very chewy, bar cookie, sparkled with flavors of orange and dates and a touch of lemon.

1/2 cup butter (1 stick) at room temperature
  1 cup sugar
  2 eggs
  2 tablespoons grated orange peel
1/2 teaspoon vanilla

  1 cup flour
1/2 teaspoon baking powder
   pinch of salt

  2 cups chopped dates
  2 cups chopped walnuts or pecans

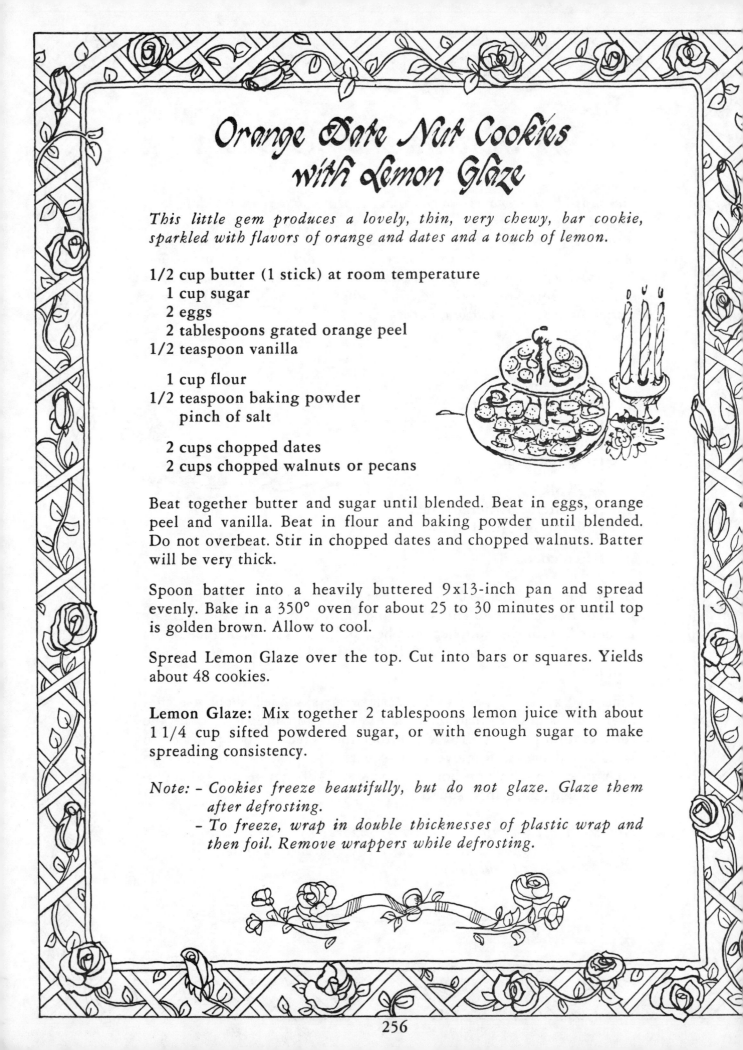

Beat together butter and sugar until blended. Beat in eggs, orange peel and vanilla. Beat in flour and baking powder until blended. Do not overbeat. Stir in chopped dates and chopped walnuts. Batter will be very thick.

Spoon batter into a heavily buttered 9x13-inch pan and spread evenly. Bake in a 350° oven for about 25 to 30 minutes or until top is golden brown. Allow to cool.

Spread Lemon Glaze over the top. Cut into bars or squares. Yields about 48 cookies.

Lemon Glaze: Mix together 2 tablespoons lemon juice with about 1 1/4 cup sifted powdered sugar, or with enough sugar to make spreading consistency.

Note: - Cookies freeze beautifully, but do not glaze. Glaze them
*   after defrosting.*
*   - To freeze, wrap in double thicknesses of plastic wrap and*
*   then foil. Remove wrappers while defrosting.*

Chocolate Fudge Brownie Cookies with Chocolate Frosting

This is a super easy, super moist fudgy brownie, that is assembled and frosted in literally minutes. It is a wonderful little gem for an evening when you are running late and want to please a chocolate lover (it could be you).

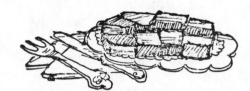

   4 eggs
3/4 cup flour
3/4 cup cocoa
   2 cups sugar
1/2 cup (1 stick) butter, melted
   1 teaspoon vanilla
      pinch of salt

In a bowl, combine all the ingredients and stir by hand until mixture is blended. Pour batter into a 9 x 13-inch pan and bake at 350° for about 20 to 22 minutes, or until top looks dry. Do not overbake. Now sprinkle on top.

3/4 cup semi-sweet chocolate chips

Return pan to oven for 1 minute, no more. Remove from oven and spread chocolate chips (now melted) evenly over the brownies. Allow to cool. Cut into squares and serve. Yields 24 brownies.

Orange Raisin Butter Cookies

   2 eggs
2/3 cup sugar
2/3 cup flour
   3 ounces butter (3/4 stick), at room temperature
   2 tablespoons grated orange peel
1/4 cup finely chopped walnuts
1/2 cup yellow raisins, chopped

Beat eggs with sugar until mixture is light and fluffy, about 2 minutes. Stir in the remaining ingredients until blended. Place about 1 teaspoon dough for each cookie on a greased cookie sheet. Flatten cookies with a flat-bottom cup to measure about 2 inches. Bake in a 350° oven for about 8 to 10 minutes or until the edges are golden brown, Yields 4 dozen cookies.

Chewy French Macaroons with Dates & Walnuts

3 egg whites at room temperature
1/2 cup sugar

2 cups coconut flakes
3/4 cup chopped walnuts
1 cup chopped dates
1 teaspoon vanilla

Beat whites with sugar until whites are creamy. Add the remaining ingredients and stir until blended. Drop batter by the tablespoonful on a generously greased cookie sheet. Bake at 350° for 15 minutes or until tops are nicely browned. Remove from cookie sheet immediately and place cookies on a brown paper bag to cool. Yields about 36 cookies.

French Macaroons with Orange & Almonds

3 egg whites at room temperature
1/2 cup sugar

2 cups coconut flakes
3/4 cup toasted sliced almonds
2 tablespoons grated orange peel
1/4 cup flour
1 teaspoon vanilla

Beat whites and sugar about 1 minutes at high speed or until mixture is creamy. Add the remaining ingredients and stir until blended. Heavily grease a 12x16-inch cookie sheet and drop batter by the tablespoonful onto the pan. Bake at 350° for 15 minutes or until tops are nicely browned.

Immediately remove cookies from pan and place on a brown paper bag to cool. Yields about 36 cookies.

Note: – If cookies are not removed immediately from the pan, they will harden and be difficult to remove. Then they must be returned to a 350° oven for about 30 seconds to soften.

Velvet Lemon Cheesecake with Raspberry Syrup

This is my very favorite cheesecake. Light, delectable, with a creamy velvet filling with a hint of lemon. The crust is the perfect accompaniment, delicately flavored with lemon and vanilla.

Lemon Vanilla Crust:

1 1/2 cups vanilla wafer crumbs
   3 ounces butter (3/4 stick)
1/2 cup finely chopped walnuts
   1 tablespoon grated lemon peel
   4 tablespoons sugar

   1 package (10 ounces) frozen raspberries in syrup

Combine the crumbs, melted butter, walnuts, peel and sugar and mix until blended. With your fingers, press the mixture on the bottom and 1 inch up the sides of a 10-inch springform pan. Bake in a 350° oven for 5 minutes.

Pour Velvet Lemon Cheese Filling into prepared crust and bake in a 350° oven for about 50 minutes to 1 hour, or until a cake tester inserted 1 inch off center comes out clean. Do not overbake. Cool in pan and refrigerate for several hours or overnight. Remove from pan and serve with a spoonful of raspberries in syrup. Serves 10.

Velvet Lemon Cheese Filling:

2 packages (8 ounces, each) cream cheese
1 cup sugar
3 eggs
3 cups sour cream
2 teaspoons grated lemon peel
2 tablespoons lemon juice

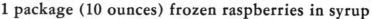

Beat together all the ingredients until mixture is thoroughly blended.

Note: – Freezes beautifully. Defrost in the refrigerator overnight.

Country French Cherry Cheese Custard

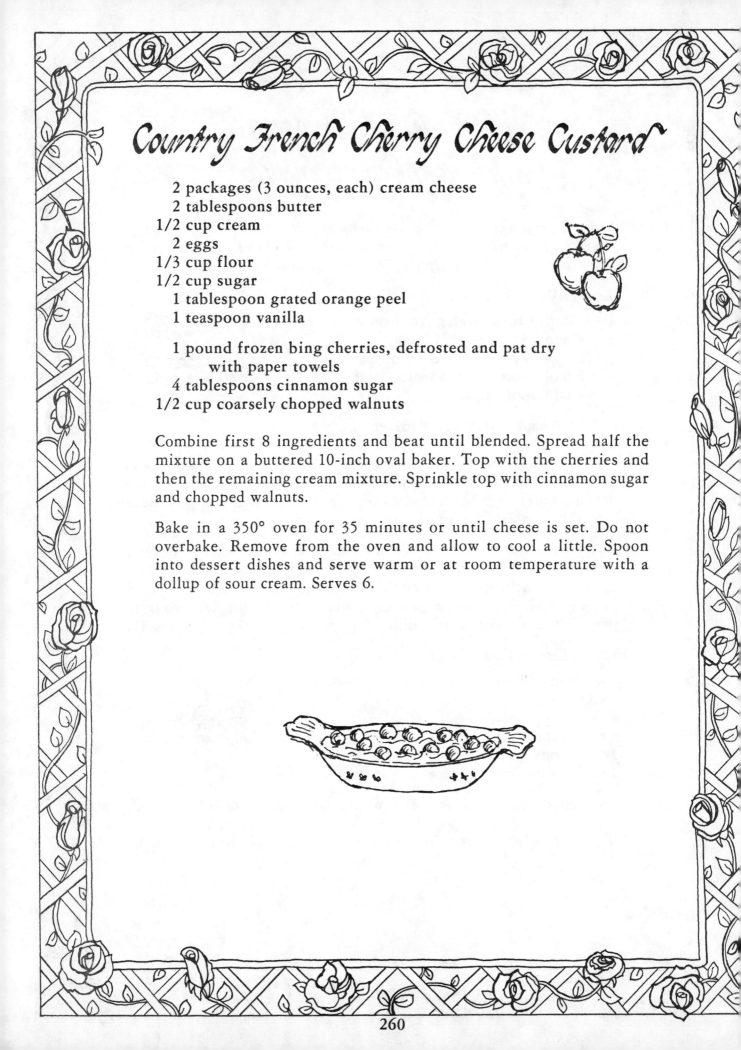

          2 packages (3 ounces, each) cream cheese
          2 tablespoons butter
    1/2 cup cream
          2 eggs
    1/3 cup flour
    1/2 cup sugar
          1 tablespoon grated orange peel
          1 teaspoon vanilla

          1 pound frozen bing cherries, defrosted and pat dry
              with paper towels
          4 tablespoons cinnamon sugar
    1/2 cup coarsely chopped walnuts

Combine first 8 ingredients and beat until blended. Spread half the
mixture on a buttered 10-inch oval baker. Top with the cherries and
then the remaining cream mixture. Sprinkle top with cinnamon sugar
and chopped walnuts.

Bake in a 350° oven for 35 minutes or until cheese is set. Do not
overbake. Remove from the oven and allow to cool a little. Spoon
into dessert dishes and serve warm or at room temperature with a
dollup of sour cream. Serves 6.

Classic Creme Brullee

This classic custard is rich and refreshing. Traditionally flavored with vanilla, it is also good with liqueur, rum or coffee.

6 egg yolks
3/4 cup sugar

2 1/2 cups cream
2 teaspoons vanilla

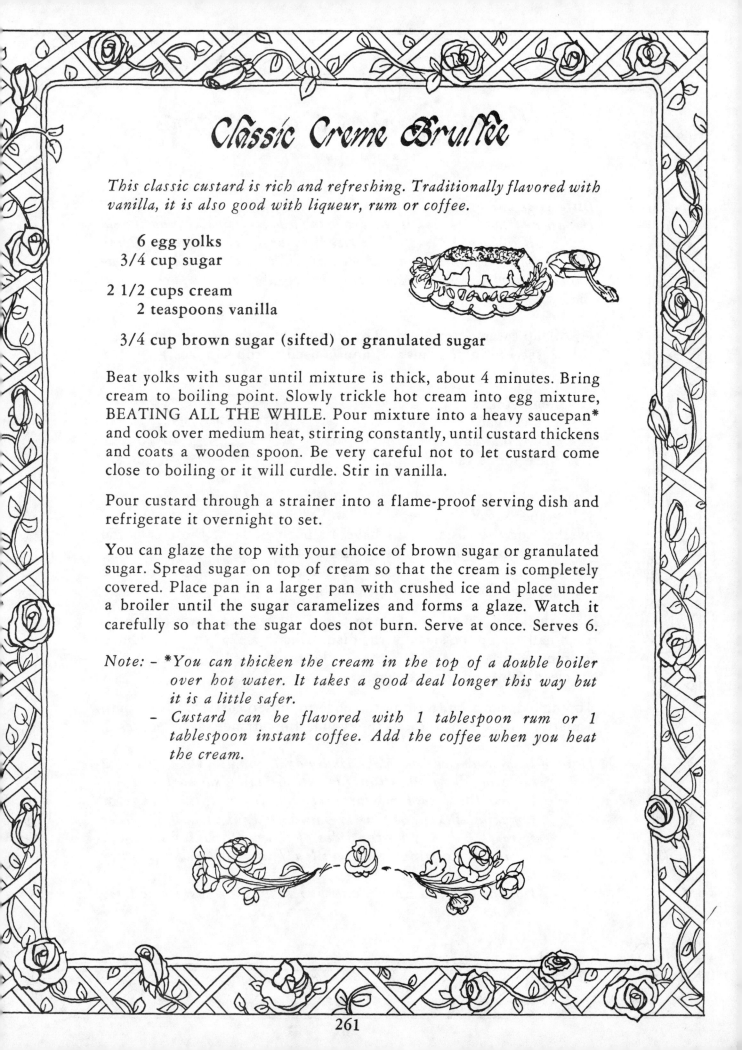

3/4 cup brown sugar (sifted) **or granulated sugar**

Beat yolks with sugar until mixture is thick, about 4 minutes. Bring cream to boiling point. Slowly trickle hot cream into egg mixture, BEATING ALL THE WHILE. Pour mixture into a heavy saucepan* and cook over medium heat, stirring constantly, until custard thickens and coats a wooden spoon. Be very careful not to let custard come close to boiling or it will curdle. Stir in vanilla.

Pour custard through a strainer into a flame-proof serving dish and refrigerate it overnight to set.

You can glaze the top with your choice of brown sugar or granulated sugar. Spread sugar on top of cream so that the cream is completely covered. Place pan in a larger pan with crushed ice and place under a broiler until the sugar caramelizes and forms a glaze. Watch it carefully so that the sugar does not burn. Serve at once. Serves 6.

*Note: – *You can thicken the cream in the top of a double boiler over hot water. It takes a good deal longer this way but it is a little safer.*
– Custard can be flavored with 1 tablespoon rum or 1 tablespoon instant coffee. Add the coffee when you heat the cream.

Crème Renversée au Caramel

(Caramel Custard)

This French custard is made with a lining of caramel which is just a little tricky. You must be careful not to burn the sugar which will impart a bitter taste, and if you are using a porcelain dish, you should preheat it so that the sizzling (melted) sugar does not crack it. Using the prepared caramel topping avoids all the pitfalls and Creme Caramel becomes an exceedingly simple dessert and very good, indeed.

3/4 cup caramel topping. (This is sold near the ice cream
      section in your market and is used to top sundaes.)

4 eggs
4 egg yolks
3/4 cup sugar
3 cups half and half
1 1/2 teaspoons vanilla

Coat a 1 1/2-quart souffle dish with the caramel topping. Beat eggs, yolks and sugar together until well blended and light. Do not overbeat or the custard will have air bubbles. Heat the cream and vanilla just below the simmer. Beat the cream in a thin trickle into the egg mixture until blended. Pour the cream mixture through a strainer into the prepared souffle dish.

Place the souffle dish in a baking pan. Pour boiling water in pan to reach halfway up the sides of the dish. Bake in a 325° oven for about 50 minutes or until a cake tester or knife inserted in center comes out clean. Cool and then refrigerate.

To unmold, run a knife along the edge to loosen custard. Invert onto a platter with a rim to catch the wonderful caramel sauce. Serves 6.

Note: – If you desire to make individual molds, then place 2 tablespoons caramel topping into 6 individual custard cups. Divide the cream mixture between the 6 custard cups or ramekins. Place them in a pan with enough boiling water to reach half way up the sides of the cups. Baking time will be about 25 minutes or until a knife, inserted in center comes out clean.

*   – Do not allow water in the pan to boil or custard will be coarse.*

Chocolate Pots de Creme with Rum

(Rum-Chocolate Custard)

Served in little covered pots, this elegant, lovely French custard is exceedingly simple to prepare and very, very delicious.

    1 bag (6 ounces) semi-sweet chocolate chips
1 1/2 cups cream
    2 eggs
    2 egg yolks
    1 to 2 tablespoons rum
    1/2 teaspoon vanilla

Place chocolate in blender container. Heat cream to boiling point and pour into blender. Blend for 1 minute or until chocolate is melted and mixture is smooth. Blend in remaining ingredients. Pour mixture into 6 individual custard cups, ramekins or chocolate pots.

Place cups in a pan with enough boiling water to reach 1/2 up the sides. Bake in a 325° oven for about 25 minutes or until a cake tester inserted off center comes out clean. Do not overcook. Cool and then refrigerate. Serve with a dollup of whipped cream or a tablespoon (or two) of Creme Vanilla.

Note: – For an exciting touch place 1 or 2 tablespoons of rum-soaked macaroon crumbs on bottom of each custard cup. Pour chocolate mixture over and proceed as above.

Creme Vanilla

1/2 cup cream
1/2 cup sour cream

    2 tablespoons sugar
    1 teaspoon vanilla

Stir together cream and sour cream in a glass jar. Leave at room temperature for about 4 hours or until thickened. Add the sugar and vanilla, stir, cover jar and refrigerate. Use to spoon over cakes, puddings or fruit. This is a lovely dessert sauce to have on hand. Yields about 1 cup sauce.

Note: – You may substitute 2 teaspoons of rum for the vanilla.

Fresh Fruit with Raspberry Lemon Cream

On a large platter, arrange attractively, various freshly sliced fruits. Cut them in wedges, such as apples and pears, in slices, balls, sticks. Dip all fruit in orange juice to prevent it from darkening. This lovely dressing is especially good with bananas, peaches, strawberries, melons, apples or pears. Decorate the platter with lots of green leaves and set the dressing where it is surrounded by fruit.

RASPBERRY LEMON CREAM

    1 package (3 ounces) cream cheese
    1 teaspoon grated lemon peel
    1 tablespoon lemon juice
1/2 cup frozen raspberries, drained. Reserve syrup.
1/2 cup cream, whipped
    1 tablespoon sugar

Beat cream cheese until light and fluffy. Add lemon peel, lemon juice, raspberries and about 1 tablespoon of the syrup to loosen cream cheese. Beat cream with 1 tablespoon sugar and fold it into the raspberry mixture. Refrigerate until serving time. Yields about 1 1/2 cups dressing.

Note: – Dressing can be made earlier in the day and refrigerated. Do not prepare the day before.

Poached Apples in Orange Butter Glaze

This delightful dish made such a hit at our house, that I couldn't wait to share it with you. Everyone oohed and aahed and unanimously agreed it was the best cooked apples they had ever tasted. Poaching the apples in the orange-butter sauce was next to the easiest thing and the results were, I must agree, very good, indeed. The syrup adds a deep and wonderful flavor to the apples.

1/4 cup butter
1/2 cup sugar
1/2 **orange, grated, plus 1/2 cup orange juice**
1/2 teaspoon vanilla
1/4 cup coarsely chopped walnuts
1/8 teaspoon cinnamon

3 Golden Delicious apples, cored and cut in half

In an 8x2-inch round pan, simmer together, uncovered, the butter, sugar, orange, vanilla, walnuts and cinnamon for 5 minutes at a very slow bubble. Add the apples to the pan and continue cooking over low heat until the apples are tender. Turn once or twice during the cooking time. Do not overcook the apples, but don't leave them too firm, either. Cooking time should be approximately 20 to 30 minutes, depending on the size of the apples.

Serve them warm, with a spoonful of walnuts and syrup in each. A faint sprinkle of cinnamon is very nice, too. These are excellent as an accompaniment to the French Chicken Pie with Mushrooms and Herbs, or a lovely quiche.

Note: – Apples can be made 1 day earlier and stored in the refrigerator. Reheat in a 350° oven until warmed through.

Wine-Poached Pears with Oranges & Honey

This is a light and lovely dessert. The poached fruit also serves beautifully as an accompaniment to chicken crepes or quiche. The flavor of the wine and orange is lovely with the pears. To prepare, it is the essence of simplicity, but the taste is deep and rich.

3/4 cup orange juice
1/4 cup white wine
   3 tablespoons honey
   3 tablespoons butter
1/2 teaspoon vanilla
   1 tablespoon grated orange peel

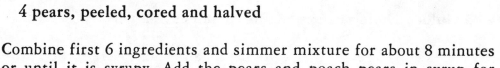

   4 pears, peeled, cored and halved

Combine first 6 ingredients and simmer mixture for about 8 minutes or until it is syrupy. Add the pears and poach pears in syrup for about 10 minutes or until pears are tender.

Place pears in a shallow porcelain baker and drizzle with the syrup. Serve warm or refrigerate and serve cold. Serves 4.

Note: – An excellent optional would be the addition of 1/4 cup coarsely chopped walnuts to the syrup.

Iced Cream Grand Marnier with Apricots in Brandy Syrup

There are few desserts that are more grand than this lovely iced cream served with apricots sparkled with brandy. It is also exceedingly simple to prepare and can be frozen for a week before serving.

1/2 cup water
1/2 cup sugar
  1 tablespoon grated orange peel

  4 eggs
  4 tablespoons Grand Marnier

  1 cup cream
  2 tablespoons sugar

In a saucepan, heat water, sugar and orange peel and bring to a boil. Boil for 5 minutes without stirring.

Meanwhile, beat eggs for 5 minutes until thick and pale colored. Now add the hot syrup in a steady stream, beating all the while, until the eggs are very light and airy. Beat in liqueur.

Beat cream with sugar until stiff. On low speed, beat cream into the egg mixture until it is nicely blended.

Spoon cream into 12 paper-lined muffin cups and freeze. Store in double plastic bags until serving time. To serve, remove paper liner and place in a lovely stemmed glass or dessert dish. Serve with a spoonful of Apricots with Brandy Syrup. Serves 12.

Apricots in Brandy Syrup

  1 package (6 ounces) dried apricots
  1 cup orange juice
1/4 cup sugar
  4 tablespoons Cognac

In a saucepan, cook together apricots, orange juice and sugar for about 15 or 20 minutes or until apricots are soft, but not mushy. Place apricots with syrup and Cognac in a glass jar with a tight-fitting lid. Refrigerate until serving time.

Orange Iced Cream
with Strawberry Orange Sauce

This delightful frozen cream is the essence of simplicity. Simply beat lightly and freeze.

  1 cup cream
1/2 package (3 ounces) frozen orange juice
      concentrate, undiluted
  4 tablespoons lemon juice
  2 teaspoons grated lemon peel
1/3 cup sugar

In a large mixer bowl, place all the ingredients and beat at low speed until mixture is slightly thickened. (Do not beat stiff as for whipped cream, but rather, lightly whipped cream.)

Divide mixture between 6 paper-lined muffin cups and freeze until firm. When frozen, store in double plastic bags. To serve, remove the paper liners and place in a lovely stemmed glass or dessert dish. Serve with a spoonful of Strawberry Orange Sauce. Serves 6.

Strawberry Orange Sauce

1 package (10 ounces) frozen strawberries in syrup
4 tablespoons frozen orange juice concentrate, undiluted
1 tablespoon Grand Marnier Liqueur

Combine all the ingredients in a bowl and stir until blended. Store in the refrigerator until serving time.

Note: – *Iced cream can be made 1 week earlier and stored in the freezer.*
  – *Sauce can be made earlier in the day and stored in the refrigerator.*

Almond Meringue Torte with Chocolate Dipped Strawberries

Plump, juicy strawberries, dipped in chocolate are just beautiful on this spectacular dessert. An almond meringue layer, topped with chocolate, swirls of whipped cream and the chocolate strawberries is an ultimate dessert. Add chocolate leaves ... a masterpiece.

Meringue Layer:
    1 cup sliced almonds (or 3/4 cup almond meal
        from health food stores)
  1/2 cup sugar
    1 tablespoon cornstarch

    3 egg whites
    pinch each of salt and cream of tartar
1 1/2 tablespoons sugar
  1/2 teaspoon vanilla
    few drops almond extract

In a blender or food processor, place almonds, sugar and cornstarch and process for about 30 seconds or until almonds are finely ground.

In the large bowl of an electric mixer, beat egg whites until foamy. Add salt, cream of tartar and sugar and continue beating until whites are stiff and glossy. Beat in vanilla and almond extract. Fold almond mixture into egg whites, by hand or on the lowest speed of mixer, 1/3 at a time. Do this with a gentle hand.

Grease and flour a 10-inch springform pan. Scrape the meringue mixture into the pan and spread to even. Bake meringue in a 300° oven for about 40 minutes or until top is dry and just beginning to color. Pour Chocolate Fudge Frosting over the layer. Decorate with swirls of Grand Marnier Whipped Cream and Chocolate Dipped Strawberries. Remove metal rim but leave dessert on metal bottom. Beautiful! Serves 8.

Chocolate Fudge Frosting: Place 3/4 cup semi-sweet chocolate chips in blender container. Heat 1/2 cup cream to boiling point and pour into blender. Blend for 1 minute or until chocolate is melted. Beat in 1 teaspoon Grand Marnier Liqueur.

Grand Marnier Whipped Cream: Beat 1 cup cream with 1 tablespoon sugar and 1 tablespoon Grand Marnier until cream is stiff.

Chocolate Dipped Strawberries: Clean and pat dry 1 pint strawberries. In the top of a double boiler, over hot, not boiling water, melt 1 cup semi-sweet chocolate chips. Holding on to the green leaves or piercing hull with a toothpick, dip strawberries into chocolate, covering half the fruit. Place on wax paper to cool and then refrigerate to firm up. And while you're at it, spread about 2 teaspoons of chocolate on the back of scrubbed and dried camellia leaves, and refrigerate with the strawberries. Peel the leaves off and Voila! beautiful chocolate leaves to decorate this masterpiece.

Meringue Clouds with Chocolate Fudge Mousse

This very delicate dessert is a literal cloud of meringue and cream, filled with a thin layer of chocolate fudge. While it sounds terribly rich, it is a rather light dessert. It presents beautifully and is exciting and dramatic.

Meringue Shell:
- 4 egg whites
- pinch of salt
- 1/8 teaspoon cream of tartar
- 1 cup sugar

Beat egg whites until foamy. Continue beating and add salt, cream of tartar and sugar (1 tablespoon at a time) until the meringue is stiff and glossy. Scrape meringue into a 9-inch springform pan that is greased. Smooth the meringue with a spatula and build up the sides just a little to form a shell. Bake in a 275° oven for 1 hour and cool.

Pour Chocolate Fudge Mousse into cooled shell and spread to even. (Reserve 4 tablespoons mousse to decorate top.) Mound whipped cream over the top and drizzle reserved mousse in swirls over the whipped cream. Refrigerate until serving time. Remove ring and place this heavenly creation on your loveliest footed platter. (Leave the dessert on the metal bottom.) Serves 10.

Chocolate Fudge Mousse:
- 3/4 cup chocolate chips, semi-sweet
- 3/4 cup cream
- 1 teaspoon rum

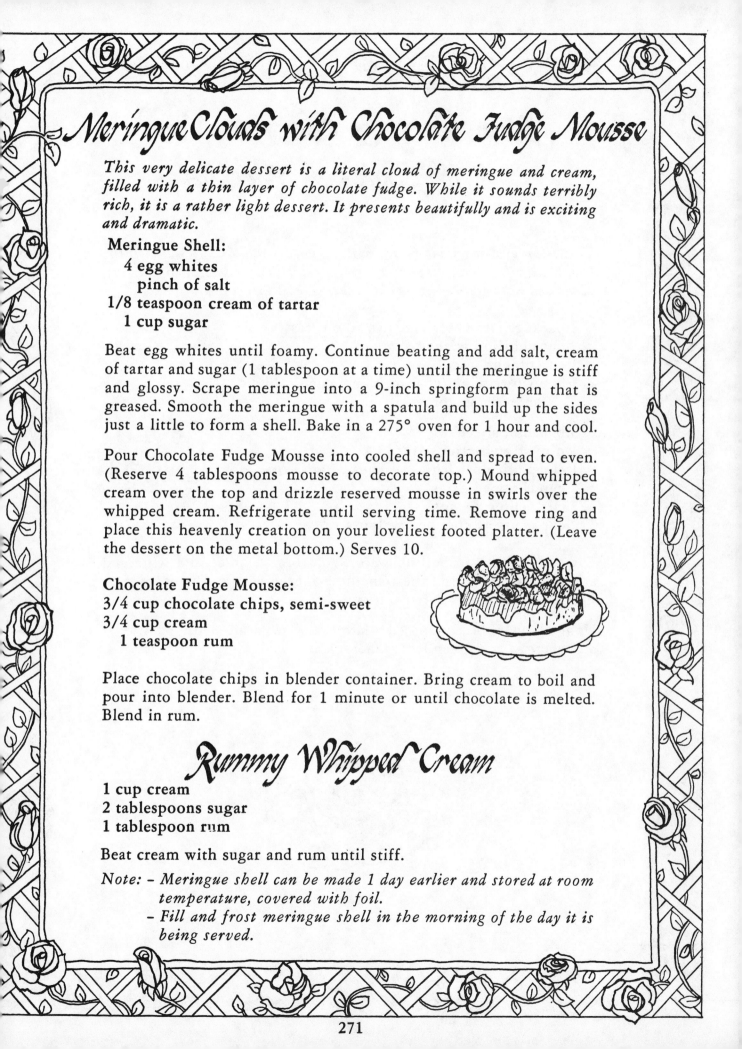

Place chocolate chips in blender container. Bring cream to boil and pour into blender. Blend for 1 minute or until chocolate is melted. Blend in rum.

Rummy Whipped Cream

- 1 cup cream
- 2 tablespoons sugar
- 1 tablespoon rum

Beat cream with sugar and rum until stiff.

Note: – Meringue shell can be made 1 day earlier and stored at room temperature, covered with foil.
– Fill and frost meringue shell in the morning of the day it is being served.

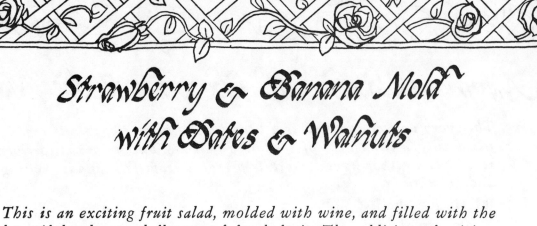

Strawberry & Banana Mold with Dates & Walnuts

This is an exciting fruit salad, molded with wine, and filled with the beautiful colors and flavors of fresh fruit. The addition of raisins, dates and nuts adds a marvelous texture and interest.

1 package strawberry gelatin (6 ounces)
2 cups boiling water
1 cup orange juice
1 cup white wine (chablis blanc, chenin blanc,
    or sweet sauternes)

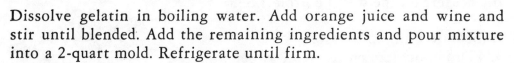

3 bananas, sliced
1 pint strawberries, sliced
1 cup additional fruit, peaches or apricots
1/2 cup chopped dates
1/2 cup yellow raisins
1/2 cup coarsely chopped walnuts

Dissolve gelatin in boiling water. Add orange juice and wine and stir until blended. Add the remaining ingredients and pour mixture into a 2-quart mold. Refrigerate until firm.

Unmold on a pretty footed platter and decorate with additional strawberries and green leaves. Serves 8.

Easy Raspberry Bavarian Cream with Lemon Creme Fraiche

    1 package (6 ounces) raspberry gelatin
1 1/2 cups boiling water
    6 ice cubes
    1 tablespoon lemon juice
    1 package (10 ounces) frozen raspberries
        in syrup, defrosted

    1 cup cream

Dissolve gelatin in boiling water. Stir in the ice cubes until melted. Stir in lemon juice, raspberries and syrup.

Whip cream until stiff and fold it into the raspberry mixture until thoroughly blended. (This can be done in your mixer, on low speed.)

Pour into a 2-quart mold and refrigerate until firm. You can spoon the cream into 8 or 10 individual stemmed glasses and refrigerate until firm. Serve with a dollup of Lemon Creme Fraiche or a spoonful of raspberries in syrup. Small, tart lemon cookies are a nice accompaniment. Serves 8 or 10.

Lemon Creme Fraiche:
1/2 cup sour cream
1/2 cup cream
    2 tablespoons lemon juice
    3 tablespoons sugar
    1 teaspoon grated lemon peel

In a glass jar with a tight-fitting lid, combine all the ingredients and stir until blended. Store in the refrigerator until ready to serve. Can be made 2 or 3 days earlier. Yields about 1 cup sauce. Can be used on puddings and fruit tarts.

Note: – The addition of 1 tablespoon rum to the whipped cream adds a party touch to this dish.

Easy Strawberry Bavarian Cream

Follow the directions above, except substitute 1 package of strawberry gelatin and 1 package of frozen strawberries in syrup for the raspberry counterparts.

Creme Mousse au Chocolat

8 ounces semi-sweet chocolate chips

1/2 cup (1 stick) butter, cut into 4 pieces

8 egg yolks
1 tablespoon Grand Marnier liqueur

8 egg whites
1 tablespoon sugar

Melt chocolate in the top of a double boiler over hot, not boiling water. Stir in the softened butter, one piece at a time until blended. Stir in yolks and liqueur until well blended. Remove pan from hot water and set aside.

Beat whites with 1 tablespoon sugar until stiff. Fold half the egg whites into the chocolate. Fold in the remaining whites until blended. Pour mousse into a pretty footed glass bowl or into individual crystal glasses. Refrigerate until set. Yields 10 servings.

Cognac Mousse with Macaroons, Raspberries & Chocolate

1 tablespoon gelatin
1/4 cup Cognac

4 eggs, at room temperature
1/2 cup sugar

1 1/4 cups cream, beaten until stiff

6 macaroons, crumbled
6 teaspoons raspberry syrup from package listed below

1 package (10 ounces) frozen raspberries in syrup,
   defrosted
grated chocolate

Soften gelatin in Cognac and place over hot water until gelatin is liquefied.

Meanwhile, beat eggs with sugar until eggs are thick and lemon colored, about 8 minutes. Beat in the gelatin mixture. Beat in the whipped cream.

In each of 6 lovely stemmed glasses, place 1 crumbled macaroon. Pour about 1 teaspoon raspberry syrup over each macaroon. Divide mousse between the six glasses and sprinkle grated chocolate over the top. Refrigerate until firm. Overnight is good, too. Serve with a spoonful of raspberry sauce on top. Serves 6.

'Note: – *To grate chocolate, take a vegetable peeler and run it down the side of a bar of chocolate that has been chilled in the refrigerator.*

   – *To make chocolate curls, take a vegetable peeler and run it down the side of a bar of chocolate that is at room temperature.*

Chocolate Amaretto Mousse Pie

If you are ever looking to lavish your guests with a gastronomical treat, you would do well to consider this dessert. It is perfect for dinner parties because it can be made up to 1 week ahead. Make certain that all the ingredients are at room temperature so that the chocolate does not congeal when the egg whites are added.

1 10-inch Chocolate Almond Crumb Crust

1 package (12 ounces) semi-sweet chocolate chips
3/4 cup cream

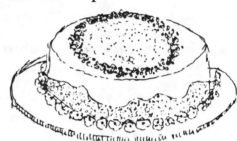

6 egg yolks
3 tablespoons Amaretto Liqueur
1 teaspoon almond extract

6 egg whites
2 tablespoons sugar

Place chocolate chips into a blender container or processor bowl. Heat cream to boiling and pour into the blender. Beat for 1 minute or until chocolate is melted and nicely blended. Beat in yolks, Amaretto and almond extract. Set aside to cool a little.

In the large bowl of an electric mixer, beat egg whites with sugar until stiff. Gently fold beaten whites into chocolate mixture so as not to deflate the egg whites.

Pour mousse into prepared crust, cover with plastic wrap and freeze. Remove from the freezer about 1 hour before serving. Cut into wedges and serve with a dollup of whipped cream and the faintest sprinkling of cocoa. Serves 8.

Chocolate Almond Crumb Crust

2 cups chocolate cookie crumbs (use a delicious cookie)
1/2 cup butter (1 stick), melted
4 tablespoons sugar
1/4 cup finely chopped almonds

Combine all the ingredients and mix until blended. Pat crumb mixture on the bottom and 1-inch up the sides of a 10-inch springform pan. Bake crust at 350° for about 7 minutes. Spread 1/3 cup seedless red raspberry jam on crust. Set aside to cool.

Mousse of Chestnut Cream in Chocolate Cups

2 tablespoons gelatin
1/4 cup rum

5 eggs, at room temperature
1/2 cup sugar

1 cup chestnut puree, sweetened, at room temperature
1 cup cream, beaten until stiff, at room temperature
1 package (10 ounces) frozen raspberries in syrup
   shaved chocolate

Soften gelatin in rum and place pan over hot water until gelatin is liquefied.

Meanwhile, beat eggs with sugar until eggs are very thick and lemon colored, about 10 minutes. Beat in the gelatin mixture. Beat in the chestnut puree. Beat in the whipped cream.

Spoon mousse into chocolate cups and refrigerate until firm. Sprinkle top with shaved chocolate and a teaspoon of Raspberries in Syrup.

Chocolate Cups:

1 bag (6 ounces) semi-sweet chocolate chips
1 tablespoon rum

In the top of a double boiler over hot, not boiling water melt chocolate. Add rum and stir until blended. Place paper liners in 12 muffin cups. You will need 1 muffin pan, 12 muffin capacity. Place about 1 tablespoon warm chocolate into each paper cup. With the back of a spoon, spread the chocolate on the inside of the cup, making certain to cover the paper completely. Place cups in muffin pan. Refrigerate until firm. Carefully peel off paper liners.

Note: – While this recipe is truly simple, it is a little tricky. If you beat cold whipped cream into the gelatin mixture you run the risk of firming up the gelatin before it is well blended. This will impart a grainy quality to the finished mousse, which is less than satisfactory. It will taste delicious but not look very pretty. To avoid this, make certain that all ingredients are at room temperature.

Easiest & Best Mousse au Chocolat with Rum

Who can resist a velvety, rich, temptingly delicious chocolate mousse? There are few desserts that are as sinfully extravagant, so keep the portions small. Add a buttery cookie and dessert will feel and taste "heaven sent."

    8 ounces semi-sweet chocolate chips
1/2 cup (1 stick) butter, cut into 4 pieces
3/4 cup whipping cream
    1 tablespoon rum
    1 tablespoon sugar

ALL INGREDIENTS MUST BE AT ROOM TEMPERATURE. (Yes, even the whipping cream. If any of the ingredients are cold, in folding, chocolate will harden and not blend properly.)

Melt chocolate in the top of a double boiler over hot, not boiling, water. Stir in the softened butter, one piece at a time, until blended. Remove pan from hot water, and set aside.

Beat cream with rum and sugar until stiff. Fold half the cream into the chocolate mixture. Fold in the remaining cream until blended. Pour mousse into a pretty glass bowl or into individual crystal glasses. Refrigerate until set. Yields 10 servings.

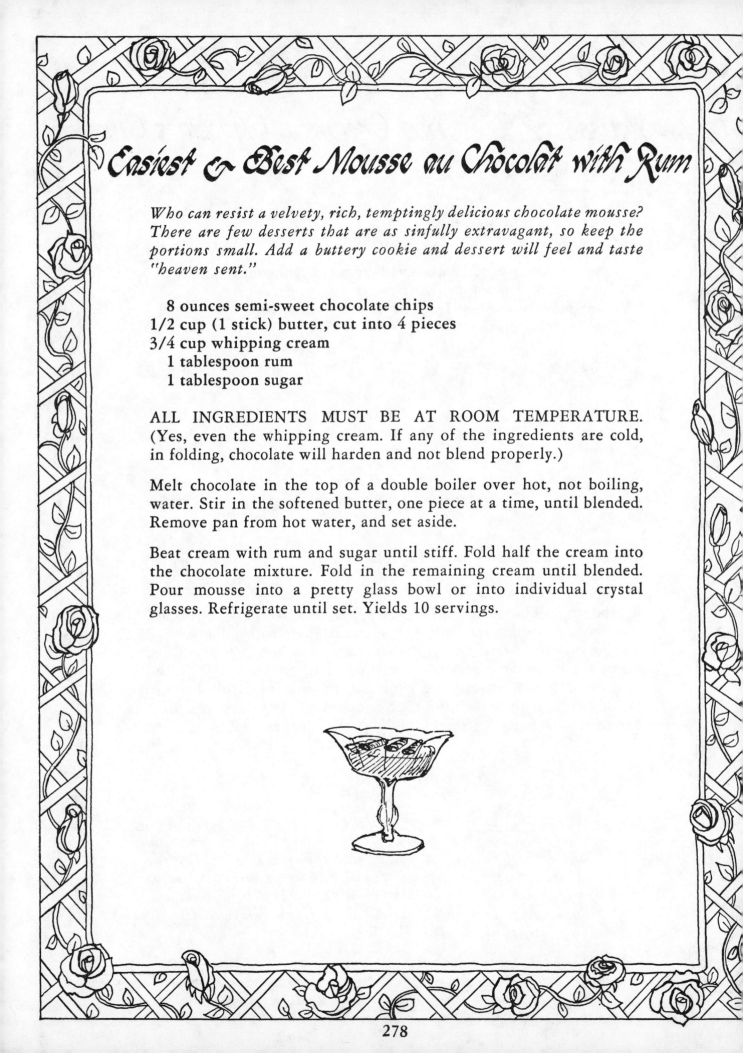

Mousseline of Chocolate with Creme Fraiche

Not quite a mousse, nor a custard, nor a cheesecake, but a little of each, this incredible mousseline is the stuff chocolate dreams are made of.

1 package (12 ounces) semi-sweet chocolate chips
3 tablespoons rum

6 eggs, at room temperature
9 tablespoons sugar

1 1/4 cups whipping cream
   1 tablespoon sugar
   1 teaspoon vanilla

In the top of a double boiler, over hot not boiling water, melt chocolate. Set aside.

Beat eggs with 9 tablespoons sugar and rum for 10 minutes or until they are thick and light and tripled in volume. Beat in the melted chocolate.

Beat the cream with 1 tablespoon sugar and vanilla until stiff. Fold cream into chocolate mixture. Pour mixture into a 9-inch spring-form pan that has been buttered. Place a sheet of heavy duty foil (18 inches) on bottom of pan and crease it up the sides of pan to prevent any seepage.

Place pan into a larger pan with 1-inch of hot water and bake in a 350° oven for about 45 to 55 minutes or until a cake tester inserted in center comes out clean. Allow mousseline to cool in oven, remove foil and refrigerate. Remove ring and place on your loveliest footed platter. (Do not try to remove cake from the bottom of pan.) Decorate with a faint sprinkling of sifted powdered sugar and serve with a dollup of Creme Fraiche (optional, but very good). Serves 12.

Creme Fraiche

1/2 cup sour cream
1/2 cup whipping cream
  2 tablespoons sugar
1/2 teaspoon vanilla

Place creams in a glass jar, stir and leave at room temperature for 3 hours, stirring occasionally. Add sugar and vanilla and stir until blended. Refrigerate until serving time. Yields 2 cups.

Jody's Elegant Strawberry Cream Cheese Pie in a Nut Crust

2 1/2 cups pecans
    7 tablespoons sugar
    4 tablespoons melted butter

2 cups cream
1 package (8 ounces) cream cheese, softened
1 cup sifted powdered sugar
1 teaspoon vanilla

1 package (10 ounces) frozen strawberries
    in syrup, defrosted

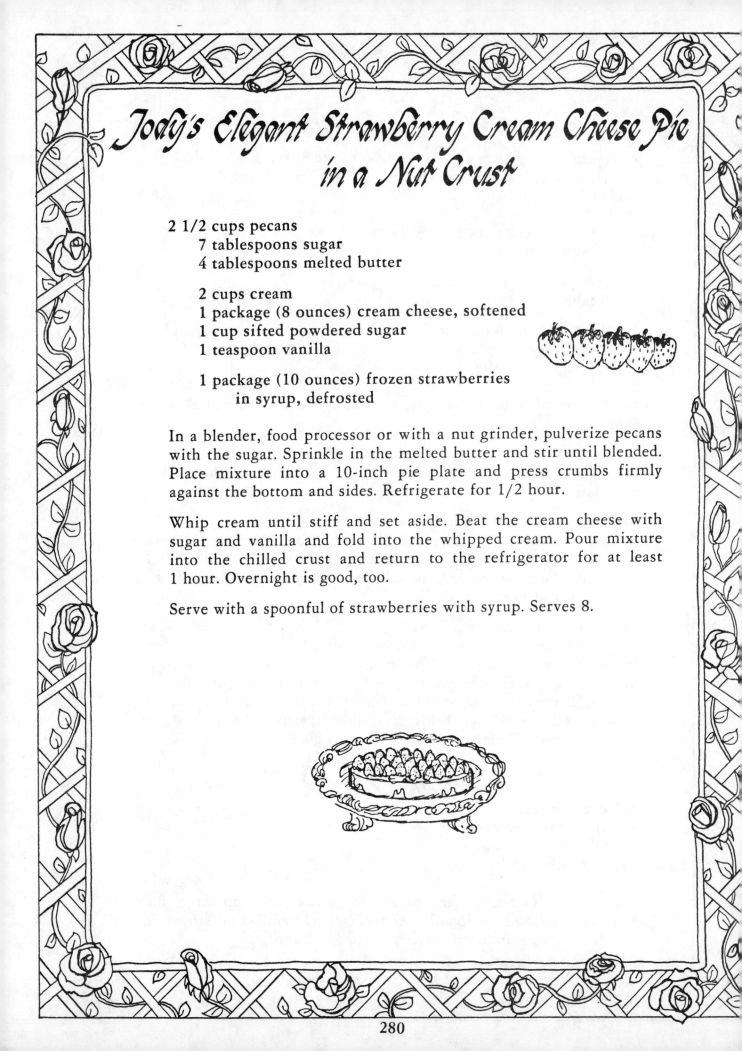

In a blender, food processor or with a nut grinder, pulverize pecans with the sugar. Sprinkle in the melted butter and stir until blended. Place mixture into a 10-inch pie plate and press crumbs firmly against the bottom and sides. Refrigerate for 1/2 hour.

Whip cream until stiff and set aside. Beat the cream cheese with sugar and vanilla and fold into the whipped cream. Pour mixture into the chilled crust and return to the refrigerator for at least 1 hour. Overnight is good, too.

Serve with a spoonful of strawberries with syrup. Serves 8.

Apple Tart with Almond Custard

     4 apples, peeled, cored and cut into 1/8-inch slices
     2 tablespoons lemon juice
 1/2 cup yellow raisins
     3 tablespoons butter
 1/3 cup apricot jam

     3 eggs
 1/2 cup cream
 1/2 cup sugar
 1/2 cup ground almonds
     1 teaspoon vanilla

     2 tablespoons cinnamon sugar
 1/4 cup sugared almonds
     1 Vanilla Crumb Crust
       melted apricot jam

In a skillet, cook together the apples, lemon juice, raisins and butter for about 15 minutes or until apples are almost tender and liquid is absorbed. Add the apricot jam and stir until blended. Place mixture into prepared crust.

Beat eggs with cream, sugar, almonds and vanilla until blended and pour mixture over the apples. Sprinkle cinnamon sugar and sugared almonds on the top.

Bake in a 350° oven for 40 minutes or until custard is set and apples are tender. Brush top with melted apricot jam. Serves 8.

Vanilla Crumb Crust

 1 1/2 cups vanilla wafer crumbs
     3 tablespoons melted butter
     3 tablespoons cinnamon sugar

     4 tablespoons melted apricot jam

Line a 10-inch springform pan with foil on the outside. Combine crumbs, butter and sugar and mix until blended. Pat mixture on the bottom and 1-inch up the sides of a 10-inch springform pan. Bake in a 350° oven for about 8 minutes or until top is very lightly browned. Drizzle melted apricot jam evenly in pan. Pan is now ready to be filled.

Deep Dish Apple Pie
with Raisins & Sour Cream

(Tarte aux Pommes)

1 9-inch deep dish frozen pie shell, spread bottom and
    sides with apricot jam
5 medium apples, peeled, cored and thinly sliced
1/4 cup butter (1/2 stick) melted
3/4 cup sugar
1/2 cup yellow raisins
1/2 cup apricot jam
   2 tablespoons lemon juice and 1 teaspoon lemon peel
   2 tablespoons flour

Topping:
1 cup sour cream
1 egg
4 tablespoons sugar
1/2 teaspoon vanilla

1/2 cup chopped pecans
   cinnamon sugar

Combine apples, butter, sugar, raisins, jam, lemon juice, peel and
flour and toss until mixed. Place mixture into the prepared pie shell.
Place shell on a cookie sheet and bake in a 375° oven for 30 minutes.

Beat together sour cream, egg, sugar and vanilla, and pour mixture
over the apples. Sprinkle top with chopped pecans and cinnamon
sugar.

Return to oven and continue baking for about 30 minutes or until
top is golden brown and cream is set. Serve warm or at room
temperature. Delectable! Serves 6.

*Note: – Traditionally prepared in a tart pan; if you allow the pie
shell to defrost for 10 minutes, you can remove the shell
and place it into a 10-inch buttered tart pan. In this case,
you will need only 4 apples.*

282

Tarte de Demoiselles Tartin

This is a variation of one of the truly great apple desserts. Caramelized apples on a bed of puff pastry is total simplicity ... yet elegant and grand. As many times as I have served this dessert, there has been no limit to the ooh's and aah's and m-m-m-m-'s.

   1/2 cup butter, melted
1 1/4 cups sugar
    6 large apples, peeled, cored and halved

1/2 package frozen patty shells (3 shells), defrosted

Place melted butter and sugar in an 8 x 2½-inch round baking pan. Arrange apples, cut side up, in an attractive fashion in the pan. Simmer apples over medium heat until syrup is golden in color, about 45 minutes.

Stack patty shells and roll them out to an 8-inch circle. Place dough over the apples, pierce the crust with the tines of a fork, and bake in a 400° oven for 30 minutes or until crust is golden.

Invert tart on a serving platter. With a spatula, arrange apples, if some have fallen away. Serve with a dollup of whipped cream. "Natural" is very good, too. Serves 6 to 8.

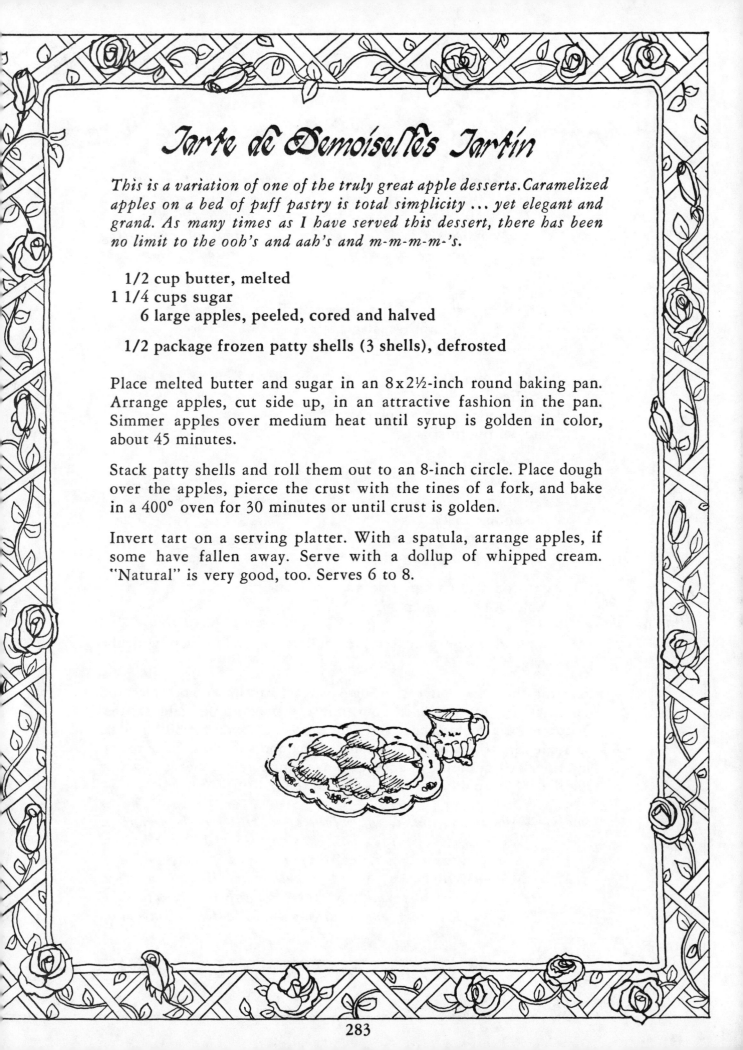

French Apple Pie with Sour Cream & Pecans

If you are an apple pie fiend, like me, there never seems to be enough variations to satisfy my taste buds. There is nothing better than a homemade apple pie with a flaky crust and mouth-watering juicy apples. Add some raisins, tart apricot jam and an interesting combination of sour cream and pecans and get ready for a delight and a joy.

1 9-inch, frozen, deep dish pie shell. Bake pie shell at
  350° for 8 minutes. Brush sides and bottom of
  shell with 3/4 cup apricot jam.

1 can (21 ounces) apple slices, drained; or 2 cups
  sliced apples
3 tablespoons brown sugar
1/2 cup yellow raisins

2 cups sour cream
2 eggs, beaten
1/2 cup sugar
1 teaspoon vanilla
1 1/2 tablespoons fresh lemon juice
1 teaspoon grated lemon peel

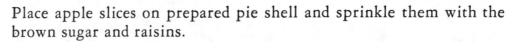

1/2 cup coarsely chopped pecans
1 tablespoon cinamon sugar

Place apple slices on prepared pie shell and sprinkle them with the brown sugar and raisins.

Beat together the sour cream, eggs, sugar, vanilla, lemon juice and lemon peel until blended. Pour mixture over apples and raisins. Place pie on a cookie sheet and bake in a 400° oven for 30 minutes. Sprinkle top of pie with pecans and cinnamon sugar and bake for an additional 10 minutes or until cream mixture is set. Serve any way you like it . . . cold or warm or at room temperature. Serves 8.

Note: – While you are at it, you might enjoy this simple variation. Make a Crumb Topping with 1/3 cup flour, 1/4 cup butter, 1/2 cup brown sugar, 1/2 cup chopped pecans and 1/2 teaspoon cinnamon mixed together until the mixture resembles coarse crumbs. Sprinkle on top of pie after the 30 minutes baking and continue to bake for 20 minutes longer.

Cream Cheese Pie with Raspberries & Chocolate

There are few pies that I have ever made that measure close to this rapturous combination of whipped cream cheese, plump tart raspberries all topped with little chunks of grated chocolate ... my favorite things.

    1 package (8 ounces) cream cheese
3/4 cup powdered sugar, sifted
    1 teaspoon vanilla
    1 cup cream

    1 9-inch Vanilla Crumb Crust

    2 packages (10 ounces, each) frozen raspberries in syrup,
        defrosted and drained. Reserve syrup for another use.
1/2 cup seedless red raspberry jam, heated

1/4 cup semi-sweet chocolate chips, coarsely crushed

Beat together the cream cheese, sugar and vanilla until the mixture is light and fluffy. In another bowl, beat the cream until it is stiff. Beat the whipped cream into the cream cheese mixture (on the lowest speed) until blended. Pour into prepared crust.

Stir together raspberries and melted jam until fruit is coated evenly. Gently spread raspberries over cream mixture. Refrigerate pie for several hours. Serve with majesty and pride. Serves 8.

Vanilla Crumb Crust

1 1/4 cups vanilla wafer crumbs
    1/2 cup finely chopped pecans
    1/3 cup melted butter
      3 tablespoons sugar

    1/3 cup semi-sweet chocolate chips

Combine all the ingredients, except the chocolate, and mix until blended. Pat mixture on the bottom and sides of a buttered 9-inch pie pan. Bake in a 350° oven for about 8 minutes. Sprinkle chocolate chips in pan and return to oven for 1 minute, to melt the chocolate. Remove from oven and spread melted chocolate evenly on crust, forming a thin chocolate layer. Set aside to cool.

Country French Peach Dessert with Cinnamon & Walnuts

(Clafouti aux Peches)

1 can (21 ounces) peach pie filling
4 tablespoons cinnamon sugar
1 cup coarsely chopped walnuts

3 eggs
1 cup half and half
2/3 cup flour
1/2 cup sugar
2 teaspoons vanilla

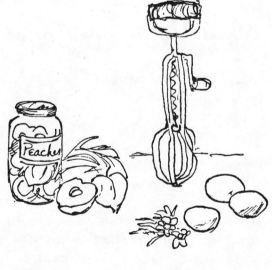

Butter a 14-inch oval baker and spread peach pie filling evenly over the bottom. Sprinkle with cinnamon sugar and walnuts.

In a mixer, beat together the remaining ingredients for 3 minutes. Pour batter over the peach filling and spread it evenly. Bake at 350° until batter is set and top is golden. Spoon into dessert dishes and serve warm or at room temperature with a dollup of whipped cream and a sprinkling of cinnamon.

Bread Pudding with Apple Custard & Raspberry Sauce

(Pain Perdu aux Pommes)

Literally translated "lost bread with apples" and what a delightful way of using a few slices of stale bread. This lovely dessert can be prepared in advance and warmed before serving.

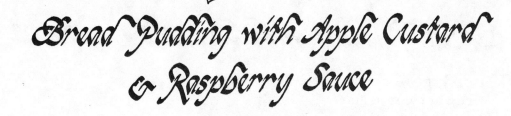

   3 apples, cored, peeled and thinly sliced
   2 tablespoons lemon juice
   3 tablespoons butter

   3 eggs, beaten
2/3 cup sugar
1/2 cup sour cream
1/2 cup cream
   1 teaspoon vanilla

   3 slices stale bread, crusts removed and cubed

   2 tablespoons cinnamon sugar
1/4 cup chopped walnuts
   1 package (10 ounces) frozen raspberries in syrup

In a skillet, place apples, lemon juice and butter, and cook apples for about 15 minutes or until apples are tender and liquid is absorbed.

Beat eggs with sugar, sour cream, cream and vanilla until mixture is blended. Stir in the bread cubes and softened apples. Place mixture into a greased 2-quart souffle dish or casserole and sprinkle top with cinnamon sugar. Bake at 325° for about 20 minutes. Sprinkle top with chopped walnuts and continue baking for about 15 minutes or until pudding is set and slightly puffed.

Spoon into pretty glass dessert dishes and serve warm with a spoonful of raspberry sauce. Serves 6.

Bread Pudding with Apricots & Raisins

    1 package (6 ounces) dried apricots
    1 cup apricot nectar
1/2 cup yellow raisins
    2 lemon slices

    3 eggs
2/3 cup sugar
1/2 orange, grated. Remove any large pieces of membrane.
    1 cup cream or half and half
    3 tablespoons melted butter
    1 teaspoon vanilla

    4 slices stale bread, crusts removed and cubed

1/4 cup seedless red raspberry jam, heated
1/4 cup sugared toasted almonds

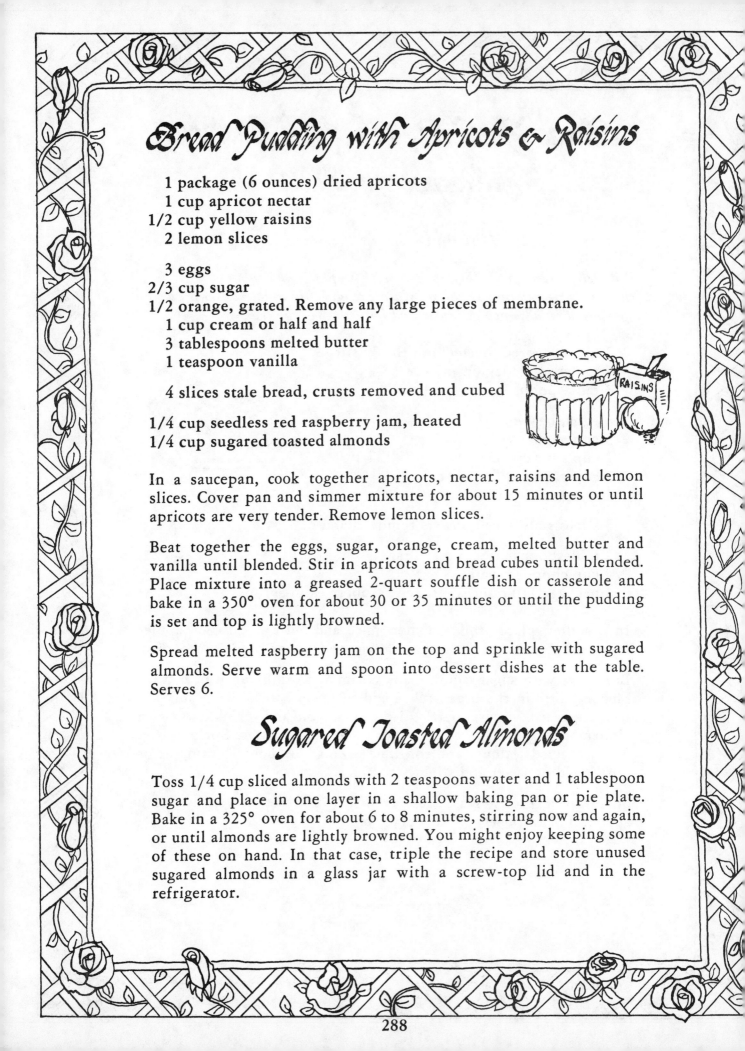

In a saucepan, cook together apricots, nectar, raisins and lemon slices. Cover pan and simmer mixture for about 15 minutes or until apricots are very tender. Remove lemon slices.

Beat together the eggs, sugar, orange, cream, melted butter and vanilla until blended. Stir in apricots and bread cubes until blended. Place mixture into a greased 2-quart souffle dish or casserole and bake in a 350° oven for about 30 or 35 minutes or until the pudding is set and top is lightly browned.

Spread melted raspberry jam on the top and sprinkle with sugared almonds. Serve warm and spoon into dessert dishes at the table. Serves 6.

Sugared Toasted Almonds

Toss 1/4 cup sliced almonds with 2 teaspoons water and 1 tablespoon sugar and place in one layer in a shallow baking pan or pie plate. Bake in a 325° oven for about 6 to 8 minutes, stirring now and again, or until almonds are lightly browned. You might enjoy keeping some of these on hand. In that case, triple the recipe and store unused sugared almonds in a glass jar with a screw-top lid and in the refrigerator.

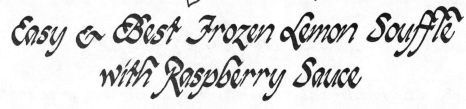

Easy & Best Frozen Lemon Souffle with Raspberry Sauce

This souffle is as smooth as satin. Light and refreshing, it is an excellent finale to dinner.

6 egg whites
    pinch of salt and cream of tartar
1/2 cup sugar

2 cups cream
1/2 cup lemon juice
1/2 cup sugar
2 tablespoons grated lemon zest

Beat egg whites until foamy. Beat in salt, cream and tartar, and 2 tablespoons of sugar at a time until whites are beaten stiff. Set aside.

In another bowl, beat cream until soft peaks form. Beat in remaining ingredients until blended. With mixer on low speed, beat together whites and cream mixture until blended.

Divide mixture between 24 paper-lined muffin cups and place in freezer. When frozen, cover with double thicknesses of plastic wrap.

When ready to serve, remove paper liner and place souffle in a lovely stemmed glass. Serve with a few fresh raspberries or a teaspoon of frozen raspberries in syrup. Yields 24 servings.

Note: – There are many variations to this recipe. First, you might enjoy serving it in a souffle dish and mound it high with a collar of foil. Of course, if you serve it this way, it will be necessary to spoon the dessert at the table.

– Another lovely variation is to line a spring-form pan with lady fingers and pour the lemon souffle over these. Freeze until firm. When serving, remove ring, but leave souffle on metal base. Cut in wedges as you would a cake.

– In both cases, spoon a teaspoon or two of raspberries in syrup over the dessert when serving.

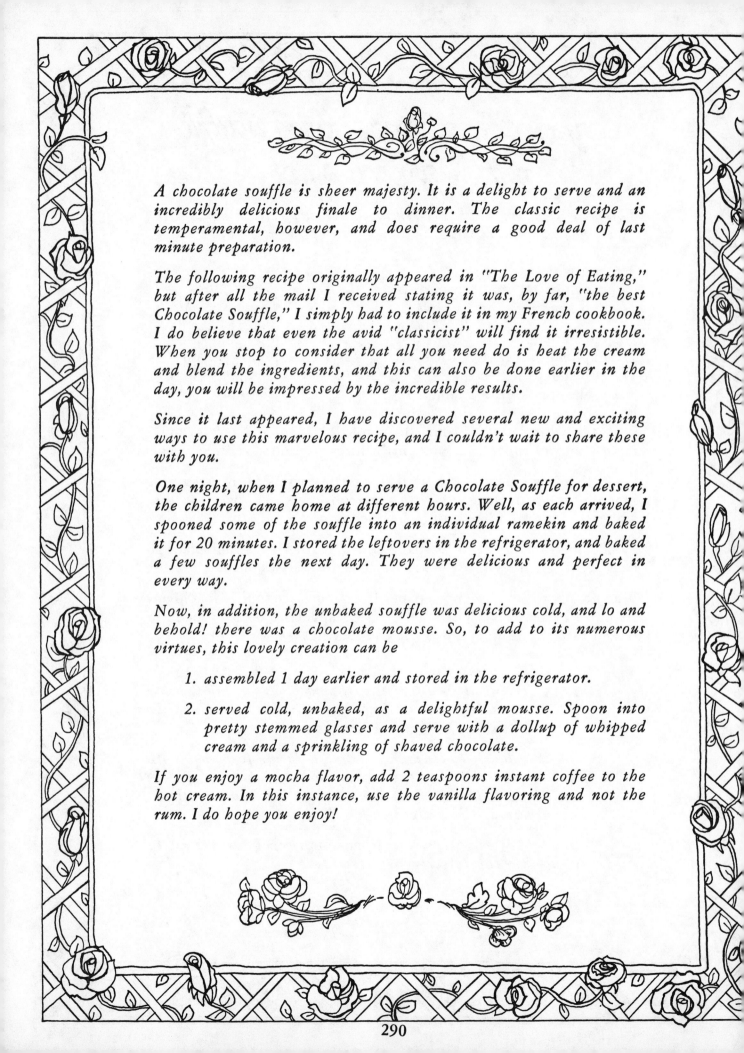

A chocolate souffle is sheer majesty. It is a delight to serve and an incredibly delicious finale to dinner. The classic recipe is temperamental, however, and does require a good deal of last minute preparation.

The following recipe originally appeared in "The Love of Eating," but after all the mail I received stating it was, by far, "the best Chocolate Souffle," I simply had to include it in my French cookbook. I do believe that even the avid "classicist" will find it irresistible. When you stop to consider that all you need do is heat the cream and blend the ingredients, and this can also be done earlier in the day, you will be impressed by the incredible results.

Since it last appeared, I have discovered several new and exciting ways to use this marvelous recipe, and I couldn't wait to share these with you.

One night, when I planned to serve a Chocolate Souffle for dessert, the children came home at different hours. Well, as each arrived, I spooned some of the souffle into an individual ramekin and baked it for 20 minutes. I stored the leftovers in the refrigerator, and baked a few souffles the next day. They were delicious and perfect in every way.

Now, in addition, the unbaked souffle was delicious cold, and lo and behold! there was a chocolate mousse. So, to add to its numerous virtues, this lovely creation can be

1. assembled 1 day earlier and stored in the refrigerator.

2. served cold, unbaked, as a delightful mousse. Spoon into pretty stemmed glasses and serve with a dollup of whipped cream and a sprinkling of shaved chocolate.

If you enjoy a mocha flavor, add 2 teaspoons instant coffee to the hot cream. In this instance, use the vanilla flavoring and not the rum. I do hope you enjoy!

Soufflé au Chocolat with Creme de Vanilla

1 1/2 cups semi-sweet chocolate chips
  1 cup heavy cream

5 eggs
8 ounces cream cheese, cut into 4 pieces
  pinch of salt
1 teaspoon vanilla or 1 tablespoon rum

Place chocolate chips in blender container or food processor bowl. Heat cream to boiling point and pour into the blender.

Blend for about 1 minute. Add eggs, one at a time, while the blender continues running. Continue blending, adding the remaining ingredients, until the mixture is nicely blended, about 1 minute.

Pour mixture into a buttered and sugared 1 1/2-quart souffle dish and bake in a 375° oven for about 50 minutes to 1 hour. Top will be slightly cracked. Serve with Creme de Vanilla spooned over the top. Serves 6.

Note: – If you prefer using the individual souffle dishes, divide the mixture between 6 ramekins and bake for about 20 minutes.
– Entire dish can be assembled earlier in the day and stored in the refrigerator, unbaked. Place into the oven about 1 hour before serving.
– If you enjoy a mocha flavor, add 2 teaspoons instant coffee to the hot cream. In this instance, use the vanilla, not the rum.

Creme de Vanilla

1 cup cream
1 tablespoon sugar
1 teaspoon vanilla

1 cup vanilla ice cream, softened

Whip cream with sugar and vanilla until stiff. Fold together whipped cream and the ice cream. Refrigerate until ready to serve. Can be prepared 2 hours before serving.

Soufflé au Cappucino with Creme de Kahlua

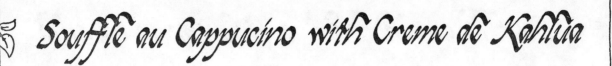

This dessert is very impressive and coffee lovers will find it delectable. When you consider that it assembles in minutes, can be assembled in advance and popped into the oven before serving, you won't reserve this little gem for "dressy" occasions, but will use it often.

      5 eggs
      1 package (8 ounces) cream cheese, cut into 4 pieces
  3/4 cup cream
      4 teaspoons instant espresso coffee
      2 teaspoons cocoa
  3/4 cup sugar
      3 tablespoons Creme de Cacao Liqueur
      1 tablespoon Cognac

Place all the ingredients in a food processor or blender container and blend for 2 minutes at high speed. Pour the mixture into a 1 1/2-quart soufflé dish that has been buttered and dusted lightly with sugar.

Bake in a 375° oven for about 50 minutes or until top is crowned and a cake tester inserted in the side to the center comes out clean. Serve immediately with Creme de Kahlua on the side. Serves 6.

Note: – If you are planning to assemble the soufflé earlier, then pour egg mixture into prepared soufflé dish and store in the refrigerator. Remove from the refrigerator about 10 minutes before placing in oven to bake. Then bake as above. You cannot bake soufflé in advance, for like all soufflés, it will fall.

Creme de Kahlua

1 cup cream
2 teaspoons Kahlua Liqueur
1 teaspoon Cognac
1 tablespoon sugar

Whip cream until foamy. Add the remaining ingredients and continue beating until cream is stiff.

2~Minute Soufflé au Grand Marnier with Chestnut Whipped Cream

One day, when you have nothing better to do and are looking for a standing ovation or to be swept off your feet, or seriously looking for a grand finale for dinner, you would do well to consider this totally indescribable majestic dessert. When you consider that it takes 2 minutes to assemble and it can also be assembled in advance, you will keep this little treasure handy.

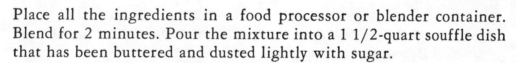

   5 eggs
   1 package (8 ounces) cream cheese, cut into 4 pieces
3/4 cup cream
1/4 cup Grand Marnier Liqueur
1/2 cup sugar

Place all the ingredients in a food processor or blender container. Blend for 2 minutes. Pour the mixture into a 1 1/2-quart soufflé dish that has been buttered and dusted lightly with sugar.

Bake in a 375° oven for about 50 minutes or until top is crowned and golden brown. Serve immediately with a spoonful of Chestnut Cream or lightly whipped cream. Serves 6.

Note: – Not the least of its glorious virtues is that this soufflé can be assembled several hours earlier and stored in the refrigerator. Remove from the refrigerator about 10 minutes before baking. Bake as described above.
– Serve at once or soufflé will fall.

Chestnut Whipped Cream

   1 cup cream, whipped
1/4 cup sweetened chestnut puree (purchased in a can)
   1 tablespoon Cognac

Whip cream until stiff. Beat in the chestnut puree and Cognac.

Note: – If you do not have the time to whip the cream, serve the soufflé with a teaspoonful of defrosted raspberries in syrup. Don't feel for a moment that this isn't a lovely optional . . . stuck as it is on the bottom of the page.

Old-Fashioned Cinnamon Date Nut Roll

Cream Cheese Pastry:

1/2 cup butter
    4 ounces cream cheese
    1 egg yolk
    1 cup flour
    pinch of salt

In the large bowl of an electric mixer, beat together the butter and cream cheese until the mixture is blended. Beat in the egg yolk. Add the flour and salt and beat until the mixture is blended. Turn dough out on floured wax paper.

Form dough into a circle, wrap it in the wax paper and refrigerate it for several hours or overnight.

Divide dough in half. Roll out one part at a time to measure a 10-inch square. Spread 1/2 of the Cinnamon Date Nut Filling over the dough. Roll it up, jelly-roll fashion, to measure a 10 x 3-inch roll. Bake rolls in a 9 x 13-inch teflon-coated pan. (If you do not use a teflon-coated pan, then butter the pan generously.) Bake in a 350° oven for 30 minutes or until the top is lightly browned. Cool. Cut into slices and serve with a sprinkling of powdered sugar. Yields 12 slices.

Cinnamon Date Nut Filling:

  2 cups finely chopped dates
1/2 cup chopped walnuts
  6 tablespoons cinnamon sugar

Mix together all the ingredients until the mixture is well combined.

Nutcracker Torte
with Strawberries & Cream

Incredibly easy and incredibly delicious, this dessert always adds excitement to dinner.

   3 egg whites
   1 cup sugar
   1 teaspoon vanilla

20 Ritz crackers, crushed into crumbs
   1 cup chopped pecans (or walnuts)

   1 cup cream
   1 tablespoon sugar
   1 tablespoon Grand Marnier Liqueur

   1 pint strawberries
1/3 cup currant jelly

Beat egg whites until foamy. Continue beating, adding sugar until whites are stiff. Beat in vanilla. On low setting, beat in crackers and nuts, until blended. Place mixture into a greased 9-inch pie plate and bake in a 350° oven for 30 minutes. When cool, frost with 1 cup cream, beaten with sugar and liqueur until stiff. Refrigerate overnight.

Several hours before serving, heat currant jelly until melted. Dip strawberries in jelly and place attractively over the whipped cream. Drizzle remaining jelly on the top. Refrigerate until serving time. Serves 8.

Note: - This nut pie freezes beautifully. Wrap in double thicknesses of plastic wrap, then foil. Defrost in the refrigerator.
- You can add 1/2 cup chocolate chips to the batter, and some grated chocolate on the top.

Date & Walnut Torte with Creme de Vanilla

       3 eggs
       1 cup sugar
   1/4 cup flour
       1 teaspoon baking powder

       1 cup vanilla wafer crumbs
       1 cup chopped dates
       1 cup chopped walnuts

Beat together eggs and sugar for about 5 minutes or until eggs are light and fluffy. Beat in the remaining ingredients until blended.

Pour mixture into a 9-inch lightly greased pie plate and bake at 350° for 30 minutes. Frost torte with Vanilla Whipped Cream and refrigerate overnight. Serves 8.

Creme de Vanilla

       1 cup cream
       2 tablespoons sugar
       1 teaspoon vanilla
   1/3 cup sour cream

Beat cream with sugar until stiff. Beat in remaining ingredients until blended.

299

Additional Copies of
THE JOY OF EATING FRENCH FOOD
*can be purchased at your local bookstore or
directly from:*
RECIPES-OF-THE-MONTH CLUB
P. O. Box 5027 • Beverly Hills, CA 90210